Statue of Saint Michael in the parish church at Garabandal.

I want to love you, Mother, and make others love you
as you love us.   CONCHITA

Star

on   the

Mountain

by   M. LAFFINEUR
M. T. le PELLETIER

Translated by

Service De Traduction Champlain, ENR.
Quebec, Canada

———————

Sheila Laffan Lacouture
Latham, New York

Published by
Our Lady of Mount Carmel of Garabandal, Inc.
Box 451, Newtonville, New York 12128

To our mother of Carmel
so as she will carry us
to the top of her mountain.

The Authors

Quebec, 1 Fevrier, 1968

(Quebec, February 1, 1968)

Fifth Printing, May, 1974

Published with the permission of ecclesiastical authority.
November 20, 1967
Library of Congress Catalog Card Number: 68–28493
Star on the Mountain by Laffineur-Noseda, M. and le Pelletier, M. T.
OUR LADY OF MOUNT CARMEL OF GARABANDAL, INC.
Box 451, Newtonville, New York 12128

Printed in the United States of America by
The Hamilton Printing Company.

Total Copies printed to date—38,000

> If it concerns prophetic revelations, the Pope is
> the sole Judge.
>
> LEO X—5TH COUNCIL OF LATTERAN

Preliminary Declaration:

The authors declare that they employ the words "apparition," "vision," "miracles," etc., only in submission to the decrees of Pope Urban VIII and without wishing to anticipate the decisions of the Church.

N.B. The prophetic revelations of Garabandal are of prime importance, as you will read here.

TABLE OF CONTENTS

viii

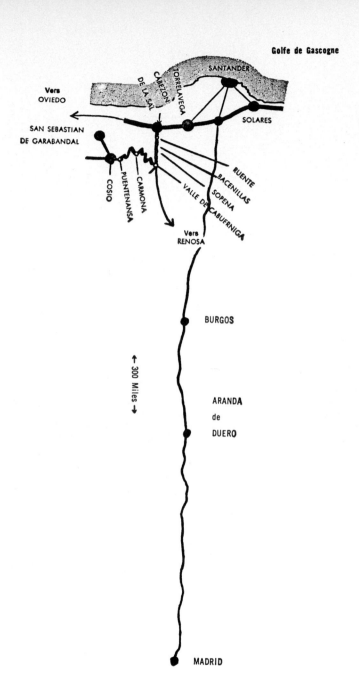

Golfe de Gascogne

SANTANDER

Vers
OVIEDO

TORRELAVEGA
CABEZON
DE LA SAL

SOLARES

SAN SEBASTIAN
DE GARABANDAL

RUENTE
BACENILLAS
SOPENA

COSIO

PUENTENANSA

CARMONA

VALLE DE CABUERNIGA

Vers
RENOSA

BURGOS

← 300 Miles →

ARANDA
de
DUERO

MADRID

Flight from New York to Madrid

xi

I

GARABANDAL AND RELIGIOUS AUTHORITIES

A few precise and chronological details:

The English brochure, "The Apparitions of Garabandal," bears the Imprimatur of the Bishop of Southwark (England). The Italian Brochure, "L'Ultimo Ammonimento," was put out with the juridicial approval of the Bishop of Sora (Italy). The book of M. Sanchez-Ventura was published with the moral approval of the Archbishop of Saragossa.

In January 1966, Conchita was greeted with the utmost kindness for two and a half hours by the Holy Office.

Shortly after, she was received most affectionately by Padre Pio at San Giovanni-Rotondo.

Upon her return to Rome, the Holy Father said to her, "I bless you, and with Me, the whole Church blesses you." (pages 140–143 and 259–261)

On July 8, 1966, the following letter was published in Mexico:

TRANSLATION

To:
Rev. Gustavo Morelos,
CITY
Dear Father:

Having in mind the indications of the Holy See and of His Excellency the Bishop of Santander, as well as required by Canon Law, we approve and bless the spreading, in our Archdiocese, of the Message of the Most Blessed Virgin Mary at San Sebastian of Garabandal, knowing in the light of Divine Revelation, we are urged of the need of prayer and sacrifice, devotion to the Holy Eucharist and to the Most Blessed Virgin

1

Mary and of obedience, love and faithfulness to the Vicar of Christ and the Holy Church.

Therefore, we find nothing in this Message, attributed to the Most Blessed Virgin Mary, that is contrary to Faith or morals; rather do we find opportune, useful and beneficial admonitions to attain eternal salvation.

Prompt and filial obedience to the dispositions of the Church has been characteristic of the persons that have been privileged in these apparitions and therefore this is a sure sign of God's presence.

The prudence of the Holy Church in relation to these important events has been manifested by careful study and pastoral vigilance; and the Church did not issue any kind of prohibition or rejection.

One of the Officials of the Sacred Congregation for the Defense of the Faith, Msgr. Philippi, stated to the Rev. P. Elias, Superior of the Carmel in the City of Puebla, who consulted him in Rome about the Apparitions, that the fact that Padre Pio, well known for his virtue, knowledge and faithfulness to the Holy See approved these apparitions and encouraged the four Visionaries to spread the Message of the Most Blessed Virgin, was a great proof of their authenticity.

Given at Jalapa of the Immaculate, July 8, 1966.

Manuel Pio Lopez, Archbishop of Jalapa (Mexico)

FOREWORD

"One must not believe in apparitions. . . . It is not a dogma of faith. . . . It is a superstition . . . unworthy of modern minds."

These expressions that we hear so often have become a sort of cliché in the hands of "progressive Catholics" of every walk of life intending to turn away simple souls from what they call "the naiveté of ignorants."

Yet, when we open the Gospel, we hear Jesus say, "I praise you Father, Lord of Heaven and earth, that you did hide these things from the wise and prudent, and did reveal them to little

2

ones. Yes, Father, for such was your good pleasure." (Matt. XI 25–26. Knox version.)

So, let us leave the wise to their wisdom and, in the simplicity of our own hearts, let us try to discover whether the things we have seen and heard at Garabandal do not contain a few of the secrets truly understood only by "little children."

Therefore, we address these lines only to those souls humble enough to put aside their prejudices when faced with marvelous events; strong enough to consider them calmly, through reason enlightened by faith, without impulsive enthusiasm, or self-consciousness.

It is true that Marian apparitions are no dogmas of faith, in the strict sense of the word. But it is nonetheless true that if Our Lady actually takes the trouble to appear on this earth, it would be a very great discourtesy on our part not to inquire humbly of the reasons for her visit and not to welcome her with love.

And if, as in certain apparitions of the past, she arouses our fears by reminding us that our sins violently offend Divine Justice, is it not supremely imprudent not to listen to her?

Disbelief in Marian apparitions may not be a sin against faith, but who can assure that in certain cases it is not a sin against love, gratitude, devotion and courtesy towards the Blessed Virgin Mary, or quite simply, against the most elementary prudence, both Christian and human?

Indeed, if the Gospel were not what it is, it would seem logical that divine revelations should be reserved for the Pope, the Bishops, the doctors and theologians of the Church.

Of course, there is the possibility that the Hierarchy, as individual members, and according to their degree of humility and interior simplicity, may be more enlightened than other people through a supernatural charismatic knowledge.

But the exercise of reason, enlightened by faith, is their normal manner of acquiring knowledge.

Granted this, the fact remains that at the beginning of Christianity, the news of the Nativity was given by the Angel at Bethlehem to humble shepherds, and not to members of the Jewish priesthood.

Nowadays, in the matter of apparitions eventually recognized and approved by the Church, frequently shepherds and children receive the first revelations of a message. And as in Bethlehem for the coming of Jesus, so today an angel announces or prepares the coming of the Queen of Heaven. It was the case at Fatima; it happened again at Garabandal in Spain.

II

THE SCIENTIFIC METHOD

It is the task of duly qualified investigators to examine the testimony of the children.

First of all, competent doctors and psychologists will tell us if the children are healthy, normal, well-balanced, and truthful. They will see if there is any question of hysteria, hallucination or hypnosis; in other words, whether the subjects examined show any signs of mental illness. They will investigate the family and social background.

Then, men of religious science will play their part. One would not consult medical doctors on a matter of theology, nor theologians on physiological reactions or on the nervous system.

In the last analysis, it will evidently be the theologians who, using their reason enlightened by faith, and in all humility, will be able to judge and say, "It seems to us reasonable to believe, or not to believe, that these apparitions are supernatural."

The "data" which will enlighten their judgment, a judgment that eventually will be either confirmed or disapproved by the Bishop of the diocese and by Rome, is plentiful.

We spoke earlier of the "physical and psychological normality" of the visionaries examined by men of natural science, doctors and psychologists.

The theological investigation will deal first and foremost with "extraordinary" facts readily observed by anyone: ecstasies, their nature and process; the doctrinal contents of these ecstasies, the subsequent miracles confirming their supernatural character.

4

The theologians will verify the fulfillment of the children's eventual "prophecies."

They will consider the spiritual impact, the influence of the "facts" on the souls and on the religious behaviour of the visionaries.

They will not overlook the religious influence of the apparitions on the children's families, on their social environment, and on visitors.

Nothing will escape their inquiry; neither eventual physical miracles, such as cures, nor moral miracles, such as remarkable conversions of unbelievers or non-Catholics.

The amount of documentation is vast indeed, so vast, particularly in Garabandal, that it will take years and years for the theologians to complete their task and before any Commission, truly canonical, can make a statement concerning their work and conclusions.

III

OUR PRESENT PURPOSE

Our purpose in this account is neither to take the place of the teachers or theologians nor to submit a scientific or theological report on Garabandal.

We only wish to relate in a simple manner what we have seen with our own eyes and heard with our own ears and to give an account of the evidence we received from the children themselves, from their families and immediate neighbors who saw and heard the things that took place at the village.

We shall relate the facts in the light of our three visits to Garabandal. The first one took place during the apparition period when we actually witnessed the children in ecstasy; the second, in March 1963, when we were able to extend our visit to the village, sharing the life of the mountain folks and the children; the third, during the summer of 1963.

5

We shall speak simply and truthfully as befits lay people. And to put our readers at ease, we invite them to meditate on the remarkable statement Cardinal Suenens made at the 53rd Council session:

"The Church is not only an administrative organization; in the broad sense, she is also a charismatic body. The time of the Church is the time of the Holy Spirit which is not given to pastors only, but to each and every Christian.

The whole Church is essentially a reality inspired by the Holy Spirit, built on the foundation not only of the Apostles, but also of the Prophets.

What would our Church be today without the charisms of teachers or theologians; without the charisms of prophets; that is, of men who, speaking out insistently on all occasions, convenient and inconvenient, remind the pastors of the reality of the Gospel? It was not only in the time of St. Francis that the Church was in need of charisms; she needs them today as well and needs them always.

Charisms in the Church without the ministry of pastors would certainly be inappropriate, but, on the other hand, it is the duty of pastors to listen to and converse with those who possess these gifts.

If the faithful owe respect to their pastors, the latter, in turn, owe respect to the faithful and to the gifts of the Holy Spirit which they have received.

Consequently, says Cardinal Suenens, may the Church give a place to charisms, to prophets and teachers, the freedom of the sons of God." (La Croix, October 23, 1963)

IV

FROM IRUN TO GARABANDAL

Crossing the Spanish border at Irun, the traveler is rather surprised by the very extended harbor of San Sebastian which, at first sight, makes the surrounding countryside rather unattractive. But how delightful when he views the coast leading from San Sebastian to Santander through Bilbao.

This very modern city would nevertheless be of no interest to the pilgrim on his way to a humble village lost in the mountains, beyond Torrelavega. Once he leaves this town, he passes through a number of villages along the Oviedo road which he leaves either at Virgen de la Plata or at Cabezon to follow a steep and winding countryside road to Carmona, Puentenansa, etc. . . .

Another mile to go . . . and he reaches Cosio, where the mule's path—somewhat improved since the apparitions—leads to Garabandal. . . . Only a few cars succeed in reaching the mountain; others give up, having never experienced such dangerous stones or steep slopes.

V

GARABANDAL BEFORE THE APPARITIONS

Garabandal is a humble little village which lies in the Cantabrian mountains, about 2000 feet up, about 56 miles southwest from Santander. Each day, some womenfolk set out with their donkeys on the rough path that leads to Cosio in order to get the necessary supplies. It is out of the question for any one to bicycle it, for, according to a road surveyor we met at the village, it is the stoniest spot of all Spain.

The parish priest, Don Valentine, lives in the valley, in Cosio proper. When possible, he goes to the village on horseback on Sunday evenings for a late Mass, after hurriedly hearing the confessions of a few parishioners.

The doctor answers emergency calls on foot, but the peasants, strengthened by a hard life, are not concerned about their health; in fact, they are quite robust.

People and things remain simple and unspoiled. Of course, as in any other town, they may have their own little family quarrels and parish differences. In this extremely poor area, they also

The Village of Garabandal.

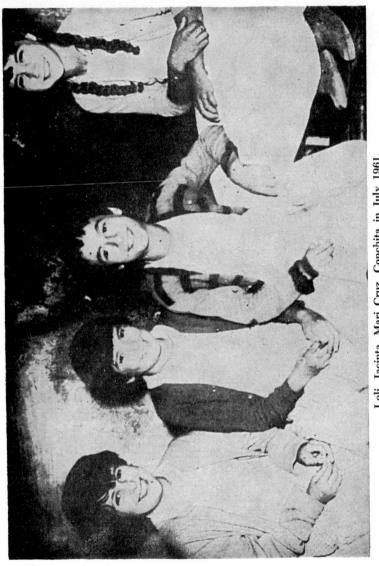

Loli, Jacinta, Mari Cruz, Conchita in July 1961.

face difficult problems of survival, as people feed on corn, potatoes, and milk from a small herd of sheep or goats. Those who cannot raise a pig kill a goat and we were able to watch the making of sausages, black pudding, and "chorizos" (Spanish sausages with red peppers).

Young men who do not tend the herds on high pastures leave the area or work in the city. The young girls, after schooling is over (at about 14), transport manure and the harvest on donkeys' backs and climb each day to mountain pastures—which means several hours' walk—to bring the mid-day meal to their fathers or brothers.

As in all rural areas, people get up early and, as is customary in Spain, they retire late at night. The evenings are spent in endless conversations and family life. Spaniards have only a few hours of sleep.

The people are healthy, religious, with a peculiar touch of anti-clericalism. Every evening, the women, dressed in black, with a kerchief or mantilla on their head, go to church and pray the rosary. The children run ahead, playing as they go, and a few men join them in church. They pray very quickly, making little signs of the cross on the forehead, the lips and the chest, "to chase the devil." They do not mind the abundance of prayers, rosaries, litanies, the stations of the cross, Paters and Aves in groups of six for this or that intention; they go through them all. . . . At the end they say a few invocations in honor of Our Lady who truly appeared in the mountain, (Nuestra Señora bien apparecida en la montana) a devotion that goes back to the 17th century and was particularly dear to the former Bishop of Santander, who passed away shortly before the apparitions. Some are even hinting that this saintly old bishop, very partial to Garabandal, obtained upon his arrival in Heaven, that Our Lady select the mountains of his former diocese as the site of her apparitions.

Spanish children, not unlike any other children, readily boast, tease and argue. They are cheerful, pure of heart, and ingenuous; their faults are those common to all children of their age.

The village has three hundred inhabitants. There are two public schools, one for boys and one for girls, with less than 20 children in each. Religious instruction is given at school and supplemented at home. It appears rather rudimentary. One detail: before the apparitions, the children had never heard of Lourdes or Fatima.

The church, rather poor, contains a few statues. St. Michael, dressed as a Roman soldier, and crushing the dragon, is typical. The life-size statue of Our Lady, next to the main altar, like the one of St. Michael, does not resemble the apparitions the children will describe to us later on.

In this setting, nothing, on the eve of June 18, 1961, could foreshadow the strange events that would drastically change the life of this peaceful little village of San Sebastian of Garabandal.

VI

THE VISIONARIES AND THEIR FAMILIES

Let us pause for a while and become better acquainted with the four children at the beginning of the apparitions.

The eldest, Conchita, just 12 years old, is a pretty brunette, full of life and zest, and the only daughter of a widow, Aniceta Gonzalez. She has three older brothers: Serafin, Aniceto and Miguel. The family owns a small herd tended by two of the boys on the mountain, while the eldest works in the mines, in the Province of Léon.

They live in a small house at the very end of the village. The kitchen, with its raised open fire, is poorly furnished. It is there that we were to witness one of the child's most striking ecstasies.

Maria Dolores, called Loli, is the second of six children. Her father, Ceferino Mazón, is mayor of the village and its real authority in every respect. He keeps a small café which is the men's rendezvous. Loli, smiling, quiet, obedient, helps her mother and will later take full charge of Guadelupe, her baby sister. Loli is also twelve years old.

Jacinta is a charming and lovely little girl. Her parents are among the most destitute in the village and their home is particularly poor. Nevertheless, they are always very hospitable. The father, a hard-working man, is also remarkable for his staunch faith. The mother, Maria Gonzalez, is charming like her daughter.

Shy and retiring, Jacinta is 12 years old. She is the most reserved of the four girls and, perhaps, the most profound.

The fourth girl, Mari Cruz, although one year younger, is as tall as her companions. She is less expansive and her family, less fervent; they say her father rarely goes to Mass.

Later, she will have—at least apparently—the most profound, painful, and less frequent ecstasies. After September 12, 1962, her face will show her deep sorrow of no longer seeing the Virgin.

Of average height and weight for their age, the four children are robust mountain girls. The doctors who examined and re-examined them agreed that they have no physical defects.

If we compare them with city children, we must realize that the development of their intelligence is two or three years behind. There are so many things they do not know as yet, because they never left their native village . . . Garabandal, of course, has neither television nor movies.

VII

THE APPARITION OF ST. MICHAEL

At San Sebastian de Garabandal June 18th, 1961, was a Sunday just like any other one. There was no unnecessary manual work of course, and with Mass and Vespers in the crowded little church. A rest in the shade, with the old folk sitting on their door-steps; the young people smiled at each other as if they had met by chance. The children, in the charge of an older sister, danced together while others played hide and seek, or marbles with little stones on the roadway.

Suddenly at dusk, four little girls disappeared without being noticed. Where did they go? To pick green apples from a tree growing beside the path leading up to "the Pines." They went out on a rather innocent plundering expedition. Here they were, laughing happily and digging their teeth into the far from ripe fruit, on an 18th of June.

Little girls! Silly little girls! Had you no thought of the forbidden fruit tree in the lost Paradise? Yes, of course they had, for suddenly they heard a noise as loud as it was unexpected! They look up, astonished, gazing to the right and to the left. "It sounded like thunder," they cried. Then Conchita, realizing that their plundering was wrong, added: "What a very naughty thing we have done! The devil is pleased and our guardian angel is very sad." Then they told us: "We started picking up stones from the pathway and throwing them as hard as we could to the left of us, where, we said, the devil was!" After throwing quite a lot of them and playing a game of marbles for a time they saw . . . the Angel!

What an extraordinary story! It almost begins like the Bible!

Conchita was the first to see the angel and fell to her knees, strangely pale, and remained in a rapture, her hands together and uttering "Ah! Ah!"

The others thought she had a "fit," and were scared. They wanted to go and warn Conchita's mother, when suddenly, looking in the same direction, they too caught sight of the angel, and in their turn fell to their knees in rapture.

However, the four of them recovered from the trance quite quickly and ran off to hide behind the church, deeply moved and trembling in awe, ashamed of their pilfering but indefinably happy about their wonderful vision.

Their first reaction to the apparition is absolutely normal; very frightened at first and most disturbed, with an uncontrollable desire to see the beautiful angel taking hold of their hearts while at the same time their hearts are torn between admiration, fear and joy.

They were soon to learn that this was St. Michael, though he did not look at all like the familiar statue of the centurion in helmet and armor in their little parish church.

"The Angel came wearing a long blue robe, hanging loose and without a seam. His wings were rosy-hued, transparent, large

13

The *Cuadro* and the Pines' road which were often descended
on knees or backwards.

and very lovely. His little face, neither round nor long . . . his
nose was very beautiful, his eyes black and his skin dark. His
hands were very finely shaped with well-trimmed nails, and his
feet were invisible. He seemed to be about 9 years old. So young,
yet he gave an impression of invincible strength."

Such was the heavenly being who appeared to them on the
evening of June 18th, 1961 . . . a Sunday never to be forgotten.

On the 19th, the angel did not appear. They saw him again
on the 20th. And, as at this time the neighbors were not yet
taking any notice, Conchita noted in the diary which she wrote
later on, and with exquisite simplicity, "On these two days there
was no one else with us. There were just the five of us: the Angel,
Loli, Jacinta, Cruz and I."

They saw the angel again on several of the following days and
in the presence of ever-growing numbers of witnesses, and on
Saturday, June 24th, he appeared with a mysterious placard bear-

14

The 4 little girls at the *Cuadro*. Each occupies the exact place they had on the first apparition on June 18th, 1961, Jacinta, Loli, Mari Cruz and Conchita.

ing letters and Roman figures, which they could not understand.

On June 24th, some doctors were there who carried out many experiments during the raptures. Completely without sensation, the girls became aware of this only when the rapture was over. "It did not hurt us, but the marks remained," said Conchita.

During the next week, there were only three apparitions.

Then on Saturday, July 1st, the Angel announced to them that the Blessed Virgin Mary would come the next day, Sunday, under the title of Carmel. They asked him the meaning of the writing on the placard, but he replied: "Our Lady will tell you that herself."

15

VIII

THE APPARITION OF OUR LADY
OF MOUNT CARMEL

At last came the "happiest day of their lives," Sunday, July 2nd. Our Lady appeared to them at about 6 o'clock in the evening.

Here we cannot do better than copy, literally, from the precious "diario" (the diary written by Conchita the following year).

"At each side of her there stood an angel. One was St. Michael; we did not know the other but he was dressed in the same way; one would have said that they were twins.

Beside the angel on the right, on a level with Our Lady, we saw a very large Eye, which seemed to us to be the Eye of God.

On that day, we said a lot to Our Lady, and she to us. We told her everything. We told her how we went to the fields, for hay making, that we were sunburnt, and that we had the grass in heaps. She laughed as we were telling her so many things.

We recited the Rosary, looking at her at the same time. She recited it with us to teach us how to say it properly.

Just as we finished, she said that she was going away.

We told her that she ought to stay just a little longer, for she had spent so little time with us. She laughed.

She told us she would come again on Monday, and when she went away it made us very sad.

When she had gone people came to kiss us and to ask us what she had said.

A few others did not believe in it, in her having come, because we had talked about so many things. But the majority did believe in the Virgin because, they said, she is like a mother whom her daughter has not seen for a long time. In such a case the daughter tells all. With greater reason for us,

who had never seen her; and more so because it was the
Mother in Heaven.

Thus ended Sunday July 2nd, a very happy day because we
had seen the Virgin for the first time.

With Her we can always be, because we love Her even
without seeing Her."

IX

OUR BLESSED LADY CAN BE PRESENT IN "APPARITIONS" AND ALSO BY SUPERNATURAL FAITH AND LOVE

We cannot resist making a short commentary on that admirable little sentence: "With Her we can always be, because we
love Her, even without seeing Her."

"Lucky little girls to have seen Our Lady" we might say, envy-
ing their good fortune. . . . But in a few very simple words they
reply: "You too can remain with Her always, because you too can
love Her without seeing Her!"

To plumb the depths of their remark, we may make a comparison; up in the mountains on a misty day, there are no longer
any snow-capped summits to be seen, no magnificent countryside. The land is of a uniform grey. A traveler arriving on Mont
Blanc can only be told that "the country is magnificent, that over
there is the sparkling summit and down there the deep valley."

He is obliged to believe the statements of his informants.

It is the same with supernatural realities.

When we live in a state of grace, Jesus and Our Lady are
always present in our souls, each in Their own way. They may
be even nearer to us than they were to the girls during the apparitions. But we can reach out to them only by love, just as
we can believe in their presence only by opening the eyes of our
faith. By faith we are aware of them, without seeing them. It is
our spiritual heart which loves the object of our faith which, in
a mysterious way, is present in it.

17

X

DESCRIPTION OF OUR LADY
OF MOUNT CARMEL

Here is the description of the apparition, just as Conchita tries to portray it.

"Our Lady comes wearing a white robe and blue cloak. She has a crown of golden stars: her feet are not visible. Her hands are slender with a scapular on her right wrist. The scapular is reddish. Her hair is long, wavy and dark brown, parted in the middle. Her face is long, her nose is long and slender and her mouth is dainty and very lovely; her lips are just a little bit thick. Her complexion is quite dark but lighter than the angel's. Her voice is different from the angel's and it is a very beautiful voice, very unusual. I cannot explain it. There is no woman who is like Our Lady, either in voice or in any way at all.

Sometimes she carries her Child Jesus in her arms. He is quite tiny, as tiny as a new-born baby. He has a round face and appears to have the same complexion as Our Lady, with a sweet little mouth. His blond hair is rather long; His hands are very small and He is dressed in a sort of sky-blue tunic. Our Lady seems to be about 18 years old."

Do not be surprised; it is really Our Lady of Mount Carmel who is described. On making inquiries we found that when she appeared to the Carmelite St. Simon Stock in 1251, she was indeed wearing a white robe and blue cloak. It was in comparatively recent times that she was portrayed as wearing the brown habit worn by her sons and daughters in Carmel today. Besides, to make the matter clear, Conchita quite definitely says that the scapular is brown.

Talking about the scapular, the children were for a long time surprised to see on the one side of it a mountain which they could not understand at all. In fact, it is the custom in Spain to talk of "The Virgin of Carmel," and not, as in France, of "Our Lady of Mount Carmel."

It is only in November, 1962 that we had the pleasure of giving them the real meaning of this mountain. On that day, too, Conchita described the shape of the scapular worn on Our Lady's wrist; it is more like the maniple worn by the priest at Mass than the ordinary scapular that we know now.

XI

THE MESSAGE

On July 3rd, Our Lady came again, and on the 4th she agreed to explain the enigmatic notice carried by the angel. It contained the first letters of an important message which Our Lady ordered the children to make known, and the date of its announcement which was to be only on the following 18th of October (1961). Here is the message: *

"Many Sacrifices must be made and much penance. Visit often the Blessed Sacrament.

But above all it is necessary to be very good. If it is not done, a chastisement will come upon us.

Already the chalice is filling, and if we do not change, the chastisement will be very great."

Later on, people seeking more details put this question to the children, "For whom was this message given, for you or for the whole world?" They answered: "Oh, for the world, for the whole world!"

From that day on many things have happened at Garabandal; some of them we shall mention now, others will be known in their right time. But the children, and Conchita especially, al-

---

* Hay que hacer muchos sacrificios y mucha penitencia y tenemos que visitar mucho el Santísimo. Pero antes tenemos que ser muy buenos y sino lo hacemos nos vendrá un castigo muy grande; ya que se está llenando la copa y sino cambia vendrá un castigo.

ways insist on what they consider as essential: "the most important of all is the MESSAGE." All the rest, even the events that can be said to be miraculous, take place for one reason only, and that is to give credit to the Message and to urge people to carry it out.

XII

COLLECTIVE RAPTURES

After her first apparition on July 2nd, 1961, Our Lady continued her visits, appearing either to the children collectively or to one or the other of them separately.

What is precisely the behavior of the children during these raptures?

Here is what we ourselves observed in November, 1962 and we are telling it in order to give a clear idea of the type of apparitions which occurred at Garabandal, anticipating other events which will be described later and which took place in the same environment.

Whether the rapture be individual or collective, it starts with three interior "calls" by the children. The first sometimes comes a long time beforehand, the second nearer the time and the third is sudden, imperious and sets the children running to the place of their heavenly "rendezvous." *

When the raptures were collective people tried the experiment, more than once, of keeping the children apart from each other, in separate houses, so that they might verify the reality and simultaneity of these "calls." Indeed, the children had no watches, but they always did meet again, moved by the irresistible force which called them at the very same second and caused them to meet at the same time and in the same place.

* The three "calls" preceded apparitions of Our Lady, not those of the Archangel Michael alone. (Translator's note.)

21

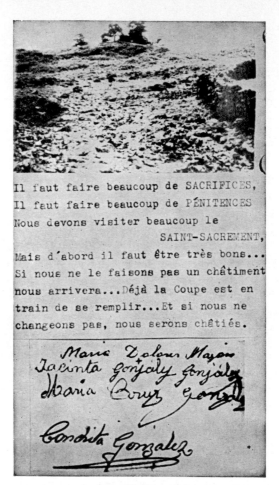

Il faut faire beaucoup de SACRIFICES,
Il faut faire beaucoup de PÉNITENCES
Nous devons visiter beaucoup le
                    SAINT-SACREMENT,
Mais d'abord il faut être très bons...
Si nous ne le faisons pas un châtiment
nous arrivera...Déjà la Coupe est en
train de se remplir...Et si nous ne
changeons pas, nous serons châtiés.

The "Message."

As soon as they caught sight of Our Lady, wherever they happened to be, even on the sharp stones of the roadway, they would fall suddenly to their knees with such force that their bones rattled like old wooden clogs being smashed up on stones. Sometimes, we are told, they fell with such force that they went flat on to the ground. But at all times onlookers were struck by the dignity, nobility and beauty of their pose, which never at any

22

Loli, Conchita, Jacinta and Mari Cruz in ecstasy.

time appeared immodest, unseemly, nervous, or convulsive.

During November, 1962, when we were present at some of the collective raptures, these began after the recital of the Rosary in the church. Immediately after leaving the church with all the people to go home, three of them were suddenly caught up in rapture: Conchita, Maria Dolores and Jacinta. The three girls ran through the village, arm in arm and carrying crucifixes. Their upturned faces were singularly beautiful in the light of the torches. Completely insensible to what was going on around them, even unconscious of the fact that they themselves were moving, they were followed by villagers, who were reciting the Rosary with them or singing hymns. They went up quickly to "the Pines" which stand high above the village, and came back down the particularly steep, stony path, faces still upturned, walking backwards, risking death a hundred times!

Back to the church steps, they walked round the Church, and

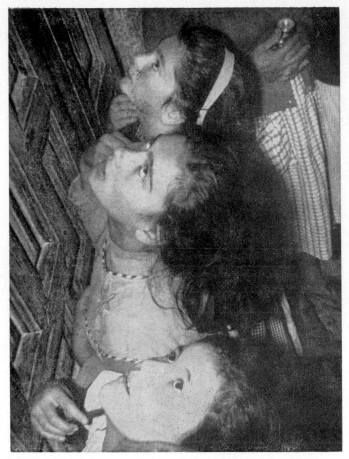

An ecstasy of Jacinta, Conchita and Maria-Dolores (Loli) is about to terminate. The children are kneeling down, during the night, at the doorstep of the closed church.

then suddenly gave a peal of laughter, surprising laughter, which seemed almost luminous and at the same time sounded like the ringing of little bells, a laughter which shocked us first of all. . . . Indeed, how could one laugh in Our Lady's presence, even though the laughter was so lovely?

Baffled by it, we asked Conchita the reason for it later on.

24

— Why, Our Lady herself was laughing!
— Whatever for?
— Because we were singing so badly out of tune!

And that was perfectly true as the tape recorder revealed!

That night they went through the village as many as five times, always in rapture, and followed by a devout crowd of people. Once they stopped to pray at the cemetery, doubtless out of pity for the souls in purgatory. Then, coming back a last time to the closed door of the church, they lifted each other up in turn to kiss the Blessed Virgin whom they could see above them and to receive a kiss from her. Finally, falling to their knees against the door, even more abruptly than at first . . . as is shown by one of the finest photographs we have of the little girls in rapture . . . and without any period of transition, they became again all of a sudden the simple, smiling children that we knew. The mysterious glow which transfigured their faces when in rapture had gone. But they announced, with a charming smile: "Our Lady will come to see us again tonight, in our homes."

XIII

INDIVIDUAL RAPTURES

When Our Lady announced her forthcoming visit in this way, neither the little girls nor their parents went to bed. We spent some evenings with Conchita, her mother, her brother Serafin and other visitors. That evening, or on one of the following days, we met a captain of the civil guards, a lady from the Philippine Islands, Dr. Ortiz from Santander (an important witness) and Mrs. Ortiz; a German industrialist (formerly a Protestant but miraculously converted at Garabandal) and his Spanish wife, along with many other people.

Who could possibly describe the charm of those evenings, those nights of waiting, interspersed with prayers and hymns

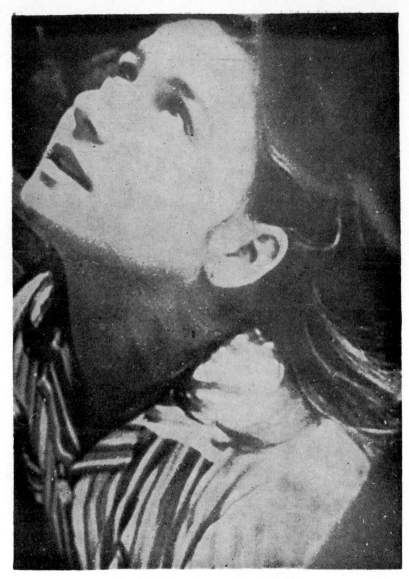

Conchita in a trance state in 1962.

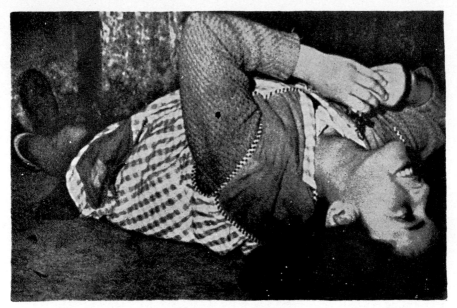
Loli in a trance state, lying on her back, with her face transformed.

and stories in which each gave thanks to Our Lady for her bound-
less attentions?

In the morning, when she finished saying the Angelus, Conchita suddenly fell to her knees. She had become dazzlingly
beautiful, out of this world. Her face, which was naturally pleasing, had become more refined, shining with a kind of interior
light; she seemed to be all love, straining towards the one above
her, who was holding her attention. Yet her body was so amaz-
ingly heavy that one of the bystanders, and a strong man at that,
could not lift her when he held her under the elbows.

Other witnesses had told us: "When they were in a rapture
four men tried to lift one of them but found it impossible."

Getting up again she took her crucifix in her hands and made
on herself a majestic sign of the cross as Our Lady had previously
taught her. She offered the crucifix to Our Lady to kiss and then
held it to each of us, to our lips.

Then without looking around she went upstairs and, at the

27

request of Our Lady, offered her a little statue of the Infant of Prague to kiss, and came back down to the kitchen.

It is impossible to describe the poise of the little girl as, with eyes looking upwards and never a glance at the stairs, she came down with what may be called a "queenly carriage." The apparition ended as abruptly as it had begun.

Then the child went up to one of the women present, saying: "Our Lady gave me a message for you." Then she went to look for a holy picture on which she wrote a few words which referred to the interior thoughts of the stranger, thoughts which had been completely unknown to the child.

This account of November, 1962 indicates the atmosphere and reveals the way in which collective or individual raptures occurred at Garabandal.

XIV

THE GREAT FUTURE MIRACLE

Now let us go back to the beginning of the apparitions.

Between July 2nd and October 18th, 1961, they were most significant and very numerous. They were also accompanied by amazing events. Let us single out a few of them.

In the month of August an eminent Jesuit,* whom people called "the Saint" and "the Theologian," still a young man, was standing beside the girls in rapture up at "the Pines." Suddenly he was heard to murmur, "Milagro, Milagro, Milagro, Milagro" ("A miracle, a miracle, a miracle, a miracle"). Strange to say, he was then, and was to remain, the only one to see unfolding before him in a vision the famous Miracle which Conchita was to announce later, although she herself had not seen the vision yet.

The priest left Garabandal that same night, his heart over-

---

* Father Luis Andreu, S.J. (Translator's note.)

flowing with love, gratitude and joy, and never tired of telling his fellow travelers of his jubilation of soul. He fell into a peaceful sleep, woke up with a smile on his lips, and . . . died . . . literally, of joy, in the car which was taking him back to Reinosa, at 4 o'clock in the morning.

We must insist on this fact; the children themselves had not yet seen a vision of this "Miracle." Conchita, who was the only one to prophesy it, gave us the following details: "It will take place on a Thursday, at half past eight in the evening. It will be more convincing than the miracle of the sun at Fatima.

"It will not happen on one of Our Lady's Feast Days, but on that of a young martyr of the Eucharist. It will not be on the 18th of the month, either. It will last about a quarter of an hour. It will be visible from all the mountains around Garabandal. The Holy Father will see it from the place where he is at the time (desde donde este). Padre Pio shall also see it.

"During this miracle those who are ill among the onlookers will be cured and the unbelievers among them will be converted."

Although the learned and holy Jesuit of whom we have spoken died of joy on seeing this miracle, Conchita replied to all questions, "We ourselves will not die of happiness because we shall receive a special grace to enable us to bear it." She added: "This Miracle will be the proof of the tender love of God and of Our Lady for the world. And after the Miracle God will permit a 'sign' to remain, to remind us of it."

It was Conchita alone who announced this great future Miracle, indefatigably and imperturbably, with absolute certainty and serenity. Nothing on this point could disturb her. She even declared: "Whether I am at Garabandal or not, the Miracle will still take place."

As for the other girls, they said: "It is true, since Conchita has said so."

It is not surprising that since this Miracle was announced more than a year ago, some people have become excited about it and imaginations have run riot!

Several people have imagined that they had found the future date . . . but the secret has been well-kept and all such predictions are condemned in advance. To the questions which are as indiscreet as they are never-ending, the child replies: "Our Lady does not wish me to reveal the date, though I already know it. I may only announce it eight days before it will occur. It will be linked with a very important ecclesiastical event."

Finally, we have just learned from an absolutely reliable source that "Conchita has revealed the date of the miracle to her Bishop, the Bishop of Santander."

XV

THE NATURE OF THE "APPARITIONS"

Now that we have spoken of the Miracle, we can once again tell of some surprising events from a new point of view. In the early days of the apparitions the girls were seen one day to be making movements that indicated that they were passing some mysterious object from one to the other, and they seemed to rock it to and fro.

The rapture over, they explained that Our Lady had put the Child Jesus into their arms.

Having heard of this from Jacinta's mother, we questioned Conchita:

— If you held the Child Jesus in your arms, you will have touched Him?

— Oh, no, you can never touch Our Lady or the Child.

— But you held Him in your arms?

— We could not bring our arms close to our breast.

— Was He heavy?

— He was weightless.

— And when you kissed the Blessed Virgin Mary, could you feel the freshness of her face?

Taking the hand of a woman standing by, Conchita raised it up to the woman's face, covering but not touching her mouth and eyes. "Try and understand; in this way, you see that you are kissing your hand. Well, it's just like that: we see that we are kissing her, but we do not touch her."

— It is indeed Our Lady whom we are kissing, but we do not feel the freshness of her face nor anything else.

— How is that possible?

— We do not know. But that is how it is.

— If we try to put our hands on Our Lady, we cannot put our hands any further because she is there. Yet we can feel nothing, although she is just in front of our hands!

One day, however, they wanted to offer the Child some small stones to play with. The stones fell to the ground as had the caramels, given to them by a visitor and which they wanted to give to Him on another occasion. He smiled to thank them, but the caramels were found on the ground.

It is for the theologians to give us an adequate explanation.

XVI

SIGNS IN THE HEAVENS

Here are two other astonishing events recorded by Conchita in her diary.

"At the time of our apparitions, Loli and I were coming down from 'the Pines' together with many people. Suddenly, we saw 'something' mysterious in the clouds. It looked like fire. It was daytime. I saw it, Loli saw it. And also many people around us saw it with us, even people who were not near us, who had remained at the village. When this stopped the Blessed Virgin appeared to us. We asked her what it was. She told us, 'It is in that fire that I came to you.'"

"Another day at the time of the apparitions, there were again the two of us, Loli and I. It was the Feast Day of Our Lady of Pilar (Our Lady of Saragossa). As we were in rapture looking at Our Lady, we saw a red star with a very long tail below Our Lady's feet. We asked Our Lady what it meant, but she did not answer."

Many people saw this star too, at the same time.

Before we had read the diary, we did not know of the sign of the "chariot of fire," but witnesses had spoken to us of "the star with a very long tail" which they, too, had seen on the Feast of Our Lady of Pilar.

XVII

OUR LADY AND THOSE WHO WITNESSED THE RAPTURES

As early as 1961 Our Lady began to reveal in different ways her compassionate love for those who witnessed the raptures. During the individual raptures, she started kissing rosaries, medals, holy pictures, crucifixes and even wedding rings.

She did not kiss all the objects which visitors asked the children to offer her, but only those which she herself pointed out to the children to hold up to her lips.

The Madonna would herself choose, by pointing to them, the objects they wore pinned to their clothes or which had been put on the kitchen table.

She would have them returned, often during the rapture, to the lucky owners whom the little girls did not even see. Generally the souls of the owners were, at the same time, given great graces of conversion or consolation.

May we be allowed to insist on this point.

The children's actions often had, for the owners of these objects, a definite meaning which the little girls could not possibly suspect. That remains a precious secret between those who were so favored and their Heavenly Mother.

Reliable witness of this is given by an unknown woman who came to Garabandal anxious to know her right vocation. A widow, she was wondering whether it would be better to retire from the world or else to live and love Jesus in her present circumstances. By kissing the wedding ring on the widow's hand Our Lady enlightened her about her future and worked a real conversion in her soul.

Here is another incident. One day someone put a precious powder compact on the kitchen table in Conchita's house.

The little girls and the onlookers wanted to remove it, saying that Our Lady never kissed a profane object. In spite of this the powder compact remained where it had been placed.

Scarcely was the child caught up in a rapture than, neglecting the other objects of piety, she offered the powder compact to Our Lady first.

Of course those present began to murmur against such strange behaviour, "How can we admit that Our Lady would kiss this object of feminine vanity! No, that is not like Her!"

When the rapture was over, Conchita explained, "Our Lady said to me, 'Give that to me for it belongs to my Son'" . . . without making any further explanation.

Soon the reason for it became quite clear. During the Spanish Civil War, between 1936 and 1938, this powder compact had been used to carry consecrated Hosts to give Holy Communion secretly to the prisoners who were going to die at the hands of the reds. It had been used as a ciborium!

One other incident was the conversion of the Protestant industrialist whom we mentioned earlier and who was completely changed after Our Lady had kissed his wedding ring. From Garabandal he went to make a retreat at Loyola. On the third day, while those around him were receiving Holy Communion, he was converted.

Last of all we have recently heard that several friends of Garabandal have met at Burgos for the baptism of a young Jewess, also miraculously converted at Garabandal.

XVIII

HUMAN WISDOM INTERVENES

Let us reread the text of the Message, which is, as it were, the very heart of Garabandal:

"Many Sacrifices must be made and much penance. Visit often the Blessed Sacrament.

But above all it is necessary to be very good. If it is not done, a chastisement will come upon us.

Already the chalice is filling, and if we do not change the chastisement will be very great."

On October 18th, 1961 in accordance with Our Lady's wish, this Message was proclaimed near "the Pines" which crown the hill above the village. It was not done exactly in the manner prescribed by Her, the children and their parish priest being obliged to submit to another person's judgment.* Already the adversary was in this place, fighting against Heaven. Ah! these men who are afraid of the foolishness of humble obedience, and who think they are wiser than Our Lady and who are weighed down with considerations they think to be "prudent"! Who can tell what would have happened if, fearful of the rain which was beating down on the crowd, they had not seen fit to defy the wish of the Queen of Heaven, and attempt so feebly to thwart the publication of this message which is so Gospel-like?

Fortunately the apparitions did not cease on that account, neither did the miracles.

---

* Our Lady had prescribed that it should be read at 10:30 p.m. But the Special Commission appointed by the Bishop of Santander to investigate the apparitions, consisting of two priests and two doctors, said that it would be better to read it at 8:30 or 9 p.m., because of the rain. (Translator's note.)

XIX

THE SIGN OF SIGNS IS PROPHESIED

In this message Our Lady asks for frequent "visits" to the Blessed Sacrament. She asked the girls for more than this; she asks for frequent Communion.

Is it because people in Spain go to Holy Communion relatively less often, especially in the mountain regions of Cantabria, where some traces of Jansenism still persist? That may be.

In any case, after he had prepared them in proper fashion, St. Michael came, ever more frequently, to bring Holy Communion to the children, the Host remaining invisible to those present.

Furthermore, as early as July 3rd, 1962, Conchita announced—with the same assurance with which she predicts what she calls today the "great Miracle for the conversion of the world"—that on the following July 18th the Archangel would give her Holy Communion and that this time the Host would be visible on her tongue.

However, July 18th, the annual Feast Day of the village, was a day of dancing at Garabandal. There was a large crowd of people, but not all of the same mind. Some had come for the dancing; others, and far more numerous, had come for the miracle which had been announced. These latter wandered around, disappointed, for the dancing still went on; it was now late at night and the miracle had not taken place.

There are authentic letters written in her own hand, dated July 8th, 1962, in which Conchita announced this miracle in formal terms to people she invited to be present for it. We have two separate photocopies of them.

Do not be surprised at these invitations from Conchita. At this time the apparitions had been occurring for more than one year. The raptures had multiplied in an unheard-of way. Everybody had been able to examine them and study their doctrinal

35

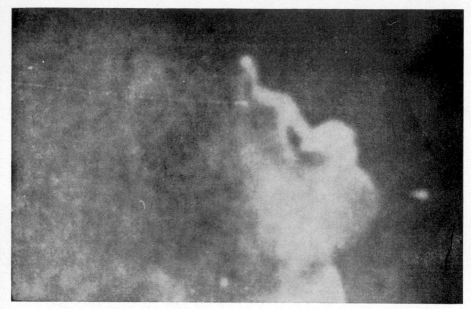

The photograph of the miracle of "The Forma" taken from an amateur movie taken by Mr. Damans, of Barcelona, at the right moment, and with a flashlight.

content. Amazing conversions had been recorded. Cases of ill health—of which we shall talk later—had made some improvement, to say the least. Some of the prophecies made by the girls had been fulfilled. Father Luis Andreu had died of supernatural joy. The crowds had seen, with their own eyes, the "chariot of fire" from which Our Lady of Mount Carmel had descended one day, and another time "the Star with a very long tail," which had risen from her feet.

As for the village people, they had experienced the two nights of the "Gritos" which are the terrible visions of the punishment of which we shall be talking further on. Alas, these "signs in the sky" like all the other events, had not been enough for the families, the villagers, the people, their religious superiors and others. And they all plagued the children, without realizing, we hope, that such an attitude would one day seem to be a baffling intellectual blindness: "A miracle, a miracle, we must have a miracle!"

In Fatima, in 1916, The Angel was
miraculously giving Holy Communion
to the children.

This miracle which the "spiritual greed" of other people was
demanding, the little girls had already requested of Our Lady
and "the Angel" many times. "So that they may believe" is what
they repeated.

On June 23rd, 1962, St. Michael replied to Conchita alone,
exactly as follows: "At my intercession and at yours, God will
do it—so that they may believe. On that day the Host will be
visible to all present on your tongue. You will be told the date,
15 days in advance."

That is why, having announced it at Garabandal as early as

37

the 3rd of July, Conchita wrote to her friends on the 8th of the month.

At about one a.m. the dancers had gone to bed and, with the visitors full of doubts about the child, the astonishing miracle took place.

XX

THE MIRACLE OF THE "FORMA"

Here for the sake of accuracy we shall give fuller evidence of this extraordinary and irrefutable miracle. Here is Conchita's account:

"When ten o'clock in the evening arrived, I had a 'call' and at midnight another one, and at two o'clock the Angel appeared to me in a room in my house. There was my mother, Aniceta, my brother, Aniceto, and my uncle Elias and my cousin Lucina and a lady from Aguilar, Maria del Carmen Fontenada. And the Angel was with me for a little while and said the same to me as on the other days, 'Recite the "Yo pecador" and think of Whom you are going to receive' and I did so. Afterwards he gave me Communion. He told me that I should say the 'Alma de Cristo' and should make a thanksgiving and that I should keep my tongue out, with the Sacred Host, until the time when he would go away and Our Lady would come, and I did so, and when Our Lady came she said to me, 'Todavia no creon todos?' (Do all of them still not believe?)"

We have questioned many witnesses about this miracle which we think is so important and which is for us the irrefutable proof of the authenticity of the events and the message of Garabandal.

The most important of all the witnesses is actually Pepe Diez, a stone mason who was doing some work in Conchita's home when the apparitions began. His own house, at the bottom of the lane where the Angel appeared at the beginning, makes an excellent watch-tower. He was able to overhear Conchita's replies when she was talking to the Angel on June 23rd, 1962, the day when he announced the miracle of the Host which was to take place in the future.

Thus warned, Pepe wanted to be in the first row of onlookers, and he succeeded. Kneeling down a few inches away from Conchita's face, he held a flashlight which he focused on the child's mouth as soon as she knelt down.

When he was questioned he took two coins out of his pocket, one about the size of a half penny and the other like a half crown. Then he said:

"I saw Conchita put out her tongue. It was clean and spotless. She did not take it in again at all. Suddenly there appeared a 'white substance' on her tongue, the size of this little coin. Then this 'thing' began to grow in size. It became as big as this larger coin. Then it thickened until it looked like a piece of bread.

As soon as Conchita put out her tongue, I shone the flashlight on her mouth and I followed the scene from very near. After about two or three minutes Conchita withdrew her tongue again."

Another witness told us, "On seeing the miracle I experienced such an amazing, wonderful joy that I wouldn't change it for millions of dollars; and this joy came to me not because I had seen 'something white' on Conchita's tongue, but because I felt that I was in the presence of the living God." A third said, "If you let a drop of oil fall on to blotting paper it will spread. Well, I saw the 'thing' spread and spread and spread!" A fourth said, "I would compare it to a flake of snow. Little at first, I saw it grow larger, wider and thicker."

In our files we have other evidence, as well as films, photographs and written testimony on the miracle of the Host.

It is for the theologians to explain for us "the Host," the "Thing," the "Forma."

To facilitate their obviously difficult task, we can add to all this what Conchita has said and repeated again and again, "The Host given to me by the Angel was 'igual,' that is, the same as other Hosts. It was the same as those the Angel gives us at other times, the same as those we receive in church when we go to Holy Communion."

XXI

GARABANDAL AND THE HOLY EUCHARIST

The Holy Eucharist is, without a shadow of a doubt, one of the most important preoccupations in the mind of Our Lady of Mount Carmel at Garabandal.

In the message she asked for frequent visits to her Son, present in the Sacred Host. We have already told of the "Sign of Signs" of July 18th, 1962, which had been foretold on the 3rd of that month.

Again, if the Angel, both before and after this famous miracle for Conchita, often came to place an invisible Host on the tongues of the four girls, could it be because they were deprived of It, since the parish priest lived so far away, coming to offer Mass at Garabandal only on Sundays and for the few funerals in the village?

Is it not clear enough by now that Our Lady wishes to remind us by the children's frequent, miraculous communions that the "centre," the "nucleus," the "spring," the "fountain" of all spiritual life is most certainly the Eucharist; visited, and above all, actually received?

❋ ❋ ❋

Obviously a number of the priests visiting Garabandal doubted the reality of these "invisible" communions, from the very beginning.

Let us listen to the priests interrogating the children: "The Angel cannot give you Holy Communion. Where would he get the Hosts?"

— From a tabernacle, of course, since an angel cannot consecrate.

— Well, then which is the greatest, the angel or the priest?

— The priest has more power than the angel, for only he can say Mass (only he can consecrate Hosts).

XXII

GARABANDAL AND THE PRIESTHOOD

Together with a devotion to the Eucharist, Garabandal teaches a great devotion for the priesthood. Our Lady teaches the girls to pray often for priests. Loli said one day, "I often pray for them, especially for those who wish that they were not priests, so that they may at least go on saying Mass."

They have the greatest reverence and affection for all members of the clergy, so much so that they are often reproached for "giving a warmer welcome to priests than to lay people."

In spite of the imprudence and upsetting hostility of certain priests, the children have never been heard to utter the least criticism of them or to show them the least discourtesy. They even make a special point of praying for them, and preferably for those who cause the children to suffer for reasons unknown to them.

To everyone expressing surprise at this, Loli replies, "When in the presence of an angel and of a priest, I would greet the priest first and it is to the priest that I would bow first of all."

That does not prevent them from being nice little Spanish girls, with a liveliness that reminds us of certain answers given by their illustrious compatriot, St. Theresa of Avila!

One theologian, a young priest, and a fine one at that, asked Conchita:

— If you think that a priest has more power than an angel, which do you prefer to see, the angel or me?

— Oh, the angel of course! He is much better looking than you!

Another cleric, deciding to put the little girls through one of these psychological "tests" so fashionable today, asked Conchita this strange question:

41

The church of Garabandal, in June 1965.

— If your parish priest were neither a man nor a woman but an animal, what kind of animal would you like him to be?
— A lamb.
— Why?
— Because he would be like Jesus who sacrificed Himself for us.

XXIII

THE VISION OF THE PUNISHMENT

The angel's message tells us of a punishment which Our Lady fears may come upon the world. What could this punishment be? Here is what we know about it.

Pepe Diez, witness of the "miracle of the Host," is also one

Jacinta, her mother, two of her brothers and their herd of goats,
in 1963.

of the chief, but not the only, witness of the following events
which happened not far from his house about one month before
the miracle of the Host.

One night in June, 1962, Loli and Jacinta went off together
as usual towards The Pines.

They signaled to the villagers who were with them to let them
go on alone. Pepe Diez then remained with the crowd at the
foot of the hill.

Suddenly cries of terror and shouts of horror pierced the air.
The two little girls were coming down the hill, trying to ward off
some terrible danger by holding out their hands in front of them.

Conchita, who was ill, was not with them, but the next day she
was there with her companions.

The same scene began again for the three little girls. Their
cries were even more sorrowful and witnesses were even able to
make out the words, "Oh! Let the little children die before it happens!—Let people have time to go to confession before hand!"

A Franciscan priest who was preaching a novena in preparation for the Feast of Corpus Christi was among those present and Pepe Diez tells us that he began to lead the people in prayer. As soon as the prayers began the cries diminished and the little girls appeared to be less pained. As soon as the prayers stopped their cries began again even more loudly than before.

The whole village was so deeply impressed by these two raptures that, with a few exceptions (five, we are told), all the inhabitants of Garabandal went to confession and communion on this Feast of Corpus Christi in 1962.

Keep in mind that this took place about one month before the "miracle of the Host" described above. Do not let us forget it, for in our opinion it also lends authenticity to these two visions of horror.

Will this terrible punishment which Our Lady fears for the world take place before or after the great future Miracle? Is it inevitable?

Conchita has written on a loose sheet of paper, carefully preserved by the owner, "This Miracle to come will take place *before* the punishment, and if the world changes its ways the latter will not occur."

What a source of hope these lines would be for us if we had not also learned that in December of 1963, Loli in a "locution" (interior words without any vision) heard Our Lady complain, "Alas, the world is getting worse."

XXIV

THE SPIRITUAL PROGRESS OF THE VISIONARIES

The continued progress in the spiritual life of these children is a sure guarantee of the authenticity of the apparitions.

Have they become perfect? No, of course not. Sanctity is at the end of a long road which is traveled stage by stage and with many a detour. Let us note only that the children are making rapid strides along the path of virtue, with a really amazing generosity and wonderful fidelity to the graces they have received.

Yet they remain children who work and who play readily, and who have to fight against their faults from time to time. If they give in to the faults they mend their ways more speedily and with more energy than do other people.

They are, we must remember, only fourteen years of age and we must not expect them to have the mentality of women matured by their sufferings and by their years. And yet sometimes we wonder whether their wisdom and generosity would not surpass the maturity of many people.

XXV

YOU SHALL NOT BE HAPPY IN THIS WORLD

Since January 28th, 1963 (the liturgical Feast of St. Sebastian, Patron Saint of the village) Our Lady's visits to the children have become less frequent. Sometimes they have only heard and not seen her, which proves that the "apparitions" have given place to what mystical theology calls "inner locutions."

But these mysterious conversations generally remain a secret between the girls and their confessor.

An important public apparition was that of December 8th, 1963.

On the morning of the Feast of the Immaculate Conception, at 5:30 a.m. while it was still dark and cold, Conchita (whose feast day it is) was irresistibly moved by a mysterious interior call, and was found in rapture at the closed door of the church. Only her mother had been able to follow her.

The rapture lasted for about ten minutes. When she came out of it she was questioned.

— Our Lady congratulated me on the occasion of my feast day. Rather taken aback because she had spoken first, I could only congratulate her in my heart. She added: 'although you will not be happy on earth, you will be happy in heaven.' Then she revealed some future events to me.

— What are they?

— I may not reveal them.

Later on a priest asked her:

— Can't you reveal this secret in the confessional?

— Our Lady did not tell me to, but I'll ask her another time.

XXVI

PROPHECY CONCERNING SAINT MICHAEL'S RETURN

Chapter XXVII will give the reader an insight on what the life in the village was between the apparition of December 8, 1963 and what follows. During this period, Conchita and Loli—perhaps, also Jacinta—had a few inner locutions. As we have insufficient knowledge on the matter, we cannot assume the responsibility of saying this is definitely so. From all evidence, the entire year 1964 was, for the visionaries, a period of secret meditation and personal recollection.

For the mountaineers and for the entire world, alerted by the spread of the Message, these twelve months were a time for reflection and awareness of each one's responsibilities.

If we dare use a familiar language, we would say that during a year, Heaven allowed earth to catch its breath. Earth responded in its own way. Then Heaven again stretched a helping hand. This was on December 8, 1964, exactly one year later.

Indeed, in a letter on January 12, 1965, Conchita writes to us:

"I very much like your brochure, 'The Mountain Star.'"

Because Conchita realized the objectivity of the brochure whose smallest detail was checked and rechecked, these few words will always be a great source of encouragement to us.

In the same letter, Conchita said:

"On the Feast of the Immaculate Conception, December 8, 1964, the Virgin wished me a happy feast, the feast of my baptismal name. (The name Conchita is indeed a diminutive of Mary of the Immaculate Conception.) She told me that on the following June 18, I would see St. Michael the Archangel. And on January 1st, 1965, I saw the Virgin at The Pines."

Her letter of January 24, 1965, confirmed this:

"I do not recall if, in my last letter, I told you that on June 18th, I would see St. Michael the Archangel. This is what the Virgin told me in a 'locution' on my feast day, the Feast of the Immaculate Conception."

        ❋   ❋   ❋

As Conchita told us, she indeed saw the Virgin at The Pines. We learned from a very good source that on January 1st, 1965, she had been seen by two young village shepherds, Joaquina, 12, and Urbano, 9, who were coming down the mountain with their sheep. According to further "cross-examination," this ecstasy must have lasted about two hours. According to testimonies, well deserving of belief, and which we shall later on refer to, the Virgin of Carmel spoke at very, very great length. Today, we shall limit ourselves to what Conchita wrote on February 2nd, 1965.

"The Virgin seemed to be the same age as the first time I saw her (July 2nd, 1961), the same age as in the past years, about 18 years old.

"She wore her white gown and her sky-blue cloak.

"A tremendous light, which does not hurt the eyes, radiated from her body and enveloped her completely.

"I do not know if (except the one on June 18) the apparitions will resume, either for me or for the four of us.

"The Virgin will give a new Message, because she said, the other one (October 18, 1961) was not heeded. The Virgin will therefore give her last Message.

"The Virgin does not allow me to tell the nature of the

47

Miracle, although I know it and I also know its date which I can announce only 8 days before.

"I cannot speak about the nature of the Punishment that the Virgin revealed to me, and also to Loli and Jacinta, except this: it will be a result of the *direct intervention of God* which is more dreadful than anything we can imagine. It would be less terrible for little children to die a natural death than to die of this Punishment. All Catholics should confess before the Punishment; the others should repent of their sins.

"THIS PUNISHMENT—IF IT COMES—AND I DO BE-LIEVE IT WILL COME—WILL TAKE PLACE AFTER THE MIRACLE."

N.B.—By "direct intervention of God" Conchita means that everyone will see that the Punishment is sent by God himself. It will not be caused, as in the case of wars or revolutions, by men's direct action; ambition, pride, hardness of heart, which usually cause our misfortunes.

❂   ❂   ❂

We are giving two excerpts from letters written after January 1st, 1965, to a prominent old religious person from Spain whose health was much impaired:

"Take good care of yourself," says Conchita, "you must live for the Miracle."

And Maria Dolores, relying on Conchita's statement, wrote to the same religious:

"I'd very much like to give you the Message which is soon going to be revealed by St. Michael. But be patient, because the Virgin knows what she is doing and we must wait for it, you and I."

XXVII

THE VILLAGE PRIOR TO ST. MICHAEL'S VISIT

For us, Garabandal is a whole unit which will be judged according to the total phenomena, according to the reactions and

48

the conduct of the visionaries, the testimony of official witnesses, the accomplishments of authentic prophecies, the miracles to come, etc.

Many details will momentarily or even permanently elude the investigators. The essential, from a scientific point of view, remains the general reconstruction of events. And to be adequate, it must include all important facts. Therefore, we feel that if a fundamental fact is missing from the structure, Garabandal as a whole could collapse.

If, for example, the apparition of St. Michael did not occur on June 18, 1965, as Conchita had announced, for more than six months previously, all the preceding "facts" would have become questionable.

＊　＊　＊

Such being our conviction, we could not afford to miss the rendezvous. All we had to do was to secure the necessary canonical authorization and we were on our way.

We were not going to keep to our regular itinerary in order to greet some friends in San Sebastian City. We had to arrive in Santander on Friday evening to meet His Excellency Bishop Beitia early the next morning.

The whole Saturday in Santander was spent in attempting to overcome the incredible barriers erected by the Episcopal Curia between the Bishop and ourselves. Without a little "miracle" of St. Michael, we would never have been able to meet His Excellency. We finally had the good fortune of finding ourselves, by chance, at the foot of the main stairs of the Bishop's palace, just as His Excellency was leaving for his episcopal rounds.

His Excellency, Bishop Beitia, appeared radiant, cordial and paternal. Without the slightest hesitation, with unusual marks of paternal affection, in the presence of three witnesses, he permitted us to go to Garabandal, blessed our mission, and defined its spirit and method: "Yes, go, act prudently as the subject demands and do not force Divine Grace."

These words were the echo of those he pronounced during our important conversation in September 1963.

Because a letter which Conchita had mailed from Puentenansa on the 9th of June (see Chapter XXXI) had not reached us, since we left the middle of France on the 10th of June, our arrival in the village became an embarrassment, both for Conchita and for us. We had arrived, and she had wished we were not there. She had written to us not to come. On the other hand, we had not let her know we were coming, because we were unaware that we were not wanted. It resulted in a painful misunderstanding for all of us. In addition, Conchita, who thought that we had read her letter, did not speak to us at all. She seemed to be deliberately avoiding us.

❋ ❋ ❋

We arrived at Garabandal Sunday, June 13, at 4 p.m.

As soon as the visionaries saw our car making its last turn in the mountain, they withdrew. When we passed by them under the porch where their little companions were dancing, they forgot to greet us. Our contact with Aniceta (mother of Conchita) and her sister Maximina, always so courteous, was more surprising still. The people from Madrid and America had rented all available rooms and we had no other alternative than to retire and cook in our car. We would have considered this a trifle if the faces of the people we talked to had not remained blank; if we had not felt that they had closed their hearts to us.

Therefore, we roamed the village, like strangers for whom there is no room in the inn.

❋ ❋ ❋

There were two possible alternatives: leave Garabandal immediately—and we thought of it—or take advantage of this mortifying setback. We felt the latter was by far the better way.

It was better to forget our French sensitivity, and to withdraw from all human affection in Garabandal, and pursue our investigations with an attitude which would assuredly, not "force Divine Grace." We would have to watch our mood and frame of mind in order not to be influenced against the events which would occur. We could have blinded ourselves to the realities because of our personal deceptions.

50

Now that it is all over, we believe that God's Providence watched over us in Santander, on Saturday and in Garabandal, on Sunday. Everyone shielded us effectively against anything that would have prevented rational thinking in the fulfillment of the task which awaited us on the occasion of June 18. The reader may be assured of it.

✿   ✿   ✿

Let us go back in our story.

What happened in Garabandal and around the village during the past twenty-one months?

First of all, the village had undergone a slight change. Some land and houses, some barns also had been bought by Spaniards from outside. Bricklayers bustled about and the construction of two new houses was half completed. Here and there, small living quarters had been provided for visitors. Often they were nothing more than an old whitewashed stable. But the cleanliness of the places made you overlook the donkey, the goat or the cow that had given up their abode, except for the evenings when the animals, in keeping with their old memories, came to poke their heads into the half-open doors to greet the new occupants.

The inside of the Church had been completely redecorated, including the gilding, so much in favor throughout Spain, thanks to American generosity, as they said. Some statues had been removed and they did not hesitate to relegate St. Michael's to the most obscure corner behind the baptismal font. Yes, even the statue of the archangel of the apparitions, the archangel who was to return, had not found favor in the eyes of modern iconoclasts.

Of course, the statue did not resemble the vision seen by Conchita and her three companions. But how is it that these humble people, so admirable in 1962, had not as yet realized that such offhand manner toward the messenger of Our Lady of Carmel was probably the cause of the moral and intellectual ordeal whose entire scope we would be able to measure.

Undoubtedly, psychological reality had been a sequel to material changes in the village.

Peace of heart was only apparent. Only the old ladies' wrinkled,

51

Corpus Christi at Garabandal on June 17th, 1965 (eve of the apparition).
In front: Ceferino, Father Laffineur and Pepe Diez.

faded faces had retained their smile and the loving spark in
their eyes. Some families were divided, through jealousy. The
apparitions had no longer a unanimous response.

Hesitant souls were impatient for the famous Miracle, thinking it required too long a wait. These people who, during two
years, had been laden with favors; these men and women who
had tirelessly followed the four visionaries in ecstasy; these very
people with the exception of their silent elders—and of a certain
number of steadfast souls—were unable to recall what they had
seen, heard and touched. They were unable to relate their certainties with past events. These people once more greedy—even
insatiable—for miraculous realities suffered from unconscious
spiritual blindness which was once more to astonish the visitor.

If some of their peers, unable to judge them, would raise the question, "what about the apparitions?" they would answer shamelessly, "Well, we don't know what to say."

But one thing still baffled these men and women and forced them to see the light; i.e. the objects kissed by Our Lady during the ecstasies.

We recall that at the beginning of the apparitions Our Lady asked the children to present to her lips some pebbles from the road. Later on, she asked for medals, rosaries, crucifixes, devotional pictures, wedding rings, etc.

Each home in Garabandal owns one or several of these treasures. If any *villager* was asked to part with one of these treasures and to offer it as a souvenir to the visitors, you may rest assured that the so-called unbelievers of Garabandal will immediately change the subject.

✿ ✿ ✿

What was the psychological aspect of the village on the eve of June 18, the day for St. Michael's return as prophesied by Conchita? There were dissensions, discussions, criticisms, hesitatations, follies, impertinent remarks toward the celestial visitor, masking an unjustified dependence upon a secret hope of seeing the famous apparition again. In other words, the people were wondering if something would happen at the village because nothing had happened during the past two years.

Reluctantly we state these things because we dearly love these mountaineers whose hearts are as good as gold. Many were of the same mind as Maria, Jacinta's mother, who in September 1963, made a confession, which was most surprising, to say the least, "For me, when I see an ecstasy, I believe. When it is over, I no longer believe. But I would believe forever if the Miracle happened."

Her husband, Simon, smiled as he listened. Jacinta, who was present, seemed unhappy and remote. We answered, "Maria, true ecstasies are miracles in themselves. Whoever does not remember them to retain faith in Garabandal will no more believe in the Miracle to come than in the Miracle of the Host."

In short, there were many "Marias" in Garabandal before June 18th. There are still some today.

53

This is so true that we feel compelled to share with our readers a conversation reported by a Spanish lawyer, a friend of ours, who served as an interpreter during our first visit to the village.

As he was walking down the mountain to Cosio, all alone, he met at the turn of the dirt road a middle-aged woman who was climbing the hill with her donkey. Both of them stopped a while under the hot sun, seeking in vain a little shady spot and chatted while mopping their brows.

— How is everything?

— It's warm, sir.

— Of course, but I mean the apparitions.

— Ah!

— Yes, what do they say about them in Garabandal?

— Oh, nothing any more.

— What do you mean, "nothing." I was present at some of the ecstasies. What about you?

— Oh, the ecstasies. . . . At the beginning, they were true, but now . . .

— True in the beginning, and false, now?

— Yes, at the beginning, they were true, I'll prove it to you.

— I am listening, madam.

— It's like this. One evening Loli was in ecstasy in Ceferino's café. There was a crowd around the table. On it, I saw medals, rosaries, holy cards, crucifixes and wedding rings. The child was taking in turn one or the other of these objects for Our Lady to kiss. I hurried home and returned with my husband's wedding ring which I slipped onto the table. Fifteen minutes later, Loli took it, presented it to the apparition, crossed the room and put it on the finger of my husband who stood alone in a corner. He protested loudly that the child was making an error. Of course, he didn't know what I had done. I went to him and explained everything. He cried with joy. That day, sir, it was a true ecstasy. The Virgin had really appeared to Loli. Why doesn't she appear again?

XXVIII

ST. MICHAEL RETURNS

On Sunday, June 13th, Conchita caught cold. The following day, she was confined to her bed with a pulse of 100 and a fever of 101° F. At her side lay a towel all stained from a nose bleed. From time to time, she was mopping her forehead. This condition lasted three days, bringing great discomfort and making her ache all over. During these three days, some said: "Of course, she is cleverly preparing next Friday's fiasco." Others, concerned, but still hopeful, asked themselves: "Will she be up for the rendez-vous with the angel?" The question was most relevant, as it was a known fact that the doctor had recommended that Conchita should stay indoors for six more days after she had gotten rid of her cold.

Thursday was the Feast of Corpus Christi, a Holy Day of Obli-gation in Spain. The whole village was either gathered in church or singing hymns behind the priest carrying the Blessed Sacra-ment in solemn procession. Aniceta had erected a triumphal arch, whose streamer, in the colors of the Spanish flag, carried the words: "Hail, Christ the King." As for Conchita, she was in bed, praying.

＊　＊　＊

What was going to happen the next day?

The next day, Conchita arose around eleven o'clock, put on a heavy red woollen sweater and . . . appeared on the door step.

During the previous night, numerous foreign cars had arrived in the village. There were two hundred Frenchmen, one hundred Spaniards from various cities of the peninsula, ten Americans, six Englishmen, four Italians and some representing other Euro-pean or American countries. In the crowd were about ten priests in their vestments, and undoubtedly, a few in laymen's clothes.

What was the mood of this crowd? On the whole, it behaved in a remarkable, pious, modest and penitent manner. Most of those present had received Holy Communion at one of the three masses celebrated that morning. Crowded against Conchita's house or scattered in front of it around the fountain or on the grass, people were praying, singing hymns or expressing themselves in their own language in a brotherly fashion.

In our interior and almost surly isolation, we took great care in keeping our distance, observing and discovering at times someone who was there for no other purpose than to watch the goings-on in order to report and to use them for the cause he represented or served. There were emissaries of the commission of Santander, naturally; also members of some foreign police forces as well as one or another representative of the ridiculous ex-Father Collin.

At twilight, some Spanish boys and girls appeared on the scene and their free and easy manner proved that the devil also wanted to be present at the spectacle.

❊   ❊   ❊

From the very start we warned the French people whom we knew: "It is quite simple. You have good eyesight and you are intelligent. Watch Conchita and if you look closely, you will certainly be able to judge her."

Humble, her eyes often cast down, gracious, friendly, concealing her extreme fatigue, tireless, Conchita allowed herself to be "mobbed" even by the most tactless women. She smiled, autographed holy cards, allowed herself to be photographed. She answered every question, promised to pray for all intentions recommended, consoled the most afflicted and kissed the children.

This went on until dusk and we don't know if she even had time to eat anything other than a piece of bread. Shivering, she went home but let no one in; she opened the kitchen window, and, through its bars, continued to place herself at the disposal of the crowd.

At 11 p.m.—and at this point we realized that for the past twelve hours Conchita had literally been the "toy" of the crowd—we were alone, leaning against the stable door near Aniceta's

56

Conchita makes the Sign of the Cross before presenting her crucifix to the Angel, June 18th, 1965.

house. Personally, we didn't need the prophecy of December 8, 1964 and its fulfillment on June 18, 1965 to strengthen our faith in events at Garabandal, but we wished with all our heart that the ecstasy would be visible to all present and be absolutely convincing. Knowing absolutely nothing beforehand, having never asked any question of Conchita concerning the nature of the apparition, having not spoken to her the whole day, we were hoping for an ecstatic march across the village which would enable one and all to see it, to follow it leisurely and to judge it.

* * *

One of us was completely absorbed in solitary reflections when sudden silence made him realize that the crowd had disappeared and we were all alone. Then, he went to the kitchen window

June 18th, 1965, Conchita presents her crucifix to St. Michael before receiving the Message, that she will announce the next day.

where a few women still remained: "My Dear, what should we do now?"—"Go also to the *cuadro*" (the exact spot of St. Michael's apparition on June 18, 1961).

Everyone had already passed by the last houses of the village and was climbing that small and dreadful lane leading to The Pines. The entire village and the late visitors from Santander and the valley had joined the three hundred and fifty strangers who had arrived during the day. This meant about seven hundred people packed like sardines in the ravine or standing in the embanked road. Almost everyone was praying in a loud voice, alternating between French and Spanish.

The night of June 18 was most extraordinary, unusually bright, with countless stars twinkling more than ever. There was no moon, at least for the spectators.

Suddenly, everyone looked up, a new star, brighter than the others, appeared from the northwest; it traced a large circle and returned to its point of origin.

Two minutes later, another splendid star, smaller than the first one, appeared directly above Conchita's house, moved slowly in the sky and disappeared suddenly above The Pines.

Everyone was commenting on these unusual phenomena, when Conchita appeared to us, in the light of the stars and the torches, shielded by a squad of civilian guards and Spanish police. Contrary to our expectation, and our prayerful wish, we must confess, she was not in ecstasy. She was walking so fast that her guards were breathless.

When she reached us, a friend of ours told us, "I took her by the arm in place of her eldest brother, the devoted Serafin. There were forty yards to go and we would be at the right spot. At this point Conchita freed herself, took a few steps alone, looked at the ground, lifted up her head and fell in ecstasy, her knees abruptly hitting the sharp stones."

✻ ✻ ✻

Even today after six months of deep thinking on the subject, this remains a mystery to our friend. Although neither Conchita nor our friend had moved an iota, they found themselves near each other; Conchita kneeling, he standing.

The ecstasy resembled those we had previously heard of in the village, in the kitchen or in the girl's bedroom: Signs of the Cross made with indescribable piety and majesty, a countenance resplendent with interior light, pupils extremely dilated, an angelic smile and most *solemn gestures*, murmurs of half-open lips and silences of a listening soul, a tear falling slowly on the temple and leaving its crystal mark.

Her earlobes were normal, her forehead cool, without perspiration. Her hair retained its usual flexible texture. In spite of the flashes that should have blinded her forever, her eyes never blinked. Not for a moment did her eyelids vibrate and when our friend attempted to check on Conchita's weight, his efforts were useless, as she seemingly weighed two thousand pounds. On the other hand, a policeman—with similar physical strength—also attempted to lift Conchita and succeeded. We realized then that her feet did not touch the ground; her legs, absolutely stiff, kept the same angle as when she was kneeling. Through carelessness, pushed by the crowd, someone crushed her foot. Conchita had no reaction whatsoever. All of a sudden, she slowly raised her right arm and with incredible joy presented her crucifix to the Archangel. When he touched it, without kissing it, Conchita, without hesitation and with dumbfounding assurance, applied it to the lips of Rev. Father Pel, who stood at our friend's left. Then, changing hands twice, Conchita presented the crucifix to Mr. Mazure and Mr. Piqué who were at our friend's right, but behind her.

Far from expecting such a favor, none of the three men had moved his feet. Conchita did not move from her position, she simply stretched her arm. When, on the following day, in the company of Doctor Ortiz and a Scotsman, we tried to re-enact the scene on the spot, it became evident that, naturally speaking, it was impossible.

TRANSLATOR'S NOTE: Conchita, in reaching back over her shoulder to allow the two men to kiss the crucifix, had moved her arm over her shoulder in such a way that would defy all natural laws, due both to the angle at which her arm moved, and the distance between her and the men.

        *   *   *

Here is another astonishing fact: As stated above, at the beginning of the ecstasy, Conchita fell on her knees a few feet from our friend. However, though neither one made the slightest move, they felt themselves to be drawn to one another, as though they were side by side. Before the ecstasy began, Conchita did not know that Fr. Pel, Mr. Mazure, and Mr. Piqué would be there. They had arrived two or three minutes after the ecstasy had begun. Therefore, Conchita, in her normal state, was totally unaware of the presence of these three men. However, in her normal state, she knew perfectly well that our friend was there, because he was the one who had supported her left arm until they had reached the *Cuadro*.

We ask the adversaries of Garabandal to explain how it is that these three newcomers were the only ones to kiss the crucifix touched by St. Michael while our friend, who stood between them, separating Rev. Father Pel from the two other gentlemen, had to be satisfied with seeing the crucifix passing in front of him?

Things would not have happened this way if Conchita had not been in another world.

* * *

Shortly after, Conchita, already in a state of ecstasy, stood up, her eyes fixed on the vision.

At this point, we were thrilled! Our prayer was answered! Conchita would go up to The Pines! This would provide the opportunity for everybody—and not only for those whose close circle had nearly smothered her—to see her, to follow her, to touch her; in other words, to possess her.

Alas, she only took a few steps, just enough to reach the point of departure of the ecstasy and fell again abruptly on her knees

The crucific has been touched by St. Michael, Conchita then gives it to the Frenchmen, on June 18th, 1965.

The pilgrims at the *cuadro*, praying, on the day after
June 18th, 1965.

on the stones. There followed two more minutes of celestial col-
loquy and she arose very relaxed and smiling; all was over. No,
not all. Alert as ever, she shielded her eyes with her hands; the
flashes were blinding her.

*　*　*

This is what we saw, with our own eyes, on June 18, at the
Cuadro. Starting around 11:40 p.m., the apparition, which involved two motions, lasted 12 or 13 minutes in all.

What did we hear? The joy of those who were able to see the
ecstasy in this impossible ravine. . . . The disappointment of
others and dissatisfaction of a few. "It is unbelievable," they said,
"these people are savages. They nearly crushed us. Ah if we had
known!"

Then little by little, deceptions vanished and peace and calm
again reigned. People were informed that St. Michael had indeed

given the Message of the Virgin and that Conchita would make it public the next day, after the community Mass. Everyone went home.

As for the stars; they remained in their marvelous sky.

XXIX

THE LAST MESSAGE

On the morning of June 19th, Conchita's house was again invaded. As we noted in 1962, the ecstasy of the previous day had restored her vigor and health and added beauty and modesty to her countenance. Untiringly she said good-bye to everybody, autographed holy cards and photos, kissed tenderly and respectfully all objects presented to her. Then, without breakfast, we went to the church where everybody again received Holy Communion. Finally around 1 p.m., on the doorstep of the little house, someone read the text, in Spanish and in French, of the Message Conchita had given in her own handwriting.

The Message

"The Message that the Holy Virgin has given to the world through the intercession of St. Michael.

The Angel said: Because my Message of the 18th of October, 1961 has not been complied with and little has been done to make it known to the world, I tell you that this is the last one.

Before (on October 18, 1961) the Chalice was filling, now it is overflowing. (The Chalice of Divine Wrath.)

Many priests are on the road of perdition and they take many souls with them.

To the Eucharist, there is given less and less importance.

We must make every effort to avoid Divine Wrath which is pressing on us.

If you ask Him for His forgiveness with a sincere soul, He (God) will forgive you.

It is I, your Mother, who through the intercession and mediation of St. Michael, want to say that you must amend. You are already in the last warnings.

I love you very much and do not want your condemnation.

Pray to us sincerely and We shall give it to you (what you ask us) (We: God and Our Lady.)

You must sacrifice yourselves more.

Meditate on the Passion of Jesus."

(Signed) Conchita Gonzalez
June 18, 1965

✿　✿　✿

Three little notations from Conchita herself:

The priests are, to varying degrees, the fathers of souls. A greater number of priests, by following those referred to in the Message, are in danger of perdition.

The message is explicit; it does not refer to all priests, nor to a few, but to many.

St. Michael intercedes for us to God and Our Lady. Moreover, he is their intermediary to speak to us, to 'protect and to help us in every way. It was not sufficiently pointed out that the Blessed Virgin requested that a chapel be built in Garabandal, not in her honor, but in honor of St. Michael the Archangel.

✿　✿　✿

Of course, Conchita who lives in her small village, is personally unaware of the present doctrinal errors concerning the Eucharist, the hurriedly made thanksgivings, the tabernacles being removed from the main altars, the decrease in Benedictions of the Blessed Sacrament, in day and night adorations, in Forty Hours, in public processions, etc. . . .

But, what she immediately learned was the reaction of the priests of the "Puentenansa area" which includes Garabandal. The first day, they said, "It concerns us." The next day, their reaction was stronger: "It concerns all the priests." We were told that on the third and fourth day, they went to protest at the Bishop's residence in Santander.

But the "revolution" that the message concerning "many

64

priests" is bound to cause is of less importance to us than our conversation in Conchita's kitchen with her brother Serafin and two mountaineers.

On the lips, and in the hearts and souls of these three laymen, there was nothing but humility and kindness toward the clergy to whom Our Lady of Carmel was alluding. They remarked, "It is the father who educates his family. Our priests are our fathers. If some have defects or commit certain faults, it is because they are human too. May they set the example and we shall be better Christians."

❀ ❀ ❀

In order to calm their fears aroused by this message to the clergy, we answered:

> "At the beginning of Mass, the priest says first and publicly: 'Brethren, I confess to you my sins.' And the faithful answer: 'Father, we confess to you our own.' The conclusion is: we are all sinners. Moreover, the priests teach us the parable of the Pharisee and the publican. We all know that only the publican was forgiven. Therefore, all is simple and easy; let each one according to his public confession at the beginning of Mass repeat the humble prayer of the publican, the repentant sinner of the Gospel.
>
> We fail to understand how someone could take offense at this message rather than lovingly thanking Our Heavenly Mother."

As we have already noted, there were some black sheep in Garabandal amidst so many exemplary Christians; i.e., some emissaries of the ex-Father Collin.

In this respect, everyone should know that Garabandal and its Message has nothing in common with the so-called revelations of the individual, who, defying ridicule, calls himself "Clement XV." This unfortunate ex-priest, reduced to the lay state and under an interdict, uses every possible means to take over Garabandal. He went so far as to have our leaflet reprinted in Canada, adding to our signature the name and address of his partisans of Edmonton. This scandalous conduct definitely passes judgment on the man. Is it madness? Satanism?

There were other opponents to the Catholic hierarchy, some

of them candidates for the papacy or other fancied ecclesiastical dignities. Baptized either in or outside the Church, they will take advantage of the Message to attack our clergy.

May we simply ask them—even if they are priests—to "search their own souls" and realize what became of them since they left us or declared war against us.

Among children of the same family, among parents and children, the only conceivable and valid attitude toward the Message is the one expressed briefly in Conchita's kitchen, a little bluntly, but truthfully.

XXX

THE WARNING

Having received all necessary ecclesiastical permissions, with some time on his hands, and less pressed than others, our priest-friend remained three days in the village and had no other contact with Conchita other than to assure her that he was still there. He stayed discreetly in the background in favor of the June 18th visitors, to provide more opportunities to new friends of Garabandal, particularly Father Luna of Zaragossa and the famous Italian artist, Carlo Campanini, who were the most active.

This provided him with a most beautiful opportunity to pursue his investigation elsewhere. With our friend Pepe Diez, for example, who confirmed his previous historic statement concerning the Miracle of the Host.

What a loyal, energetic and intelligent witness, that one! As we asked him if he had appeared before the Commission of Santander, he answered, "Never." Because we wondered about this strange attitude and incredulity on the part of the same Commission, he concluded the conversation in the manner of a self-confident swordsman, "Because the truth does not suit them." We were to learn more astonishing things yet.

It was now the fourth anniversary of the apparitions. Yes, everything had started four years ago, on June 18, 1961. The Commission had already published three notices, and the last one, on October 1962, affirmed that the events were of a natural order. And yet, during these years, it never had the time to summon either the visionaries, their families or even the parish priest. It is inconceivable for the French people and those who know the history of Lourdes, Fatima or Beauraing. Yes, inconceivable, but alas, true, very true.

The Commission satisfied itself by sending emissaries and some of them are well known to us. We are well aware of the harm they did in this small village, left to itself in the midst of events far beyond them. They named a certain individual and we had no other alternative than to realize that his extensive activities in Garabandal were nothing less than those of a spy or a traitor. Did this show lack of intelligence or character, vanity, good faith, bad faith, intrigue, unscrupulous ambition? We believe there is a mixture of all of these. And yet, how the village trusted him until it discovered that he was two-faced!

The ecstasy of the preceding Friday had become a determining factor for the people of the village. Pepe Diez, the bricklayer, the workman who always mingled with the little people, and who kept his ear open always, noted: "Now, that it has happened, everyone believes again."

                  ❊   ❊   ❊

The three days spent a little distance from Conchita were by no means a loss of time for our friend since they provided him with the opportunity to review his investigation notes.

Moreover, he had a long conversation with the parents of Mari Cruz; Escolastico, her father, Pilar, her mother. He learned from the eldest of the village that Escolastico's father and mother had lived a good Christian life. His religious background was good, they said, and they failed to understand why he seldom practices his religion. As to Pilar, they added, while pursing their lips, she is a stranger to us, she comes from Pas, she is a "Pasiega." This origin is given as an explanation for many things apparently incomprehensible about the family.

67

An extraordinary thing happened which we relate only because we are dealing with the apparitions. One night, Julia, the mother of Loli, was suddenly at death's door. Ceferino, her husband, all upset, came to knock at our priest-friend's door. After the priest administered the Last Rites, she nearly died in his arms.

At this supreme moment, when truth appears in all its clarity, he had witnessed the extraordinary piety and heroism of this peasant woman. In the presence of her husband, of Loli, of Maria, Jacinta's mother, and another neighbor woman, while no one could actually realize what was taking place and why she was dying, Julia—who during the previous days had spontaneously made the sacrifice of her life—as a spouse and mother of a large family—renewed it at this time for the "acknowledgement" of the apparitions.

Never in his forty years of priestly life had our priest-friend wtinessed a similar sacrifice of someone, a few hours before full of life, fulfilling in Spanish style, the spiritual mediation which had became necessary because of the blindness or the lack of intellectual steadfastness of some.

Humble and smiling Julia, patient and habitually silent, who so often welcomed in your home the Virgin coming down from Heaven, you will always remain for us the heroic witness of the absolute authenticity of the apparitions of Garabandal.

✿   ✿   ✿

We could then go back to Aniceta and spend a long time with her in her little kitchen, so much so that we found her completely relaxed and smiling.

— Well, Aniceta, the six and a half months of anxiety are over?

— It's not too soon.

— Is the prophecy of December 8, 1964, well realized?

— Yes, finally.

— Are you now at peace?

— Yes, thank God.

Now it is Aniceta's turn to ask questions:

— Did you doubt of the coming of the Angel?

68

— No, not for a minute.

— Why?

— Because, since 1962, we are definitely sure of Garabandal.

— And if nothing had happened?

— Jacinta told us a long time ago: "Conchita never lies."

— Yes, but the Miracle is yet to come.

— So what?

— I can't believe it, it's beyond me.

— Aniceta, don't start your drama all over again. Everything is linked in the events of Garabandal. The past guarantees the future.

— May God hear you.

— Aniceta, it's all understood, the Virgin said so and she, above all, never lies.

* * *

At this point of the conversation, Conchita, alert and happy, invited us up to her room: "I have presents for you, take them."

It was a copy, in her own handwriting, of the Message which we didn't know thoroughly as yet, and another document, also in her own handwriting, concerning the Warning.

We were going to question her on the latter but she didn't give us a chance. She added, "The Virgin told me many, many things for a long time. But She didn't tell me to reveal or not to reveal them. Often I don't know what to do, I don't know what to reveal."

"Here is in writing the Warning that was given to me during the Apparition of January 1st, 1965, while I was alone at The Pines."

* * *

The Warning

The Warning that the Virgin will send us.

It is like a punishment to bring the good closer to God and to warn the others (either to amend or face punishment).

I cannot reveal of what the warning consists. The Virgin

69

did not tell me to say it, (Conchita doesn't write, The Virgin did not allow me) or to say anything else. (In this respect, I have nothing to reveal.) [1]

God wishes that through this warning we make amends and commit fewer sins against Him.[2]

Since we asked Conchita if this warning would cause death, she wrote the following, as a note:

"If we die from it, it will not be from the warning itself, but as a result of the emotion felt in seeing and feeling the warning."

✳ ✳ ✳

The Message of June 18 is not only the last one given, but, in the words of St. Michael, according to Conchita, it is also the last one that the Virgin will give. We should not expect any other. We are indeed in the era of the last warnings before the end of time. Conchita will note later on, *before the end of an era*, she emphasizes, *which is not the end of the world*.

Then, among these last warnings, special importance should be given to the one we have just read. It will occur before the Miracle and will be a spiritual preparation for it.

✳ ✳ ✳

We deal again with "Prophecies." Once again, Garabandal brings us back to these mysterious realities narrated so relevantly by St. Paul. May we remind you that according to the doctrine of the Fifth Lateran Council and Pope Leo X (1512), the Holy Father is the only judge of revelations of this kind.

At the same time, may we point out for those who need it that it is no longer necessary to await the Miracle in order to finally believe in Garabandal. May they simply look forward to the Warning.

Publisher's Notes: The following was told by Conchita and written down on October 20, 1968 by two members of the Newtonville Garabandal Center:

[1] "The Warning is something supernatural and will not be explained by science. It will be seen and felt. For those who do not know Christ (non-Christians) they will believe that it is a warning from God."

[2] "The Warning will be a correction of the conscience of the world."

XXXI

HESITANT MINDS

May we also recall the general outburst of the press and of the authorized spokesmen (authorized by whom?) the day following June 18: "Nothing happened in Garabandal on the set day. The priests were not allowed to go. Lemonade, exploitation of people unacquainted with the facts, tourist trap, etc. . . ." Calumnies, nothing but calumnies, which have judged and still judge their originators, so much so that as of now they neither had the loyalty nor the courage to retract their statements. For their confusion and the edification of others, we reproduce textually hereafter an unpublished letter from Conchita. It bears the postmark of Puentenansa and is dated June 9, 1965. Yes, nine days before the apparition of St. Michael, this young girl sent us the following letter which is disclosed to the public for the first time. We did not read it until June 30, because it arrived on June 13, after we had already left to witness the ecstasy prophesied for the past six and a half months.

"Ave Maria.

"I have now decided to write to you what I think about June 18.

"I believe it is better that not many people come to Garabandal on June 18, for the following reasons:

"First of all, the coming of the Angel is of concern only to me, not to the people who will be there.

"It is possible that the people—almost all of them—will leave very disillusioned. Something evil could result from it, because many people expect some kind of a miracle to happen. And this will not be the case.

"When the time comes for the Miracle, it is then they should come. But fewer people will come then, because they will say: 'On June 18, what happened was less than nothing, so it will

71

be the same thing on the day of the Miracle.' And it is far more advisable that they come on the day of the Miracle rather than on June 18, 1965.

"I fear very much that something will happen on June 18. I think it is rather risky.

"It is up to you to discourage people from coming so as to avoid promoting such an environment."

✿ ✿ ✿

Three points must be kept in mind about this letter:

1) The Angel will come on June 18 for me alone.

2) The important thing is the Miracle to come. . . . Therefore, it is on that day that great crowds must come. If some people were disappointed on June 18 because they had expected to see a Miracle while only an ecstasy, similar to many previous others, took place, they risk imagining that the Miracle will also disappoint them. They may fear that nothing will happen on the day of the Miracle which, actually, will be the essential thing.

3) If people come on June 18, I fear an indescribable something that could be rather harmful.

✿ ✿ ✿

If we are not mistaken, someone had gone to Conchita's house and warned her against "environment promoters." This vocabulary is not Conchita's, and this young girl could not have found it by herself. . . .

You may be assured that we all had our heads on our shoulders. None of the visitors present in Garabandal on that day ever expected a miracle. But several had envisioned that the ecstasy would be similar to previous public ones; that each one would be able to see Conchita in one of her ecstatic walks, for example.

The fact that the apparition occurred at the *"cuadro,"* the very spot where St. Michael appeared the first time in the ravine leading to The Pines, enabled but few people to contemplate Conchita in another world. And this—momentarily, it is true—disappointed those who were not near her. We say "momentarily," because everyone understood quickly that it was not possible to see more.

On the other hand, if a man, a priest, whose name comes readily on our lips, had not sent his mysterious envoy to influence Conchita, to warn her against imaginary "environment promoters," she would never have mentioned this, she would never have thought of it.

All these pressures did not prevent her from prophesying once more and through correspondence. Indeed, "something evil happened," but only in the heart of a few absent people. And it was on account of them, and through them, that Garabandal suffered a wave of calumnies and that an attempt was made to give it a staggering blow.

Let us review the newspaper articles on the matter, as we kept the entire collection; let us hear once more the so-called authorized spokesmen: "Nothing happened at Garabandal on June 18. The Archangel did not show up. All we saw, was business selling soft drinks, etc. . . . well-organized quackery, tourist trap, Spanish superstition, etc. The priests were not allowed to go to the village."

Who then, in God's plan according to this extraordinary young girl who said in a letter posted at Puentenansa on June 9, had such a definite "foreboding" about the future?

XXXII

THE VILLAGE AFTER THE VISIT
OF THE ANGEL

The end of our stay at Garabandal was most gratifying. After a week and a half it became evident that everyone had forgiven us for coming, in spite of Conchita's famous letter that we were to find upon our return to France.

※　※　※

It is amazing how everyone accepted willingly that the Archangel "favored the French people" and had Conchita presenting her crucifix to kiss only to three Frenchmen. The people of the town remarked: "after all, you were the most numerous and the most pious." And they added, "we were so privileged in the past, it is only fair that you have your turn." But what they didn't say— because they were unaware of it—"after all, St. Michael, is the special protector of France."

Because we did not forget it, we had given Father Valentine the large sum of money collected in France for the building of a chapel in honor of St. Michael, in Garabandal.

* * *

One morning, as we were gathered at the entrance of the church, Loli came spontaneously to us and, taking us by the arm, called us to the side and confided in us. She had that beautiful smile which reminded us of her ecstasies in her kitchen and her communions with the Host invisible on the tongue.

"Above all," said she, "do not believe Mr. X, he is a foreigner. You may be sure, very sure, that I saw Our Lady and St. Michael. Do not be concerned about the 'fracasos,' no matter what they are."

Charming Loli and, at times, so outgoing with cordiality! We didn't expect that much. The situation was very clear to us concerning these "fracasos," as they say in Spanish slang, i.e. the troubles faced by the community with regard to the apparitions. We knew about the first one which we had witnessed in March 1963 and we also knew what resulted from it during the first months of 1965.

* * *

No one missed the rendezvous, not even Jacinta, usually so reserved. More than once we saw her only from a distance, and if we had not known her thoroughly, we would have been tempted to think that she was trying to avoid us. We had to be very skillful in order to get a picture of her and yet she would not agree to it unless she was surrounded by her companions. In this particular instance, she came to us stealthily to offer a small statue of Our Lady of Lourdes which had been kissed by

74

Our Lady of Garabandal. This young girl is indeed a hidden treasure that will be known fully only in Paradise!

❀ ❀ ❀

Pilar, the mother of Mari Cruz, had forgiven us for mentioning in our writings that her husband rarely went to Mass. We had a long conversation with him in her presence and we understood that his poor health could explain many things.

As for Mari Cruz, so easily and so often aloof, she had agreed to allow herself to be photographed with a smile, and, of her own accord, had autographed a picture of the Little Flower of Lisieux. And it was not a picture chosen at random. It represented our little saint leaning against the cross, holding a lily in her right hand. The text was the main words of the offering to the merciful love of Jesus. This shows that Mari Cruz can also make a prophecy, spontaneously and unknowingly.

❀ ❀ ❀

While strolling in the village, we met a few older ladies and one of them confided with great emotion that she was the first one to know about the apparitions. Indeed, her house was the nearest to the *"cuadro"* and from it she had only to lift up her eyes to see the famous apple tree.

❀ ❀ ❀

We thank Valentina, the oldest, who, upon our arrival on Sunday, had assured us that we would not sleep in our car, but at her house, on a good soft mattress filled with the same quality wool which was drying on her balcony.

We met Ceferino and Julia, Simon and Maria; also Aurelia, the owner of our home, etc. We do not want to forget Eloisa, the Filipino, our good and devoted interpreter. We had yet to see Conchita, her mother and her brothers, Serafin, the oldest, stern but smiling; the two youngest ones, Aniceto and Miguel, friendly and silently devoted.

We said good-bye as if our coming had been without shadow. Everyone had forgotten the letter posted at Puentenansa on June 9th.

Conchita, absolutely relaxed, ran up and down stairs, and said: "this is my gift to you, here are rosaries for the three of you."

Calling one of us aside, on the threshold, she said: "here is a letter for the bishop, I entrust it to you: would you kindly give it to him personally?"

— And what about a letter for Rome that we would address directly and surely?

— I do not have another one for the time being.

※　※　※

At Cosio, Father Valentine was waiting for us. He knew that we had to stop at the bishop's house and he had some business at Santander; we kindly took him along with us.

During the trip (about 56 miles) everyone was unusually silent and even solemn. The conversation was in slow hushed tones. June 18th was the subject uppermost in our minds; as well as the four years that elapsed between the first and last apparition of St. Michael, and the present reactions of the priests of the area.

— Father Valentine, they told us at the village that you had never testified before the Commission.

— That's right.

— What do you mean, "that's right"?

— It is absolutely right.

— But, you are the pastor of Garabandal, aren't you?

— They ignore it.

— You have known the children and their families inside out for a long time; you are their confessor, their spiritual director.

— I am telling you that they ignore it.

— But, after all, you are everything in Garabandal.

— For you, maybe I am everything over there, but to the Commission, I am nothing. I do not exist.

— You are coming with us to the bishop's house?

— No, because, as I told you, I do not exist.

76

XXXIII

A PRIEST NO LONGER BELIEVES
IN GARABANDAL

On the evening of June 18, we were invited to a meeting which was to be held at Puentenansa the next day. An engineer, who introduced himself as a member of the Santander Commission, was hoping for a get-together at which he would participate with

Ceferino, Loli's father and mayor of the village,
during the apparitions.

77

Loli and her mother pray at the *cuadro*.

the priests of the area and ourselves. We confidentially informed Father Valentine Marichalar, pastor of Garabandal of this proposed meeting, but he finally objected to it.

We may have unconsciously lost an excellent opportunity to gain more information. This engineer and the group we were to meet were avowed adversaries of the apparitions. We agreed with the old Roman saying: "It is useful to be informed by your enemy."

As a reward for our deference toward the pastor of Garabandal, Divine Providence provided us with two other meetings which were far more important to us.

We shall relate now the second meeting, although it occurred four months after the first one.

We refer to a priest for whom we have great esteem and to whom we remain very grateful.

We shall never forget that it was he who, in September 1963, introduced us to Bishop Beitia, succeeded in winning his confidence and became then our collaborator in the Garabandal investigation. On June 18, through circumstances beyond our control, we were only able to meet him in front of Aniceta's house for a handshake. It was only on November 1st that we were to learn this most unusual thing. Our friend had hid in the village church during Conchita's ecstasy at the *cuadro*. There, he prayed for her and for the crowd whom he thought was in error: he no longer believed in Garabandal.

What a drastic change in one's conscience! Through the years 1962–63, he had willingly shared with us all his studies in favor of the cause. We had read them with interest. He has stayed at Garabandal often and for prolonged periods. He knew a lot of things. He was one of the most energetic defenders of the supernaturality of the apparitions and we heard him with our own ears forcefully presenting his arguments to Bishop Beitia himself.

Now, during the night of June 18, he no longer believed in his own past and he was going to make it known to the world. He was going to change camps and militate with ardor and perseverance against Garabandal, and particularly against Conchita.

❋   ❋   ❋

On November 1st, 1965, we spent two wonderful days in Spain with him. We knew his new theories very well. Our discussions were frank and open.

It will never occur to us to judge the intentions of a young priest whom we respect.

But we are in no way concerned with his person. He forced us, so to speak, to explore the reasons behind his complete "turnabout." As these motives are well known to the public, we consider them from now on as impersonal and opened to free discussion. Moreover,—and this is by far the essential—there is Garabandal, and the closest friendship must give way to the truth.

Now, our friend questions everything, doubts everything, criticizes everything, condemns everything.

To answer him point by point would mean to write a book. This situation reminds us of the trouble one gets into when unwinding a skein of wool by the wrong end. Only the scissors will help out, at the expense of the beautiful wool that becomes a mass of loose strings. No one and nothing can make up for the damage.

Moreover, we were able to note in the course of our long conversation that the most detailed answers could never satisfy his present confused state of mind and soul.

Instead, we shall consider two main ideas that explain and enlighten the whole subject both for the partisans and the opponents: the working method and the submission to Holy Mother the Church. We feel particularly free to do this, in that—our friend will certainly recall it—it was in this fashion that we summarized our personal arguments with him.

I—Working Method

To make matters easier for our readers, we shall resort again to a dialogue. The young priest opens it:

— St. John of the Cross teaches that our beliefs in the matter of "visions" must be primarily based on the virtues of the visionaries.

— We do not believe that this is the complete doctrine of the Master you are referring to, but we do know that St. Thomas Aquinas repeats over and over: "Nothing enters the mind that had not been introduced first by the senses."

— What do you mean?

— That rather than being concerned first with the virtues, the faults or condition of soul of the visionaries, we should consider the phenomena that you and I have seen, heard, touched, i.e. the ecstasies.

— I see defects in the life and the conduct of the children.

— This is a matter of surprise to us, because at one time you saw only virtues in them. Remember the day we drew your attention to some impertinence of Conchita, you tried to convince us that we were wrong.

— Won't you agree at all with me on this point?

— Of course, I agree that the children of Garabandal are also subject to the seven capital sins.

— Then?

— Then, but sinners could be favored with genuine ecstasies and no one has any right to question them, even though the visionaries would retain some of their defects, commit some fault. Doesn't the just man fall seven times a day?

— You leave me no escape on the matter.

— I disagree. You are not my prisoner, rather we are both, you and I, prisoners of the "fact." According to St. Thomas, the "fact" the "reality" here is the ecstasy which has been seen, heard, touched, duly observed; without overlooking all the other particulars of which we have already spoken in the first edition (chap. II) of "The Star on the Mountain."

— And if I were to prove that the ecstasies and the other particulars, as you called them are false?

— Then, I would agree with you, and I would follow you. But this is precisely what you do not do, what you cannot do.

✻　✻　✻

— Do you give any significance to the Virtues of the visionaries?

— Yes. I consider them an added grace from God to help us in our sincere search for the truth. But our human reason, enlightened by faith and supported by evangelic virtues, forces us to undertake our difficult and, at times, painful investigation on the basis of the reality of the ecstasies. That's why on June 18, your duty was not to pray in church, but rather to be present with me at the "cuadro" to observe Conchita in ecstasy.

Moreover, one should always keep in mind that the apparitions of the children entrusted with a message for the world cannot be compared to mystic phenomena accompanying an intense union of the soul with God, as are for example many visions of St. Theresa of Avila, St. Catherine of Siena, St. Margaret Mary.

We are dealing with two different worlds, although identical in origin and manifestation. The apparitions to the children are not part and parcel of an advanced mystical life and are not ordained for their sanctification. By them, through them, God wishes primarily, directly, immediately, to speak to the world and help it.

It would be out of place here to put the visionaries of Garabandal in the "mansions" described by the *Madre of Avila* so dear to Spain.

* * *

The young priest:

— As I told you at the beginning, I adhere to the doctrine of St. John of the Cross.

— St. John of the Cross is perfectly aware of the fundamental distinction between the grace "given as a pure gift" and the grace "which makes the soul pleasing to God."

The first grace is given to the visionaries first and foremost for the needs of humanity. The second one unites them directly to God, through supernatural love.

The apparitions of Garabandal belong primarily to the first kind. The same is true of the apparitions and "voices" of Joan of Arc, in as much as they dealt with the liberation of France, the victory of the armies and Joan's horrible death at the stake in Rouen.

— I do not understand you.

— I know it only too well. Because of that, remember that over a year ago, I sent you two long letters written in French, addressed to our interpreter and mutual friend. I reminded you then of "the working method" without which you risked to face the greatest dangers.

You reacted as did the Parisian Review: "Les Etudes Camélitaines" in 1933 with regard to Beauraing.

Because it failed to establish that very important distinction noted in theology by St. Thomas Aquinas and St. John of the Cross, this review condemned the five visionaries of Beauraing. Its readers and many others were influenced by it.

But nine years later, the canonical investigation being completed, Rome approved the conclusions and the Bishop of Namur announced to his diocese and to the world that it was reasonable to believe that the "Facts" were authentic.

II—Submission of the Investigators to the Church

The young priest resumes the dialogue:

— In my priestly life, I seek what is most perfect; I endeavor to follow the most perfect way.

— We do not question your intentions.

— The most perfect for a priest, for others also, is to obey Holy Mother Church.

— Of course, surely.

— Santander has spoken; I obey to Santander.

— What did Santander say in its last statement of July 10, 1965?

— That there was no evidence that the apparitions were supernatural and that the priests could not go to Garabandal without the authorization of the Bishop.

— That's right. I agree. But neither you nor I—and you know it better than anyone else—ever went to Garabandal without this authorization.

— That's right.

* * *

We:

— The Santander statement of October 1962 said: "the apparitions are of a natural order." The last statement is worded differently: "There is no evidence that they are supernatural."

— That's also true.

— Doesn't it occur to you that there is a tremendous difference in the wording of these statements as to the very heart of the matter?

— Of course, it is different.

— It is so different that we take the liberty of drawing your attention to this.

In the case of a genuine apparition, of a real ecstasy, the evidence is only given to the visionary.

As to the witnesses of a genuine apparition, they have in no way the evidence of the "object" seen by the visionary. They must be satisfied with the exterior signs. For example, you are in front of me, it is an evident fact. But, if for the time being, you were visible only to me, those to whom I would say that I see you would have to be satisfied with the outward "signs" that I would give and to the degree of belief that could be ascribed to them.

— What do you mean exactly?

— Exactly this: No one, we mean no one, will ever have the "evidence" that Garabandal is supernatural: no one, outside of the four visionaries. The others, you and I, will have to be satisfied with the study of the signs and testimonies. They will deny or affirm, through the sole exercise of human reason, of reasoning reason. Now, in its normal and legitimate function, reason can never get "evidence." It can make an opinion, reach a conviction, and it is tremendous, but reason can never "see."

— Then, what about the wording of the Santander statement of July 10?

— It is not relevant in terms of sound doctrine and this is a very serious matter.

✧   ✧   ✧

— The most perfect is nevertheless to obey Santander.

— We spoke in terms of intelligence. Let us now speak in terms of will. Where did you read in the Santander statement that it demands obedience on the root of the matter? To affirm— through unintentional fallacious reasoning—that the apparitions are not evident for the Commission is not to enjoin someone to accept its judgments and to conform to it his conduct. The Commission does not compel, cannot compel to think as it thinks.

— What about the interdictions?

— The Bishop of Santander forbids the priests to go to Garabandal without his authorization. The priests should comply with this disciplinary measure and see first the Bishop, provided they are received with kindness by the Bishop himself and treated with dignity.

— Why do you narrow things down thus?

— Because the Holy Office has also spoken.

— I obey the Bishop's statement of July 10, 1965.

— But the Press Release of the Holy Office came after this statement in that it is dated July 28, 1965, and Bishop Beitia had it published on August 10.

— We owe obedience to the Ordinary Bishop of the diocese to which Garabandal belongs.

— But the Bishop showed us the way by having this Press Release published a month after the Santander statement.

— What do you mean?

— That the most perfect is to obey the legitimate authority of the Church which, in the present case, is Rome and no longer Santander.

— Explain yourself.

— We do not have to remind you of the Fifth Lateran Council, or Leo X, or canon law in matters of prophetic revelations. You know it and you know that Garabandal is dependent on it. This was proved once more to you on June 18. We simply say: the commission is the commission, the Bishop is the Bishop, the Pope is the Pope.

* * *

We know through personal experience that neither the scientific method nor the strict obedience to Holy Mother Church are sufficient for belief in the apparitions.

A loyal and strenuous work may lead the priest of the Christian's human reason to the conviction that these apparitions are true, without giving him faith in them.

Why?

Because the "object" of the apparition being of a supernatural order, it is absolutely necessary that human reason be inwardly enlightened and human will be interiorly pushed, "moved" as say the theologians, by a supernatural grace.

Here, the "object" is the person, the presence and the mysterious action of Our Lady of Carmel and St. Michael. In order to

85

Simon, Jacinta's father.

believe in Her and in Him, to give them our hearts, we cannot
rely on the certainties of the reason, we need Faith, which, according to St. Catherine of Siena, is the new pupil of the eye.

❖   ❖   ❖

We did not convince our friend, we know it. Unfortunately,
he lost faith in Garabandal. And his reason has lost its foothold.[1]

[1] Today, Conchita, Loli and Jacinta have left Garabandal. Only Mari
Cruz remains in the village. A young priest (26 years) is the appointed
pastor which proves that over there the supernatural wisdom of a priest
does not depend upon age. He does not believe in the apparitions. He is
attempting the impossible, to influence the judgment of the visionaries and
the villagers. Under these conditions, what can be the legitimate basis for
forbidding the priests to go to Garabandal?

Maria, Jacinta's mother.

XXXIV

BEFORE THE COMMISSION

We were to meet the Commission June 24, 1965.

To be exact, after having spoken with the 75-year-old permanent secretary of the Bishop who, on June 9, did not conceal his hostility for Garabandal, one of us was to spend four hours with the clerk of the Commission.

The latter did not tell us that he had just interrogated Mari Cruz and her mother Pilar, but we knew this from another source.

Affably and courteously, he invited us to lunch and started his interrogation, which was precisely what he had in mind. Without preamble and without any warning as to his intentions, he took out 3 large sheets of paper containing 35 hand written questions. The questioning began during the hors d'oeuvres.

We immediately visualized the setting of a regular diocesan commission proceeding with an official investigation of past apparitions, now recognized by the church, with its court, chairman, assessors, attorney at law, notary, or clerk. We could still hear the complaints of the venerable clerk writing notes during three long hours, as this is the clerk's assignment. In this particular instance, the Santander clerk assumed the rights of the entire court.

There was no opening prayer to the Holy Spirit and the "witness" was not required to take an oath.

In view of the importance of the subject under discussion, we wondered at this point whether we should go on with the comedy and disregard its possible tragic aspects or agree with this scandalous caricature of canonical court?

On the other hand, we were given such a wonderful opportunity since the clerk is the mainspring of the commission. The 35 questions would afford us an opportunity to know him and to form a just opinion of him and upon all those at Santander who are all-powerful in the investigation of Garabandal.

— I am at your disposal, Mr. Clerk.

✿ ✿ ✿

Here are the reflections of our travelling companion:

"The interrogatory was not made in French, my mother tongue, but in Spanish, and lasted four hours."

"I kept all my personal notes and I remember very well the questions and particularly my answers. Of course, these notes are the exclusive property of the church. Moreover, I respect the priestly character of this man-Friday clerk."

"But I have no other alternative than to speak the truth."

"In view particularly of the fact that the 'clerk' has the courage of his convictions, that he defends them through every possible means, ranging from harshness to insinuations. 'Amicus, mihi, Plato . . .' would he say."

"During the four hours, I often wondered whether I was considered as a witness or as a defendant; as a young military recruit or a decorated soldier; as an apprentice or as a qualified workman; as being honest in the things of God or a mere charlatan."

"For four hours, without any right, and in accordance with the requirements involved in the questioning, the clerk played successively the role of the procurator, the assessor, the chairman in this 'restaurant-court.'"

"I have seen him 'working' on the witness, or defendant, to draw from him some information liable to be detrimental to Garabandal. If he sensed that he was dealing with a pro-Garabandal, he would at the most opportune time endeavour to extort a contradictory statement. If the 'witness'—realizing that the questions were 'slanted' and illegal in every respect—would refuse to sign the Minutes, the clerk himself would not hesitate to write the name of the one he attempted to trap, in capital letters."

"Yes, these are the true facts. I bear witness to it publicly. This astonishing clerk wrote my name because I refused to sign; because I refused to sign what I considered to be an incredible contempt of all scientific loyalty, a scandalous challenge to all canonical laws."

* * *

The clerk and the other members of the Santander Commission never believed in Garabandal since the beginning of the apparitions. Why?

Evidently—and this was noticeable from their attitude toward the children, their families, Don Valentine Marichalar, Pepe Diez —because in the first place they disregarded every truly scientific method in this matter.

Also, because at the end of July, 1961, their attitude toward Conchita was similar to the one assumed by Cauchon and his followers toward Joan of Arc in the cemetery of St. Ouen. Because for the past four years, they blindly retained the same mental outlook. Finally, because under these circumstances, it was, and is still impossible for them to obtain or receive the supernatural and free gift necessary to believe, i.e. the gift of faith, in the sense we have noted in the preceding chapter.

How can they, for the past four years, use every possible means to oppose human reasoning and canonical law?

This is their business. It was ours to expose their conduct. The above statement will enable all souls who were confused by the Commission to know what stand to take.

XXXV

A BISHOP

On June 24, at 11 a.m., Msgr. Don Eugenio Beitia Aldazabal, Bishop of Santander, received us in his office at his Residence.

First of all, he carefully read the letter we gave him on behalf of Conchita and our conversation opened in a cordial and friendly manner.

He made no mention of the June 18 events, of which he was well aware. We did not allow ourselves to refer to it except to thank him for the confidence he placed in us and to ask him a favor.

— Your Excellency, the French people understand your prudence very well. Unfortunately, the restrictions contained in the October 1962 statement make Garabandal a virtual prison. On the other hand, they give the world the impression that we are afraid to see the truth. We would welcome any control of our conduct, but leave the doors open, allow us to go to the village without special permission.

— I wish I could do that. But ten days ago, I received a letter from the Holy Office asking me to make no further statement. Through courtesy I must remain silent.

* * *

— Your Excellency, we are sorry that you resigned. We sincerely regret it.

— Well, I do not care for honors. Moreover, I am a very sick man and at the point of losing my sight. I no longer feel able physically to carry out the duties of this vast diocese. For the past two years, I have made known the state of my health to the Holy See. In two or three occasions during the Council sessions, I reiterated my request. I thank the Holy Father for having finally complied.

No one could have spoken with greater simplicity, humility and detachment. We were in the presence of a great bishop of the Catholic Church and soon, we would be in a position to say it, because he would definitely leave the See of Santander on August 16, the eve of the installation of his successor.

We could then affirm to the world that his departure had absolutely no bearing on Garabandal, thus putting an end to all insinuations to the contrary, already wildly spread.

*　*　*

We are convinced now that in this affair, the personal attitude of Bishop Beitia was correct.

When he arrived at Santander three years ago, he found the commission established by Msgr. Doroteo, the provisional apostolic administrator of the diocese. He reaffirmed the task of this commission. But, at the same time, he allowed the creation of a so-called unofficial and secret commission, whose members were favorable to Garabandal.

He acted very tactfully this way toward the public commission which was completely unaware that its sealed reports, placed on the bishop's desk, remained in his personal file. They didn't have the slightest idea of the bishop's esteem because their reports were neither answered nor acknowledged.

We have the deepest admiration for this bishop, so conscious of his personal responsibilities and professing a high respect and esteem for the unique grace of the episcopal consecration.

Indeed, even if Bishop Beitia had himself designated the official commission, he knew very well that it could act only in a consultative capacity; that it had no part in the "charisms" of the successors of the apostles. He alone received from God mission and grace to judge things. Therefore, to enlighten this judgment, prudence and wisdom demanded that he knew the pros and cons in the matter of apparitions. Apart from its avowed adversaries that formed the official commission, he owed to God, to the

Church and to himself to listen also to the consultative voices of the unofficial commission.

This he did without the knowledge of anyone; in order not to offend some nor flatter others.

This provides us with another reason to state publicly that he was a grand bishop.

❁   ❁   ❁

And he remains as such because of his unparalleled intelligence and the national responsibility he kept after his retirement.

More than once, the dean of the faculty of Canon Law, who conferred on him the Doctorate degree, used to say to his friends: "Msgr. Beitia was the most brilliant student in our university." The Spanish Episcopal Conference designated him Chairman of Press activities in Spain. And we know that he made a very great impression in America during a recent world meeting.

Such is, and always will be, the image of Msgr. Don Eugenio Beitia Aldazabal, the bishop of the apparitions in Garabandal. With Conchita, we ask Our Lady of Carmel to restore his health on the day of the Great Miracle.

XXXVI

CONCHITA ANNOUNCES HER DEPARTURE

In Chapter 31, we have asked who is Conchita? She will be better known after one reads the following letter:

> San Sebastian of Garabandal, August 18th, 1965.
> This short letter will make you aware of my great joy.
> Indeed, my mother allows me to enter the convent.
> For me, it is a great thing to offer myself to Christ, totally.
> from the early age of 16, and for life.
> I am so unworthy that I cannot understand that Jesus Christ calls me to Him.

I have no doubt as to my vocation, and I am confident that everything shall turn out right so that I will be able to enter the convent.

Pray for me, that I be very good, and that I persevere.

Here is my wish: to love God very much, and, by His will, to love the world.

Therefore, I offer myself completely to God to love Him with all my might, and, at the same time, to do something good for the world.

Pray that it becomes a reality, that everything turns out right quickly, so that I may enter as soon as possible the convent of the Discalced Carmelite Missionaries.

Ask that people pray for me, I will do the same for everybody.

My mother and my brothers greet you and I ask your prayers for them.

With the affection of one who remembers you in her poor prayers,

Conchita Gonzales

A few words of this letter appear to us as being "inspired." She writes: "Here is my wish: to love God very much, and by his will, to love the world," this teenager solves the problem of "the presence of the Church in the world."

Such is the seal of Conchita on the Garabandal events.

We shall see later, why she could not realize her formal wish to enter the convent at the set date.

XXXVII

THE CONVERSATION OF TORRELAVEGA

In the presence of witnesses, on September the 8th, 1965, we asked 45 written questions of Conchita, and to her mother Aniceta. Here are a few of her answers, the remainder being kept for future reference.

Serafin, Conchita's oldest brother.

— Yes, I have written the date of the Miracle to His Excellency the Bishop.[1]

— I have had a "locution" with the Blessed Virgin, on July 2nd: I shall write to tell you what was said. And I have had another one on July 18th, I shall also write it down.

— I am thinking of entering the convent, and my companions also. We have thought of this since the first days of the Apparitions.[2]

— This has not been suggested to us by any priest. Aniceta confirms this statement.

Conchita continued:

— The Holy Father, Pope of Rome, will see the Miracle from where he will be and Padre Pio will see it also.[3]

— Yes, the Council will be extraordinarily successful.

— After His Holiness Paul VI, there will be only two more popes

[1] This letter sent by mail, never reached the desk of His Excellency Msgr. Eugenio Beitia.

[2] We would not venture any question to Conchita, on this subject, other than that implied by the following answer.

Publishers Note: The following was told by Conchita and written down on October 20, 1968 by two members of the Newtonville Garabandal Center:

[3] "The prophecy concerning Padre Pio remains the same." Padre Pio had died in September 23, 1968.

The following was also learned: Conchita did not elaborate further on the prophecy but we feel that this was not necessary in the light of the evidence

Aniceta, Conchita's mother.

before the end of the present period, which is not the end of the world. The Blessed Virgin told me so, but I don't know what that means.

— I know absolutely nothing of the date the Council ends, the eventual difficulties, the eventuality of an anti-pope, the many types of catastrophes which were mentioned concerning Fatima.

— I am entering the Discalced Carmelite Missionaries at Pamplona. I wish to go to Africa because the kind of life the nuns lead pleases me, and because I am fond of black people.

that was shown. Conchita has in her possession a veil that covered the face of Padre Pio after his death while he lay in the coffin. The veil remained over the face of Padre Pio for several hours prior to the covering of the coffin by a glass cover to prevent the faithful from touching him directly. It is felt that the fact that Conchita has the veil, that must have been most precious to the monastery at San Giovanni Rotondo, gives evidence of the closeness of Padre Pio to the events of Garabandal. Conchita does not have to speak any further on the prophecy since the veil itself speaks clearly enough.

— My departure from Garabandal will not hinder the announcement of the Miracle. I will inform my Superior of the date, and, if necessary, I will also inform my spiritual director.

— Besides, the Blessed Virgin has the necessary means for us to know this date, even if my spiritual Director or my Superior did not mention it.

— I am entering the convent at the end of this month of September, at Pamplona . . .

Aniceta cuts in:

— She is very young . . . but God who gave her to me could well take her back. . . .

Conchita continued smilingly:

— Mother, if I were to marry, I would also be leaving. With this difference: I would be leaving with a man, whereas now I will leave with God.

We insisted:

— Why leave so young for the convent, Conchita? [4]

The adolescent smiled again.

Then her answers continue. She mentions a German group who has made rather fanciful declarations, for example, that the Holy Father would personally announce the date of the Miracle.

— The Germans are wrong, I never said that the Holy Father would announce the date of the Miracle.

Aniceta apologizes for them:

— These Germans do not understand Spanish well.

Conchita continues to answer several questions.

— A chapel will be built in honor of St. Michael, after the Miracle. I would prefer it if we didn't do as they did at Lourdes where I went on May 18th, 1963, I would prefer poverty and simplicity.

— It is very difficult for the village to remain poor and simple as at the time of the apparitions, but I wish it.

— The greatest danger to the village of Garabandal is pride.

— The principal virtue in Christian life, is humility. A soul who

---

[4] Because she did not consult us about her decision to enter the convent, we are unable to relate anything more.

is not very humble cannot love Jesus, cannot have total confidence in Him.

— When I wrote the letter of August 16th concerning my departure for the convent, with these words, "to love Jesus and by meditation on Christ do good to the world," I meant this, "Jesus gives His love to the soul, and the soul loves others through this love."

— Yes, Mari Cruz has seen the Virgin. Her recantation is due to a mysterious operation of the devil. She will reaffirm the reality of her trances after the Miracle.

She was asked:

— What will happen in Garabandal when Loli, Jacinta and Conchita have gone, only Mari Cruz will remain in the village repeating to strangers that the apparitions are false?

Conchita widens her eyes in astonishment; she had never considered this problem. She remains silent.

Last question:

— When all three of you have left, no one will go up to Garabandal?

— On the contrary, it is then that it will become necessary to go up; then people will come only for the Blessed Virgin.

XXXVIII

DIALOGUE IN THE TENT

On September 10, 1965, a French family, the parents and their eight children, set up a tent a few feet from Conchita's home.

That day, only the mother and the two youngest children remained in the tent.

To be gracious, Conchita entered the tent with the ever-devoted interpreter, Eloisa Deguia. Here is the text of the dialogue:

Conchita:

— You are fortunate to have set up your tent on this spot (behind the fountain), this is where the Virgin appeared before Mari Cruz.

Mari Cruz asked the Virgin for a sign, to make a miracle, so the crowd might believe. At this moment, a star came and perched itself on the feet of the Virgin, and everyone could see this star.

(This was previous to the "Forma" miracle of the 18th of July, 1962.)

— Conchita, my little sick child which I recommended to your prayers on the 18th of June, is not cured. Is it because my merits are not sufficient to obtain this grace?

— We do not have more or less merit. We are more or less loved. He who never heard of God does not have less merit than we have; but he is less loved.

— Just the same, the Blessed Virgin chose well, in choosing you!

— When the Blessed Virgin appears to me, her glance does not fix on me, does not pause on me. It circles the mountains, it embraces the whole world, and her face smiles to the universe. She doesn't come for me.

— The painting in the hall off your bedroom represents the Virgin. It is a nice one. Does it resemble your vision?

— No, compared with reality, it is nothing. This type of beauty cannot be reproduced.

❋   ❋   ❋

Conchita questions in turn.

— Are you acquainted with Fatima?

— A little, I've heard of the miracle of the sun.

— The miracle of Fatima is nothing in comparison with the one which will take place here. It will be much, much greater.

At this moment, the interpreter whispered to Mrs. X, "I think we will see the Virgin herself."

Conchita having heard, answered immediately:

— "No, no, it's not that."

On another occasion, she was more precise. "If we saw the Virgin, it would be an apparition, and not a miracle."

After that, raising her arms and spreading them, Conchita added:

— It will be much greater, much more powerful than at Fatima. Persons present will be so upset that no one will leave here doubting.

The whole world should be present for the Miracle, for then surely there would be no punishment, since all would believe.

❋ ❋ ❋

Mrs. X:

— Would all the sick that were present be cured?

— No, not all, nor a few. The Virgin did not say "todos," nor "unos," she said "Los": The "sick" will be cured.

On her own, the adolescent continued:

— The Virgin laughs and smiles a great deal. She is not frightening.

— So she is very kind! Kind like a mother?

— No, more than a mother. She is good like a friend, because we can tell her everything that passes through our heads. She understands, and helps us.

She laughed and even played with us. She even let Loli have her crown to play with. Loli put the crown on her head, but was afraid of being burned on the stars.

With a mother, we are not so free, nor as confiding as with the Virgin. We do not tell our mother about our mistakes nor reveal our faults!

— We are bringing you to France with us. We will show you Saint Bernadette, at Nevers. Her body, her real body, uncorrupted, is in a shrine. We see her dressed as a nun, and people come to pray before her. It would be so nice for you to see this shrine.

— Oh! when we have seen the Virgin, nothing else is nice.

The interpreter murmured to Mrs. X in French:

99

— Well, when she is dead, she will also be put in a shrine and people will come and pray to her.

Conchita, extremely intelligent, and now used to hearing our language spoken, had guessed. She burst out laughing and pointed her index to her forehead as if to say; aren't you a little crazy?

After that, her face became more and more serious and she seemed to be collecting her thoughts:

— If it be God's will, if it make people pray more, I would let it be so. But to me, that is not the important thing, it is but a small matter.

XXXIX

TESTIMONY GIVEN BY CHILDREN

The opportunity was too good. After we noted the dialogue under the tent of Mrs. X, now returned to France, we gathered around the family table, in the presence of the father and mother, five of their boys and one of their girls, and we questioned them.

We can't resist giving here their spontaneous answers; we thus have the testimony of "young people" about one of their own age group.

Bernard, age 16, said:

— I came into the tent when Conchita was saying, "we don't have more or less merit, we are more or less loved." I couldn't help exclaiming, "It's always the same thing. There are still teacher's pets in your heaven. It just isn't fair." She burst out laughing heartily.

Daniel, age 7, said:

— She loaned me her donkey. I had a tumble. Luckily, I fell beside the stones, in the grass near Conchita's feet.

Michel, 14 years old:

— And you?

— Me, nothing.

The others:

— Yes, yes go on and tell it, we won't laugh at you. Tell it, tell it.

— Well, she played a trick on me! She said, "go on up to The Pines and you will see the Virgin."

— You're joking, I answered.

— No, no go on, She is waiting for you.

— And so?

— I went. But I saw nothing. I came back down, furious.

— And you are still?

— No, now I laugh.

— And you resent her?

— Oh, no, I like this Conchita.

— You are right. You'll understand later on.

The others.

— But he already understands.

— How, why?

— Go on, Michel, keep on right to the end.

Michel hesitates, sniffs and puts his elbows on the table.

— Well then here goes. She looked at me smilingly, then murmured, 'you will become a priest.'

— Oh, that. . . .

— Yes, Oh that. It isn't funny, I hadn't even thought of it. I'm in a fine fix now.

Philippe, 15 years of age:

— Don't worry, Michel, we will see about it when the time comes.

✿ ✿ ✿

Guy, 13 years old, with the most nervous manner of all the boys, interrupted:

— What a character this Conchita is!

— And in a chorus:

101

— Oh yes, she is a character, Conchita, a good character, but genuine!

— Easy, boys, easy.

— It's just that she didn't go about doing things gently. She was very gay, simple, open, and a great tease with us. She wouldn't hesitate to tussle good naturedly with us. We used to say to her, 'you're a misplaced boy.' She would answer, 'you are but misplaced girls.' We worked at the haying with her and we certainly played roughly. We would throw hay at her and she would try and make us eat some. Just as we did to begin with.

The boys are still excited over it, we can't hear a word of what we're saying.

— Quiet, quiet children!

The eldest, who is 16 glanced at us, and concluded with these remarks:

— With all that, she is perfectly straightforward, no trouble there. Impeccable, impeccable Conchita. She went up with us to the fields, but older boys were not allowed to go with her. If all the girls were like her, there wouldn't be any temptations.

                     ❀   ❀   ❀

During the conversation with her brothers, the little sister had gotten up on the table.

— Now, it's your turn, Françoise.

— I also played with her in the grass. But mostly Conchita kept me by her side, holding my hand.

— She spoke?

— No, she would smile at me.

— No souvenirs?

— Yes, a picture. I will go and get it.

We have the picture before us. On the face of it is our Theresa of Lisieux (Teresita as they call her in Spain) dressed for her first communion, the 8th of May, 1884. These lines in French were printed on the card:

> Oh, but I loved Jesus in the Host
> Who came in the morn of my life

To be betrothed to my rapt soul!
Oh! how I opened with joy,
My heart!

On the reverse side, in Spanish: "For Françoise, as a souvenir and mark of affection from she who wishes that you love her always through Jesus and Mary. One question: who loves their hearts more, you or I? You pray for me. I pray for you.

Conchita Gonzalez

Conclusion:

We then turn to the forty-year-old father of the family, who had been attentively following the testimony of his wife and that of his six children.

— Sum up, happy husband and father!

— Garabandal! A corner of paradise! There are two Conchitas luckily, my wife's and my children's. They complete one another admirably.

XL

SOME AMERICANS QUESTION CONCHITA

What we have just read, and other equally important texts which are to follow, are evidence of the haste Conchita was in to reveal in part what was on her mind before her departure from Garabandal.

She wants to leave us what interests us at present.

Here, given rather loosely, are her answers to questions put to her in an interview with some Americans on September 14, 1965.

These answers were put down in her own handwriting and countersigned by the witnesses who were present.

— The warning is something coming directly from God. The entire world will see it, regardless of where one will be.

103

— It will be like the revelation of our sins. Believers as well as unbelievers will see and feel it.

— The Miracle will last about 15 minutes, the Virgin said so. It will happen around 8:30 in the evening, the hour at which the angel appeared to us for the first time. It is the same angel as the one we saw, before seeing the Virgin.

— The Warning should purify us for the Miracle. It is also like a catastrophe. It will make us think of the dead, in the sense that we would truly prefer to be dead rather than have to experience this warning.

— Our Lady said that the sick present in the village or on the mountains around the village itself will be cured on the day of the Miracle.

— It will therefore be necessary to go up to the village of Garabandal and not remain at Cosio, for example.

— She did not say "all" or a "few." She said "the sick."

— The Punishment—if we do not change—will be horrible, as we deserve. We have seen it (Loli, Jacinta and I), but we can't tell what it consists of, because I do not have the Virgin's permission. When I saw it, I felt terrified even though I saw the Blessed Virgin at the same time. (Even though I saw the indescribable beauty and goodness of the Virgin at the same moment as the punishment.)

— She prayed on the rosary very slowly, while facing us, as if she wanted us to pray in that manner. She said the "Hail Mary" to teach us to say it well.

— The Virgin mentioned this to me in one talk: "the body of Father Luis will remain as intact as on the day of his burial."

This referred to Father Luis Andreu, the Jesuit who died of joy after having seen the Virgin and a preview of the Miracle.

*   *   *

— Father Luis Andreu's mother, who has three other Jesuit sons, one in Spain, one in Caracas and the last in Formosa, is now a professed nun of the Visitandine order. When we visited her recently she told me:

104

"as he lay on his bed at the Reinosa clinic, my son Luis appeared to be merely sleeping. A drop of ruby-red blood was on his lips. I shuddered, asking myself if he would not be put in his coffin alive."

In the course of the same interrogation, Conchita explained that Jesus would perform miracles with objects kissed by the Virgin during the trances.

— Those who would possess these objects and use them with faith and courage, would pass their purgatory on this earth. This purgatory will correspond to the one they would go through after death because the sufferings they will endure on this earth will enable them to avoid purgatory in the beyond.

— The Blessed Virgin told me nothing concerning the perfume of flowers which, they say, emanates sometimes from objects she has kissed, but she said that the objects she has kissed would accomplish wonders and miracles.

Concerning the great miracle to come, Conchita specified:

— If I am in a convent, the Virgin will tell me how to announce the Miracle eight days in advance; it is up to her to arrange everything.

Conchita also said that the Virgin did not teach them the verses in advance which they were singing, for instance, the unknown poetic stanzas sung by the three clairvoyants at night in front of Mari Cruz's sleeping house. She helped them to "pull out of themselves" several little poems at the moment they were singing them.

These children were not repeating a lesson, they were "seemingly inspired," at the same moment, in the same manner, all three of them at the same time.

* * *

— The Warning will be recognized and accepted by the world as a sign coming directly from God. Because of this, I think that it's impossible for the world to be so stubborn as to not change.
— The "sign" will remain forever at The Pines. The day of the Miracle, it will be possible to see it, to photograph, and to tele-

vise it. But it will be impossible to feel it. It will appear as a thing not of this world, but originating from God.

— Concerning the Church, her Son and the Popes, the Virgin said in 1962, that there would be but two more Popes after his Holiness Paul VI. But this does not signify that the world will end with these two Popes.

Seventeenth question:

Many who believe in Garabandal wish (but are anxious in view of authority) to do all they can to spread the message of our very Holy Mother. What have you to tell them?

Answer:

That is very well for the Virgin. She would like us to work at spreading the Message. And it is what the Virgin wishes. But she wants us to obey the Church, and this will bring greater glory to God. She will allow time for the Message to be spread with the permission of the Church.

Last question:

Did the Virgin tell you if one of the clairvoyants would die young?

Answer:

It is something that people speak about, but the Virgin did not say so.

XLI

CONCHITA'S MISSION

The essential mission of the clairvoyants of Garabandal is to be among us, the "witnesses" of Saint Michael and Our Lady of Carmel. We have seen that Conchita, for her part, never disappoints. Furthermore, she now seems in a hurry to inform us rapidly and totally.

At the same time, this adolescent who answers little or not at all the heaps of letters she receives, has exercised a prodigious apostolate through images. She has dedicated thousands.

Since 1962, we have examined this work thoroughly.

The few phrases that she wrote hastily on these pictures corresponded to the secret state of mind of the interested person. Sometimes, these words constituted a veritable prophecy. Or else, they were an evangelical lesson, of which the receiver had an urgent need. Very often, it seemed to us that on these countless occasions, Conchita was "inspired" without knowing it. It resembled what she had said previously about the little songs. "It just came out of us, with the aid of the Virgin."

We have even noted on a series of pictures, inscriptions which tell of her own spiritual doctrine:

— Who is Jesus? Jesus is someone who let Himself be nailed to the cross to redeem us sinners. Besides, He left us His Mother as Mother to the sinners we are.

— Let us meditate and think that though we put Jesus inside ourselves, wretches that we are, while He is within us, we dare to sin against Him.

— What nothings we are and yet at what cost? Because we are the children of Mary who is mother to all of us, even the sinners.

Sometimes Conchita is crushed by the realization of her spiritual poverty. Then the Virgin summons her:

— Hallo! what are you up to?

The Blessed Mother reproaches Conchita for taking refuge in self-pity, and adds:

— You must approach me with complete confidence.

We listen again while Conchita tells us:

— She presents herself to us. (Jacinta, Loli, Mari Cruz and Conchita) not for our own benefit, nor for the village, nor for Spain, but for the entire world. Because of that, let us spread her Message throughout the universe. It is our mother, Mary, who warned us many times already that if we didn't change, her Son would punish us, but we turn a deaf ear. It is not the sorrows and sufferings of the Punishment which should grieve us, but we should grieve that we are the cause of this Punishment through our numerous sins against Jesus and Mary.

XLII

MARIA DOLORES OR MARY OF SORROWS

What an error one would make by concluding that Conchita alone sums up Garabandal.

Besides, she is hurt when a gift is made to her alone. She does not permit us to think only of her, as she is infinitely tactful with regard to her companions.

She esteems and loves them profoundly. She has tender feelings particularly where Mari Cruz is concerned.

These feelings are also returned to her by the other three.

Whatever might be the permanent or occasional tensions which might exist between their families, all four children always find the means of comforting one another when going to or coming out of church, they play together on Sunday afternoons, they walk together the way adolescents do, arm in arm among the younger girls.

Or else, they stand around to watch their little friends dance under the awning in the village.

How often Conchita asked Our Lady to appear to the others as often as to herself, to give them the same mission, not singling Conchita out for the role.

One day, when she felt crushed under the weight of her inner trials, she even said to the Virgin, "Mother, why only me? Why not share with the others?"

We have no knowledge of the extent to which these requests, these prayers of the eldest of the clairvoyants have been or will be granted. But we have come to know the other three sufficiently well to be able to speak about them favorably.

Let us then leave Our Lady her freedom of choice. One must not forget that God alone knows the exact merits of each girl and the secret or visible ways by which He leads these little clairvoyants.

* * *

Maria Dolores was sixteen on May 1, 1965. She is heavier and shorter than Conchita, with sparkling, laughing eyes in a face which has grown pleasantly longer. Her thick, shining hair falls on a pair of solid shoulders.

In the first year of the apparitions, she was apparently the most favored of Our Lady of Carmel. At the time, she would repeat to the vision: "Bring me to heaven with you right now."

Since then she is constantly weighted down from the work and worry of the large family of which she happens to be the eldest girl. At the same time, she is the diligent cook and busy waitress of the small village bar. To sit or pause is out of the question in this house, as her father, Ceferino, sees all, hears all. He is from a large family of 12 children and always on the alert when the subject of his daughter and apparitions are concerned, he begins by scrutinizing the visiting stranger, without being too obvious about it. He will deny his gullibility before anyone and is determined to not have anyone "put one over" on him, not even his Loli who must toe the mark.

Loli, who always appears to be in a good mood, even if she feels like weeping, prompted someone to write recently, after spending a week in a close contact with her: "one can sense an ardent inner life. She is the mystic of the group."

In order to realize this, one must draw her away from her time-consuming household tasks and accompany her up and down the road to Cosio.

Every other day she goes to Cosio for supplies, accompanied by one of her dearest companions, the family donkey, who carries the goods on his back. The round trip is about 9 miles.

Free at last to be herself in the midst of her mountains, Loli effortlessly reveals the secrets hidden behind the purity of her smile, her constant joviality, unchanging good humour, and the hidden bit of mischief lurking at the bottom of her nature.

On the 30th of September 1965, she left for a nun's boarding school in the province of Zaragoza, repeating to herself the

Maria Dolores (Loli) 1965.

Virgin's inner revelation, which had surprised her shortly before:
"If I no longer show myself to you, Loli, it is because the moment for you to suffer has begun."

* * *

Suffering she has known, deep and tearing.

Her mother is the only one to guess; only a very pious mother's sensitivity will perceive unspoken misery.

110

Jacinta, 1964.

We shall point out further on the spiritual struggle of a 13 and 14 year old child, distressed by intellectual contradictions as subtle as they are dangerous.

One must have personally fought with the antagonist she faced, one must know and love him to appreciate the weight of the cross Loli has to carry.

That's how things go when, in a small mountain village, an

unwise father will carelessly admit into his own house various young university students coming from different Spanish cities; especially when this student takes sides while being involved in the midst of a secret and painful crisis in his own Catholic faith.

Unknown to Ceferino, Loli has witnessed the numerous discussions between her father and the students. She heard every argument, every consideration which should have systematically destroyed all certainty about the Garabandal events. She saw, heard and measured the disastrous effect of these debates on the mind of her father, whom she respects and loves dearly.

Silently, like her mother, she has suffered beyond description, never imagining that this is how it would be when one is named Mary of Sorrows.

XLIII

JACINTA

It was said that when Loli left, she dampened two handkerchiefs with her tears.

We will never learn whether Jacinta, who accompanied her the same morning, had cried also.

Surely, the separation from her family and village tore at her heartstrings! But, this mountain child Jacinta, who had never travelled previously, is more of a "nun" than the other three girls.

She turned 16 on April 22, 1965, and she had asked for admission to the Discalced Carmelite Convent, one of those austere cloisters with double grating, similar to the one Thérèse of Lisieux belonged to. A regular community vote had admitted her, and there she would find a refuge. But in front of her, as it was in the case of Loli—and as we shall see later on concerning Conchita—there arose a sophisticated wisdom, far different from the villagers' customary practical judgment.

Despite her attraction for the Carmel, she was to go first to a boarding school run by the Sisters of Charity, in the province of Zaragoza.

For the rest of it, we shall see later on.

Let the sages bear their responsibility; today and tomorrow!

This solution probably received the immediate approval of her mother, Maria, ever kind and devoted as are all mothers of large families.

For a mother, is not a Carmel mainly a parlor behind hostile grating! . . .

Her father, Simon, a man of firm and unshakeable faith with an ingrained simplicity, had reacted, to our astonishment, in exactly the same way.

To remain permanently at a boarding school or elsewhere in voluntary retirement, with a spirit of atonement, discretion and self-effacement seems a surprising choice for the least mentioned of the four clairvoyants.

And yet, what interior fervour, behind Jacinta's silence!

It was the good fortune of many persons to be able to observe her expression during Mass, while saying grace, or assisting at night prayers.

Those rare visitors with whom she felt relaxed and at ease were also privileged to have been favored with one of her heavenly smiles. A French boy of her own age, usually grudging with compliments to girls, remarked to his mother on observing Jacinta going to the fountain; "Mon Dieu, she is beautiful, she could be taken for the Virgin herself."

Yes, she is beautiful!

No sooner did we see her, than she suddenly disappeared.

To succeed in talking with her, one would have to be a girl of her own background with a mind similar to her own!

She did however, confide in an Andalusian lady who had gone up to Garabandal on June 18, 1965. On the day following the apparition of St. Michael, she made the following disclosures:

As they both chatted pleasantly the lady asked her:

— Jacinta, are you happy about Conchita's trance?

— Very.

— Where were you yesterday afternoon?

— In front of Conchita's house.

— What were you doing?

— I answered the prayers and sang like everyone else.

— Did you expect to have a trance also?

— No.

— Do you expect to take part in the next trance on July 2nd?

— I would like to.

— Do you believe in Conchita?

— What Conchita says is true.

Then in confidence to the same person Jacinta continued:

— Sometimes, I dream that the other three are in a trance and I am left out. It hurts me very much. But one day Conchita said to me; "I was dreaming that you were in a trance, Jacinta." And this gave me great joy.

There will be more about Jacinta in a later chapter.

XLIV

MARI CRUZ OR MARY OF THE CROSS

She became fifteen years old on June 21, 1965.

We celebrated her birthday on the day following the last apparition of St. Michael at Garabandal.

Loli was present. But even her warm smile could not completely cheer up Mari Cruz, this adolescent, who bears, as well as she is able, a heavy and mysterious cross.

We have nothing to conceal one way or another concerning Garabandal.

One must take it as a whole, with its bright moments and passing shadows.

It is not our role to penetrate God's secret ways with regard to Mari Cruz's aching shoulders. But without hesitation, we can tell what we know of the matter, with all due affection and compassion.

In November of 1962, Mari Cruz no longer had trances. During that time she followed her three companions, led as usual through the village for hours at a time, by their vision. She went along on these walks, her face pale, her expression modest and attentive. She prayed and sang along with the crowd which tirelessly followed the other three girls. Mari Cruz harbored no jealousy nor doubted the reality of what was happening. Sometimes there would be a flicker of regret over losing past joys but she remained hopeful that they could return. Mari Cruz was to wait many times for the Virgin's return.

✿ ✿ ✿

In March, 1963, we were in the kitchen of local grocery store along with a friend, a Spanish lawyer. As though by chance, Mari Cruz came in, and leaning against the door frame, looked at us rather sadly.

She was 13 years old then.

Her face was pale and drooping, her brow clouded as though possessed by another self, she said, "No, I did not see the Virgin."

As she stood there motionless, her monotonous tones seemed to come from another world.

The lawyer spoke to her for a half an hour in her own dialect. She would not give any explanation and it was impossible to draw anything more from her. She kept repeating in the same tone, in the same far-off manner, "No, I have not seen the Virgin."

She left then without further word or greeting, which was unusual in the friendly village of Garabandal.

Our friend concluded, "We have seen a ghost. It was not Mari Cruz who spoke to us."

✿ ✿ ✿

In September, 1963, four persons from Seville spent their vacations at Garabandal. All the warmth and liveliness peculiar to Andalusians settled in the Cantabrian mountain!

Mari Cruz's negative reaction astounded them, because they had in their possession a highly important document which contained evidence contradicting her negative attitude.

This document, as follows, is a summary of a conversation that one of these women, Josephina, had had with the child at 9:30 on the morning of September 6, 1962, on the balcony of her house.

— Mari Cruz, how old is the Virgin?

— About 18 years old.

— Is she always alone when you see her?

— No, one day, I saw her with her Little One.

— How old is the Little One?

— Nine or ten months old.

Then Mari Cruz told how the apparitions began.

— We wanted to go and "pinch" a few apples, then we thought that our guardian angel could see these apples. So, it was then that St. Michael presented himself to us.

— Did the angel speak a great deal during the different apparitions?

— Yes, a great deal.

— What sort of clothing does the Virgin wear?

— A white dress covering her feet and a blue mantle.

— What color are her eyes?

— They are black. Her hair is long, chestnut brown in color, it hangs down on her back and has a center part.

— Do you have to pray for the world?

— Yes, it is very evil.

— Did the Virgin speak very much?

— Yes, very much.

— What does she tell you?

— I can't speak about it.

This conversation had been carefully noted and kept by Josephina. The word "carefully" must be noted, because this happened six days before Mari Cruz's last apparition.

❊   ❊   ❊

In September, 1963, one of Josephina Maria Pepa's friends wanted to get to the bottom of the matter. She returned to see

116

Mari Cruz who, by now, was denying having seen the Virgin.

— Mari Cruz, we were here last year during this same period, and you still had trances. It was on September the 12th, was it not, that you saw the last apparition?

— Yes, that was the last, the one on September 12th, 1962.

❁ ❁ ❁

June 23rd, 1965.

The last witnesses of St. Michael's apparition on June 18, 1965, were leaving Garabandal.

Among them were the same Sevillian nurses, good-hearted and fraternally inclined.

They were as devoted to the family of Mari Cruz as to the others.

Maria Pepa easily became the confidante of the troubled adolescent.

This is what she wrote about the interviews:

"At the beginning, when I would question her during a conversation about her trances, Mari Cruz would only shrug her shoulders as an answer.

"On the road to 'the Pines,' we paused near the apple tree, and I asked her how they had picked the famous apples. I had never heard the story told by any of the other clairvoyants.

"She gave me all the details, showing how they had gone about jumping over the wall to reach the tree.

"I encouraged her to have confidence in the Virgin, and not to feel afraid because she had denied having had her trances. I told her that at her age, fear can cause hesitation and indecision. I even went so far as to reveal to her a problem concerning certain scruples of mine about a private matter in which I had been involved.

"Mutual confidence between us was reestablished.

— Mari Cruz, how many times have you seen the Virgin?

Her shoulders shrug.

— My little one, this is the way children answer when they haven't learned to talk yet.

— ? ? ?

117

— My little nephew who is a year and a half, does as you do.

"Mari Cruz began to laugh and answered:

— Yes, I saw the Virgin.

— How many times? One? . . . many times?

"Relaxed, she laughed and answered: 'many times.'

"From then on the roles were reversed, Mari Cruz asked the questions:"

— Have you seen me in a trance, Maria Pepa?

— Yes.

"This answer pleased her deeply. She continued showing interest in the trance Conchita had experienced on June the 18th. Mari Cruz asked:

— Did she please you?

— Of course.

— Why?

— I explained how I felt, Conchita's joy and all the rest. Then Mari Cruz left, weeping.

"I tried to find out the reason for her tears, but she came down the road without saying another word."

＊　＊　＊

Who is Mari Cruz? She is Mary of the Cross. What is her "testimony"? It is painful mystery, yet a necessary part of the conflicts which are breaking this adolescent's heart.

Her passion, or her compassion, will end, on the day of the Miracle, as Conchita, her best friend, has said.

XLV

LATER INTERVIEW WITH JACINTA

On September 5, 1965, Jacinta was interviewed by a knowledgeable older man, who knew Garabandal to his fingertips.

Here is a part of that conversation:

Jacinta:

— Conchita informed me last Sunday, that she would write to her mother from the convent where she was going, of the date of the Miracle, when the time had come.

Mr. X:

— You are also going to the convent?

— Yes.

— Now that you have such a nice new house, are you not sorry to leave?

— Since I wish to become a nun, it's because the world means nothing to me.

— Do you not regret leaving your little village?

— No . . . have I not seen more than enough of it? In 1961, we (all four) used to say that we would leave for the convent.[1]

— Do your parents, Maria and Simon, believe in the apparitions?

— Whenever I was in a trance state, my mother would say, "Yes, it's the Virgin." When I was not in a trance state, she would say, "No."

— Did the Virgin ever mislead you?

— No! How could the Virgin be misleading?

— But what about the Miracle?

— It is very certain that the Miracle will happen.

— What do you think of those who do not believe in the apparitions?

— No one is obliged to believe! . . .

— And of those to whom proof has been given and who do not believe?

— The Virgin gave them proof to see what their faith would amount to.

— What does Father Valentine, the parish priest of Cosio and your own parish priest, say now?

---

[1] "We will be nuns," such was the answer the four clairvoyants thought they had to give to Our Lady, by 1961.

119

— When he heard that we would be leaving for the convent, he was very pleased.

— What is your most vivid memory in the apparitions?

— I, in the beginning . . . when they began, I didn't know the mysteries of the rosary, nor the litanies . . . and I still don't know how I learned them. . . .

— Did they not teach them to you in school?

— No, no, Sir, I didn't know them. . . . When Madame Serafina (the teacher) said the beads, she would say the mysteries and litanies herself. It was bit by bit every day, on seeing the Virgin, that I learned them, but I don't know how.

XLVI

RETRACTION OF MARI CRUZ AT SANTANDER

What follows is the second part of the interview Jacinta had with the same man. We consider it to be highly important in helping to understand Mari Cruz's present attitude.

Jacinta reveals herself steadfast, willing and able to cross swords and strike in the right place.

The answers Mari Cruz gave are evidence, as Conchita said long before, that she is not speaking on her own; what she is saying does not come from within herself.

Her interviewer asked Jacinta:

— Have you spoken with Mari Cruz since she simulated a trance before his Grace, the Bishop, after which she was interrogated by Canon Odriozola, clerk of the Santander Commission?

Jacinta answered:

— When we spoke of that, we were both in front of Generasa, a woman from the village. She was present during our conversation.

I asked Mari Cruz:

— What did you dare to do before his Grace, the Bishop?

She didn't answer me but attacked immediately.

— I am firm and unshakeable. If you were too, you would imitate me. Firm and unshakeable, I remain! Yes.

Tell me, is it true that you simulated a trance and that you denied at the same time having seen the Virgin? How is it possible?

— Yes, I simulated a trance . . .

So, I continued:

— Mari Cruz, when you lied in saying that you had seen the Virgin, you went to Communion every day. Now that you deny having seen the Virgin, you pretend to be telling the truth, but you no longer go to Communion. Why, Mari Cruz?

— It's all the same to me. Jacinta, do you believe you are better than I am today?

— No, no, on the contrary. By putting things at their best, I am worse than you are.

❀ ❀ ❀

At this moment, Mari Cruz showed that the interview annoyed her. I continued nevertheless:

— Why are you getting so nervous?

She became vexed, then furious:

— Because you believe you alone have seen the Virgin, because you believe that I did not see her . . . because it infuriates me when things are said which are not true.

Then she added:

— All that is due to the atmosphere in the village. Yes, Padre Odriozola explained it to me at Santander: it's the atmosphere of the village which is the cause of . . .

Jacinta concluded:

— Mari Cruz did not finish her sentence. She wanted to say, but did not dare, that Padre Odriozola attributed the apparitions to the atmosphere in the village. So I tried to change the subject. It does not please Mari Cruz to have her personal attitudes discussed. But do not believe, sir, because of this, that Mari Cruz is

121

bad. No, no, Mari Cruz is good. She does not speak by herself, on her own initiative.

* * *

Here we find ourselves once more in sight of the truth.

Mari Cruz will accept having Jacinta think that she, Mari Cruz has not seen the Virgin. Furthermore, she asserts that at Santander, she was made to understand that the "apparitions" were the result of the "atmosphere" created in the village by the natives and the visitors.

Here, we come to the rescue of Mari Cruz's memory, as her nervousness was responsible for an important omission. Had she related everything which had taken place at Santander on the 24th of June 1965, she should have admitted two of her answers, of which we guarantee the absolute authenticity:

— When I simulated a trance, at the Bishop's house, his Grace told me, after a minute: That is sufficient.

— When I was spoken to about the nature of the trances, I answered: When they were genuine, we saw nothing and heard nothing of what was going on around us. When they were false, we saw and heard everything.

Poor, dear Mari Cruz, how can she know what a real trance is?

XLVII

CONCHITA'S CROSS

Strangely enough, at first sight, Conchita seems unaffected by any hostility concerning the apparitions themselves.

She pays no attention to criticism, its place of origin, or the lies which might affect her.

She lives in a world unlike that of her detractors. She feels no concern over their attitudes, but remains pleasant with all, becoming more humble, pious, obedient and modest than ever.

Does she suffer? Yes, we would say beyond expression, if we ourselves were being subjected to her inward and outward pressures. Evidence shows that she is going through what Catholic theology knows very well; purification of the soul's sensitivity. There is no other explanation for what she terms her "spiritual misery."

"I am so bad, and have so many defects and these defects are the greatest," is what she states at present.

Her detractors cannot comprehend such a statement, and use such spoken thoughts to attack her. They are dumbfounded by a spiritual reality which is beyond them.

Should any of them go up once again to Garabandal, they could then hear Conchita explain to someone questioning her on this important point, "To those who have seen the Virgin, defects and imperfections are much more serious than to other people."

It is certain that the realization of what she calls her "inner misery" is very painful to her.

❂   ❂   ❂

Still, one is led to wonder why she should welcome such wretchedness as a good thing.

She seems to be engaged, though still very young, on the same spiritual path as St. Teresa of Avila, whose motto of, "suffer or die" is very well known.

That is why she already knows the secret that so many saints have revealed to us, that suffering which is accepted for love, becomes a loved suffering, not for itself, but because it conforms to the Divine Will.

Conchita is happy to suffer because she is living out the spirit of sacrifice of the Message. Loving the crosses she bears for the sake of the Crucified One, she was heard to say to Jesus in a thanksgiving prayer, these astonishing words, "I live without suffering."

Here is the amazing document she signed, which was delivered to us by the priest who gave her Communion on that day, in 1963.

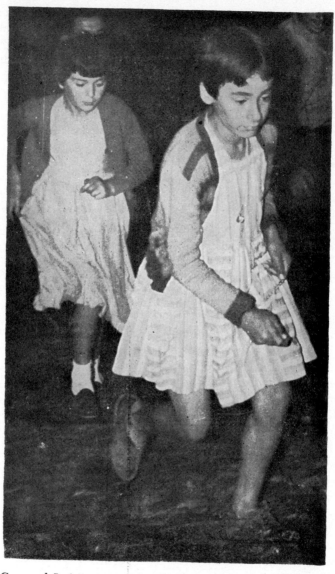

Mari Cruz and Jacinta answer the third call and run to the place where
the Virgin is expecting them.

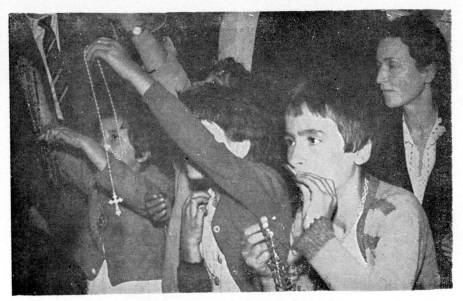

1961, Mari Cruz in a trance with the others.

— As I was thanking God, I asked Him for graces. I asked Him to let me bear the cross, because I live without suffering, except the suffering of not having a cross.

Jesus answered me:

— Yes, I will give it to you.

Very moved, I questioned further.

— What purpose will the Miracle serve? To convert many people?

He answered me:

— To convert the whole world.

— Will Russia be converted?

— It will be converted too and thus all will love Our Hearts.

— Will the Punishment come after?

He did not answer that.

— Why do you enter my poor meritless heart?

— I do not come for you, I come for all.

125

— After the Miracle, I'm afraid that they will say that only I saw the Virgin.

— By your sacrifices and great wishes, it is you who will intercede for Me to perform the Miracle.

I said to Him:

— Is it not better for the four of us to intercede, or that none of us should serve at this intercession?

— No.

— Shall I go to Heaven?

—"You will love a great deal, and you will pray to Our Hearts."

— When will you give me Your Cross?

He did not answer.

— What shall I be?

He did not answer the question.[1]

But He told me, "Wherever you are, or in whatever situation you will be, you will have much to suffer."

I continued:

— Shall I die soon?

— You must remain on earth to help people.

— I'm not much, I can't help very much.

— Through your prayers and sufferings, you will help the world.

— When we go to Heaven, are we dead?

— We never die.

— (I thought that we didn't go to Heaven before resurrecting.)

I asked Him if Saint Peter was at the gate of Heaven to receive us.

He told me no.

When I was in this oration, this conversation with God, I felt that I was no longer on earth.

Jesus also told me that today there are many who love His Heart.

He spoke to me about priests. He told me that there was much

---

[1] Jesus did not answer concerning Conchita's "Station in life."

need to pray for them, for them to become saintly, to accomplish their duty well, and make others better.

He ended with these words:

— That to those who do not know Me, they make Me known; and to those who know Me, but do not love Me, they make them love Me.

Conchita Gonzalez.

      ✿   ✿   ✿

"On previous occasions, the Virgin made me understand that the greatest Cross was the one which was borne by Her Son Who was God.

"In speaking in this way, she made me understand that we must imitate Jesus in suffering for Him and for the good of souls."

      ✿   ✿   ✿

These are awesome words. Whatever her life, wherever she may be, Conchita Gonzalez will suffer much. Jesus did not answer her question about anything immediate nor about her own vocation.

Here we are in the months of October and November, 1965. Despite her formal decision to enter the convent at the same time as Loli and Jacinta, she is still in Garabandal. This causes much comment about her, particularly on the Franco-Spanish border, in towns in a group from San Sebastian-Biarritz-Bayonne. The latter spreads fanciful rumors such as: "Conchita thinks only of fashion, it's all gone to her head; that will be the end of her going to the convent."

But then, what were the girl's feelings at this period?

Let us read a letter which she wrote to us, at the beginning of October.

"I thank you very much for your prayers on my behalf. I really need them.

"In fact, as you may well understand, wherever the Virgin is, there the devil will try to be also.

"So continue to pray for me. Thank you. Pray for me to enter the convent very soon."

She came back to the same subject in her following letter.

127

"Pray to the Virgin for me, so that I may enter the convent as soon as possible."

A third appeal for help followed a few days later at the beginning of November.

"Pray for me, as I need it greatly. Pray especially for me to enter this month, to prepare me to become a bride of Christ.

"I cannot believe that I will be such a high-ranking person as a bride of Christ. Pray for me to remain very, very faithful to Him. Now, my mother doesn't tell me when I may enter the convent."

Finally, what she believes is a last resort:

"When you write to me, tell my mother in your letter that she must let me go to the convent as soon as possible. Thank you. Adieu."

The form of trial that Conchita doesn't want, though she had asked for it from Jesus, and had not received the expected answer, was this: a demonic presence at Garabandal is the cause of her remaining at her mother's house in spite of herself.

Such was the cross of Conchita Gonzalez, in the last months of 1965.

XLVIII

OBEDIENCE TO THE CHURCH

Conchita was 16 years old on February 7, 1965. There is no point in trying to obtain information from this girl which she evidently doesn't possess.

How could she be aware of the consternation among strangers, particularly the French, facing the outward situation produced at Garabandal by the notes from the Bishopric of Santander.

These have, in effect caused Garabandal to become, for us, a veritable prison. Our impression was that in isolating us in this way, there had been a fear that we might discover the truth, all of the truth.

Conchita is completely unaware of our deep involvement in this matter. Besides, how could she, by herself, make the distinction between these notes and the Communiqué from the Holy Office? How could she understand that the date of the latter was subsequent to all the Santander notes, the Holy Office then is evidently the light which must brighten our path. We have reason to believe that she has not even read it, though even if she had, she could not have grasped the meaning of it all. She evidently has no inkling of the manner or style of the supreme Tribunal of the Catholic Church.

All that is out of her jurisdiction because, with regard to Santander, Rome and the readers, she is merely "the witness to be tried."

What interests us for the moment is her state of mind as "witness" in relation to the Authority by whom she will be judged. More precisely, we have what she has written herself on the subject. We extract this from an interrogation of which we have spoken previously in chapter XL.

The following question was put to her:

— Many of the persons who believe in Garabandal have the strong desire, while considering the question of obedience to the Church, to do all they possibly can to spread the Message of our Holy Mother. What can you tell them about this?

She answered:

— It is very acceptable to the Virgin that we should spread the Message and do as she wishes. But she wishes us to obey the Church, and this obedience will bring more glory to God. She will grant enough time for the Message to spread with the Church's permission.

Read this important text well. It reminds us of Joan of Arc standing before her judges at Rouen, victoriously discoursing on the nature of the Church and appealing to Rome.

Thus, the following is the authentic text of the Communiqué, not of a particular Church, but the Church of Rome, not a diocesan Church, but the universal Church.

129

From the See of the Holy Office,
July 28th, 1965.

To His Excellency Don Eugenio,
Beitia Aldazabal,
Apostolic Administrator of Santander.
Your Excellency,

Your letter of the 7th of this month has duly reached this Supreme Sacred Congregation, and Your Excellency informed the Holy Office on the subject of the apparitions of the Blessed Virgin Mary which, from what has been said, have taken place at the village of San Sebastian of Garabandal.

From the documentation that you submitted, it would seem sufficiently clear how prudently you have acted in this matter.

Now, I pray Your Excellency to follow this matter with a vigilant outlook in its future development. Should something new develop, please communicate it to the Holy Office.

Profiting by this occasion, I offer you the expression of my deep respect, and repeat myself to be, of Your Excellency, the very devoted.

Father Raimundo Verardo, Commissioner,
August 9th, 1965.
Eugenio, Bishop, A.A.
Let this letter be published.

This communiqué means everything it says but nothing more. It is the sentence of a sovereign Tribunal. If need be, and if it is deemed proper, the Holy Office will make further declarations later on. For the time being, it suffices.

It suffices because since the Fifth Council of Lateran (1512) and Pope Leo X (1513–1521)—that is, for 452 years—the doctrine in such matters is the following: "When there is a question of prophetic revelation (which is evidently the case of Garabandal) the pope alone is judge."

All those who have forgotten this, whoever they were, were wrong.

This communiqué will relieve the minds of men and women who are honestly working in favor of Garabandal to inform humanity in an objective way.

130

Much has been said these past years of the Holy Office. Its nature has surely been misunderstood, its role an absolute necessity. It is the Supreme Tribunal of Catholic Doctrine, the guardian of religious orthodoxy. It is also the protector of legitimate freedom within the Church.

Let us make no mistake. Without the Holy Office, the basic teachings of Catholicism could be thwarted even by a parish priest.

Do these lines surprise you? Think along these lines and remember the lessons of your experience. When a colonel is not a competent commander, all of his subordinates, from the battalion commander down to the last corporal, assume an authority which is not theirs and so the simple soldier has to suffer for it.

On the subject of Garabandal, we formally declare, in absolute loyalty: "We are struggling to prove the supernatural element of the visions. We are the fraternal adversaries, we admit, not of the Bishop of Santander, but of the Commission's methods as he found them, on taking his episcopal seat.

"Though opposed to this Commission, we nevertheless submit with mind and heart beforehand—yes with mind and heart—to the decisions of the Supreme Congregation of the Holy Office of which His Eminence Cardinal Ottaviani is secretary, and his Holiness Pope Paul VI, the Prefect."

☼　☼　☼

Is there anything reprehensible about the events at Garabandal?

Is there anything in the words the clairvoyants attribute to the Virgin which could be contrary to Christian doctrine?

Let us go back to the Note of July 8, 1965 from the Archbishopric of Santander:

"We have found no motive for ecclesiastical censureship, neither in the doctrine, nor in the spiritual recommendations disclosed on this occasion and addressed to the Christian faithful. Furthermore, this doctrine and these recommendations contain an exhortation to prayer and sacrifices, to devotion towards the Blessed Sacrament, to the cult of Our Lady along traditional, commendable lines, to a holy fear of God offended by our sins. It merely reminded us of the usual Church doctrine in this matter."

In these conditions, we of the laity do not see what harm the diffusion of the Message of Our Lady of Garabandal could do to our souls.

What harm can we do in proclaiming the urgency for conversion of the world?

Why can't our priests go freely to Garabandal and why could

Mari Cruz in a trance state.

Mari Cruz in a state of trance among the crowd in 1962, like Conchita
on June 18, 1965.

they not be authorized to remind us of the perils involved in not
obeying the Message?

Why should San Sebastian of Garabandal be a cursed place,
an object of ecclesiastical hostility?

There are many sanctuaries, for example Pellevoisin, and Ile
Bouchard, to name but those two, where it is supposed that the
Virgin must have appeared, without the Church ever having
made any pronouncement on the basis of the matter. The Church
merely permitted the erection of a chapel. Priests go there to
pray and Christians are free to gather there.

Why could it not be the same at Garabandal?

Yes, why?

133

XLIX

THE WAYS OF PROVIDENCE

"My ways are not your ways," God said.

What ways does God want? What ways will God permit? Let us respect the King's secret.

Is Conchita captive? Yes and no. Yes, as we have seen, in chapter XLVII. She had been prevented from entering the convent since September 29, 1965.

No, since Our Lady of Carmel consoles her because she couldn't leave as she wanted to.

"I had a communication from the Virgin, and she told me: 'Come to the Pines, on the 13th of November, 1965. Bring me many religious objects. I will kiss them, and you will distribute them. Through them, my Son will accomplish wonders for those who will use them in faith and confidence.'"

The letter from Conchita continued:

"In union of prayers to plead with God for the world, and especially our brothers who still do not know Christ, and do not have His divine support."

Nothing could ever hold Conchita captive, because even caged in, her spirit would always break free.

*　*　*

Is Conchita captive?

The pontifical Congregation of Propaganda in charge of missions has a statue of St. Teresa of the Child Jesus. The statue represents our "Teresita" leaning forward, the gospels held to her breast, mantle flowing, setting out in conquest of souls. The Carmelite used to say:

"Oh Jesus, I would like to travel the world over to spread the Gospel in the five parts of the world."

Conchita may not know it, but this statue of "Teresita," now in

134

the vestry of her parish church, was donated by her grand-mother.

In any case, the comparison to be drawn is that if Teresita's spirit was not confined in her cloister, neither is Conchita in her home where she is detained against her wishes. Like the saint of Lisieux, she lets her spirit travel, preferring those lands where her non-Christian brothers live, whoever they might be.

No one can curtail her excursions in spirit which go beyond ecumenism itself.

❀　❀　❀

The preceding texts were brought back from Spain to one of the editors of our international group. The "postman," who delivered them is also the printer (in French) of this book, among other things. He had just returned from Garabandal with his wife and three children.

Our printer had gone there sometime previously with his family. They had left without having any knowledge of Spanish and without any contacts in the village. Their only assets in their adventure were their faith and simplicity.

Nothing stopped them, not being bogged down in the mud, the climb on foot, nor the risky descent at night in the downpours.

However, later on they felt rewarded when they met two interpreters by chance, in the kitchen of Conchita's home. Aniceta and Conchita made them feel welcome, the latter kissing the mother and children. As for our printer, he was given a picture with this dedication: "In union of prayer to pray to God, for all our brothers who still do not know God and can't enjoy faith."

The dedication seems especially appropriate for a printer.

The printer has worked devotedly in the service of all our publications. Along with his wife, he came away with the following impressions:

His wife made the following remark:

— Conchita loves children. She adores the smaller ones and spoils them. She seems to pray for the older ones while they are there. She gave the impression that she could see something which we could not. She heaped attentions on us in every way, and yet in her presence, we feel intimidated.

135

— Why did you undertake such a trip?
Reply:
— Because on the 18th of June in Garabandal, where we were,
Our Lady of Carmel cured our seven-year-old boy.

*　*　*

The above interlude did not lead us away from Providential
route. We continue. Without the test permitted by Providence,
there would not have been any "missionary" conversation on
October 30th, 1965, and no last rendez-vous at the Pines on
Saturday, November 13th as we will read in the following pages.
Without the test, we would never have known that this young
girl was already much more of a missionary than the young
novices of the Order of Discalced Missionary Carmelites which
she was to enter at Pamplona.

*　*　*

Conchita Gonzalez! Daughter of the sun, of the wind, of the
mountains' storms!
Pure beauty of Spanish youth. Downcast eyes hiding the
reflection of the living image of Our Lady of Carmel!
Composure similar to that of the Mother of the World who
was keeping the mysteries within her heart, even when near the
Cross.
Miraculous modesty pleased only when playing with children,
especially with the youngest!
Reflection of the woman who is the Dawn arising on a world
much in need of a new Pentecost!
Prophet of a Good Friday, preceding the joy of Easter!
A star lost amongst the splendour of all the stars twinkling
above the luminous diadem of her vision.
Tomorrow, away from Garabandal, and amongst the nuns of
Pamplona, joyfully anonymous because the Virgin must grow
in importance and she must lose importance.
Conchita Gonzalez, called, protected by the archangel of the
Paradise lost before the time of Redemption.
So, without fear and reproach, humble and smiling under the
fiery wings of Saint Michael, Conchita Gonzalez appears before
the world.

No, she will never be a prisoner, no matter what!

After the departure of Conchita, the walls of the "prison" that is now Garabandal shall fall by themselves. Those who would try to retain her would resemble the soldiers collapsing around the Easter tomb!

The visionaries will have found a refuge in the silence and freedom which is their right.

Then the crowds will come up and no one can ever accuse them of having created the "atmosphere responsible for the apparitions."

Free at last, the crowds will be able to wander where they will. In the village, they will be able to find each of the places, and the traces of the passage and presence of Our Lady of Carmel. At Beauraing, one has to pray before the Hawthorn, at Lourdes it is at the Grotto. At Fatima, people pray on the steps of the Green Oak Chapel.

At Garabandal, the Virgin visited the church and almost every house. She went through all the roads of the village, from the entrance to "The Pines," without forgetting the smallest lane. She had even led the clairvoyants regularly to the cemetery.

Guided by Saint Michael, whenever they will want to go, men, women and children from all over the world will kiss the hand of She who came not for Loli, Jacinta, Mari Cruz or Conchita, nor for the village, nor for Spain, but for all of humanity:

Our Lady of Mt. Carmel of Garabandal.

L

A FRENCH DOCTOR

The following letter which was dated August, 1965, gives a good explanation of the actual atmosphere of Garabandal, and is an answer to the lies printed in certain newspapers:

"You have asked me for an account of what I saw and thought at San Sebastian of Garabandal; so it is with pleasure that I go about the task, and at the same time authorized the publication of my testimony, if you wish to do so.

So that you may better understand my social and professional position, I state that I am a pediatrician, age 52, and that I have eight children, and am a grandfather twice over.

When we left for Garabandal on the 12th of July, 1965 with two of my daughters and the fiancé of one of them, we did not have any intention, my wife and I, to go on a pilgrimage or go and invoke the Blessed Virgin under another name. We both wear the Mount Carmel scapular.

On the 13th of June, a colleague had given me an account of what he had learned about the apparitions of which, up until then, I had not been aware.

On that day, one of my sons was killed in an automobile accident with a friend of his, and another friend was left with irreparable injuries and frightful wounds. The possibilities of a cure and conversion (our two daughters are married into families who have little or no faith) had attracted us, my wife and I; but we especially wanted to look over the site in order to act as eventual guides.

We left with two rather vague and incomplete addresses, those of Father Luis Retenaga for whom we had to search a fairly long time in Renteria, and that of Doctor Ortiz at Santander. We were happy over the kindness of these two men who were truly inconvenienced because they had not received the letters we had written the previous week.

* * *

Through unforeseen circumstances, we had left by ordinary means of transportation, without any itinerary or reservations, and suddenly found ourselves in Cosio on the night of July 15th, and without planning it, we spent July 16th at Garabandal.

Contrary to what we had read in the newspapers (Sud-Ouest de Bordeaux, le Figaro and le Monde de Paris), we had enough trouble to get something to eat in Garabandal. We had a day of involuntary fasting (bread, chocolate, bananas), all of poor quality. We even had the impression that these poor, brave people were selling to us through kindness and not seeking a clientele.

Certainly, we didn't see anywhere any article, souvenirs,

138

photographs, or pious objects of any nature, even though we wandered about the small territory throughout the day while waiting till it was time for the rosary and evening service. No one offered us anything.

There were no visible signs, except for some minor vandalism sustained by one or two pine trees. Everything seemed very ordinary, humble and poverty-stricken.

A Spanish priest who spoke French well promised to introduce us to the little clairvoyants (we did not have this in mind when we came), and this promise was what made us remain till evening service.

We were pleased to see the modest condition, the simplicity of Jacinta and Loli, the kindliness and generosity of Conchita.

Don Luis Retenaga had told me that one or two physicians appointed by the Bishop of Santander, had called these children hysterical, and victims of hallucinations and imagination caused by the great poverty and isolation of any out of the way village, far from the city.

* * *

We pediatricians, sometimes have to deal with young girls (or young boys) whom we call "pithiatiques." * And we take enjoyment out of detecting them within the first few seconds of contact. Their appearance and their gaze reveal to us what conclusions must be drawn.

Well, I can state that my impression had been very much the contrary in the presence of the three young girls. It is rather that of simplicity. There was no affectation, and it still is a wonder to me that, after having been the center of attention and sought after, these children—especially Conchita, who was the most exposed to attention behaved very modestly and did not try drawing attention to themselves or playing a role, even though they were aware of being the focus of attention and that people travelled thousands of miles to see them.

Truly, the sincerity of Conchita's welcome, after what she has had to endure, the past several years, is almost miraculous.

We may add that even if the numerous trances were simu-

---

* Pithiatism: A medical term meaning: curable by persuasion or suggestion in reference to a class of conversion hysterical symptoms which can be made to disappear or reappear by means of suggestion. (Stedman's Medical Dictionary)

lated, and more so if they resulted from natural nervous phenomena, it is still a greater miracle that these girls have remained unchanged!

That night, as I said, we had gone to attend evening service and the rosary. The little clairvoyants were a few minutes late. There was an empty place beside my daughter in the pew, which Loli came and occupied. I was able to observe her during the recitation of beads and nudged my wife. The quality of her prayer was admirable.

With her gaze fixed above the altar, her lips scarcely moving, she was indifferent to everything around her, as though she could see something. She was not in a trance state, although the memory of her vision of Mary was doubtless intense enough to give her this expression.

* * *

To finish, I would like to reveal a personal impression that I brought back from Garabandal and which it pleases me to recall and which is like breathing the perfume from a flower which had been given to me.

The evening service had seemed to me very lengthy. Night had almost fallen and I was apprehensive about coming back down to Cosio, my wife having mentioned that her flashlight was about ready to burn out.

I was waiting for my wife, who was talking to a priest in the vestry and was taking a long time to come out. I happened to be right in the path of Conchita as she was coming out of church. She recognized me, since we had spent half an hour at her home in the afternoon and had spoken with her. She gave me a level look and favored me with a smile of which I keep a pleasant memory. I had already seen that smile and that look, and found them to be the opposite of anything wanton.

Without any pretention, I can say that my appearance is not that of a venerable old gentleman, and I was thinking that only one possessing genuine purity and authentic saintliness could smile at a man in such a way.

Had she been playing a role, or more simply a pupil from some "Holy School," she would have kept her gaze directed chastely to the tips of her shoes.

These are the impressions of modesty that I brought back from Garabandal.

May I add that I admire the insight of the interpreter of the

Message of June 18th? Should someone tell me it was Conchita's invention, I will know what to answer.

For the past several years, my wife and I have been annoyed by the biased opinions of certain priests. I have become hostile with regard to their doctrine, to their tendency toward belief in immanence, to a sort of neo-protestantism, hiding the light of the Church Triumphant under a bushel. We were amazed at the exactness of the diagnosis which we had formulated ourselves, though less clearly: that less and less importance is given to the Blessed Sacrament, and we "think" but little about the Passion of Jesus."

Doctor Apostolidès,
Chief of Pediatric Services,
Hospital Center, Troyes (Aube)

LI

FINAL RENDEZVOUS AT THE PINES

Aniceta could prevent her daughter from entering the convent on September 29, 1965, at the time of Loli and Jacinta's departure.

She could not—she would not have wanted to, anyway—forbid her to go to "The Pines," where Our Lady of Carmel had set a final rendezvous on November 13th, 1965.

It was a Saturday, as announced by the Virgin two weeks earlier. It was on the feast day of that extraordinary lay brother, Diego, born at Saint Nicholas del Puerto, in Andalusia, around 1400. This saint had fully lived up to his ideal, Saint Francis of Assisi.

Miracles flourished about him, and during periods of contemplation he received such deep insight on Faith that theologians were happy to gather some of the written scraps.

What anniversary could better suit Our Lady's purpose than that of this humble monk who died in New Castille, with his gaze directed to the cross.

Another coincidence: The Virgin who had wished to have the numerous objects which she had kissed distributed throughout the world, had shortly before inspired a French layman, on a pilgrimage to Lourdes, to send one hundred prayer beads and four rosaries to Conchita. . . .

* * *

This is the translation of the five pages of her notebook where Conchita relates her encounter with Our Lady.

"I awaited the arrival of this day, Saturday, Nov. 13, with great eagerness to receive those who had planted in me the seeds of God's happiness: the Virgin Mary and her Son, the very little Child Jesus, whom She carried in Her arms.

"It was raining, but evidently, that didn't matter to me in going up to 'the Pines.' I had many prayer beads with me, which had been offered to me shortly before as gifts to be distributed. As the Virgin had told me, I was bringing them for her to kiss.

"On going up to 'the Pines,' I was alone. As I walked along thinking to myself, overcome with great remorse for my faults, that from now on, I would not fall into these ways. It was because I felt ashamed to present myself before the Mother of God, without removing my defects from my soul. I was ashamed of the way I would feel after having been seen by those who see my defects. They are very big, they are the biggest.

* * *

"On arriving at 'The Pines,' I began taking out the prayer beads that I carried with me. As I was busy taking them from the parcel, I heard a very soft voice, evidently that of the Virgin. In fact, she is easily distinguished from all other women. Her voice called me by name.

"I answered Her: What do you wish?

"And I saw Her with the little Infant Jesus in her arms. She was coming, clad as usual, and smiling.

"I had chewing gum in my mouth. But after seeing Her, I stopped chewing it. I slipped it in back of a tooth. But the Virgin was wise. She 'knew' that I had it in my mouth and said, 'Conchita, why don't you remove your chewing gum and offer it as a sacrifice for the glory of my Son?'

"Shamefaced, I took it out, and threw it on the ground.

"Afterwards, she said to me, 'Do you remember what I told

142

you on your feast-day, December the 8th, 1963? That you would suffer very much on earth? Well, I am repeating it. Have confidence in Us. You will offer everything to Our Hearts, for the welfare of your brothers. And so, we will help you, and you will feel that we are near you.'

"And I said to Her, 'But I am unworthy, oh, Our Lady, of so many graces granted by you. And you come to me again today, to lift my little cross, that I am carrying now.'

"She answered me, 'Conchita, I do not come for you only, I come for all my children, hoping to draw them closer to Our Hearts.'

"She added, 'Give me all that you have brought with you that I may kiss them,' and I gave them to her.

"I carried a crucifix with me. She kissed it and told me, 'Slip it through the hands of the Little Jesus.' I did so. "He" didn't say anything.

"I said to the Little Jesus, 'I will bring this crucifix to the convent.' He didn't answer me.[1]

* * *

"After having kissed everything I offered her, the Virgin said, 'By means of the kiss which I gave to these objects, my Son will accomplish wonders. Distribute them to others.'

— "I will do so."

"After that, She asked me to present the requests for other people, the petitions they had entrusted me with. I presented them to her.

"She continued, 'Tell me, Conchita, tell me things concerning my children. I hold them all under my mantle.'

"I answered her: 'We are not all gathered under your mantle, it could not cover us all, it is very little.' She smiled.

— "Conchita, Conchita, do you know why I did not come myself, on the 18th of June, to give you the Message destined for the world? Because it grieved me to tell it to you myself. But I

[1] Once again, we note, Heaven gives no precise indication to Conchita concerning her vocation. There is never any answer to her decision to become a nun.

must tell you for your own good, if you carry it out and for the glory of God. I love you very much, and desire your salvation. I desire to see you all reunited here in Heaven, around the Father, the Son and the Holy Spirit."

"Conchita, is it not true, you will comply?'

"I said to her, 'If I saw you always, yes. But, without this favor, I am very wicked.'

— 'Do everything you can on your side. And we will help you. We will also help our girls Loli, Jacinta, and Mari Cruz.'

This apparition lasted a very short time.

She told me also, 'This is the last time that you will see me here. But I will always be with you and with all of my children.'

She added: 'Conchita, you must visit my Son in the Tabernacle more, why do you let laziness prevent you from visiting my Son more often? He awaits you night and day.'

* * *

"As I mentioned before, it was raining a great deal.

"The Virgin and the Baby Jesus did not get wet in any way. When I saw them no longer, I was wet.

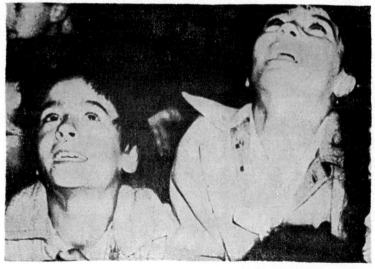

Mari Cruz and Conchita in a trance state.

144

"I made a request of the Virgin, 'Oh, I am so happy when I see you both. Why do you not bring me away with you now?'

She answered me, 'Remember what I told you on your feast-day. In presenting yourself before God, you must show your hands filled with deeds you did for your brothers and for the Glory of God. Now, however, your hands are empty.'

※　※　※

"That's all. The happy time that I spent with my Mother from Heaven and my best friend, and with the little Jesus is all over. I have ceased to see them, but I still feel them. Once again, they have spread peace and joy in my heart, with great desires to conquer my faults, and to love with all my strength, the Hearts of Jesus and Mary who love us so much."

LII

LOLI WRITES TO AN AMERICAN

Mr. William A. Nolan, one of our friends from the U.S.A., sends us a photocopy of a letter which Loli wrote to him on March 25, 1965.

"For my new and excellent friend in Christ.

"I thank you very much for your trip to Spain and your visit to this village of San Sebastian of Garabandal, province of Santander. In this village situated in the middle of the mountains where Our very Holy Mother, once more appeared to show the affection she has for the entire world.

"As a mother, she forgives us everything, if we ask her with faith.

"She shows this 'letter' in her village.[1]

'I would also say to all of you that to avoid the Punishment,

[1] Loli compares the apparitions and their content to a letter of the Virgin in which she instructs her people.

145

we must make many sacrifices, the family must say the Rosary together every day.'

"This is what our very Holy Mother asks us. She asks us also that we love one another as Our Lord loved us.

"White people should love black people and black people should love white people, for we are all Brothers.

"I will say adieu in Christ and in Mary, our very Holy Mother."

Maria Dolores Mazon Gonzalez.

LIII

CONCHITA'S LAST DETAILS

On the 10th of December 1965, the adolescent wrote:

"Before the last Apparition at 'The Pines' on November 13, 1965, the Blessed Virgin had said:

'Jesus does not send you the Punishment to discourage you, but to help you, and to rebuke you for not paying attention to Him.

'He will send you the Warning to purify you and to prepare you for the Miracle. In this Miracle, He clearly proves the love He has for you as well as His desire for you to carry out the Message.

'The Warning will be seen, will happen everywhere and to everyone. It is like a punishment, like a chastisement. We shall see how we have acted in committing sin. I think, (I, Conchita) that for we who hope, will derive great benefit from it for our sanctification.'"

On January 10, 1966, one of Conchita's confidants made the following credible remark:

"Yesterday I spoke with Conchita.

She knew perfectly well the exact date on which the Miracle is to take place at Garabandal. At present she is authorized to convey it only to the Holy Father. She will do it in a very few days, on the occasion of a personal visit.

The date she doesn't know is that of the Warning. . . . But she knows the nature of it, she is aware of what it will consist."

We must take note of this: two different events are predicted by Conchita, the Warning and the Miracle.

Conchita does not know the date of the Warning.

The purpose of the Warning is to open the eyes of all those who follow the "movement of Garabandal." In fact, the fulfilment of this "prophecy" will have as a consequence, the presence of a great number of people, at Garabandal, the day of the Miracle. Concerning the date of this Warning we know only that it will occur before the Miracle.

Therefore, Conchita does not know the exact date of the Warning, but she knows perfectly well that of the Miracle.

The Miracle will be very, very spectacular. There will remain a permanent sign of it at "The Pines." This sign will resemble a pillar formed from some unknown substance which will be visible to the naked eye and could be photographed and filmed. But it will be impossible to feel, there will be no sense of feeling on touching it.

Conchita gives this definition of it, "It will be something which will resemble a 'pillar of smoke.'" [1]

❊   ❊   ❊

At the beginning of March, 1966, Conchita had sent a special message to us through a reliable intermediary:

"Conchita asked me to write to you to urge you to continue spreading the Message, and do so more urgently than in the past.

She asked me to write to you to be sure of the coming of the Warning and the Miracle which will follow.

Publishers Note: The following was told by Conchita and written down on October 20, 1968 by two members of the Newtonville Garabandal Center who visited her in Garabandal:

[1] "The sign is something that you will be able to see but that you can not touch. It can also be likened to rays of sunlight." Conchita went on to explain that it will not be rays of sunlight or a pillar of smoke but that the resemblance is in a metaphorical sense—a pillar of smoke or rays of sunlight can be seen but not touched.

147

She told me, 'The Warning is like something very frightening which will happen in the sky.'

Do not forget this message that Conchita entrusted me to convey to you. Let the Garabandalists continue to propagate and spread the Messages.

The Virgin will reward them, she assured me."

A few months before Conchita had stressed, "Spread the Message. If it is welcomed, rejoice. If it is not well received, do not argue the matter, pass on to others, go elsewhere."

LIV

CONCHITA WRITES
TO FRIENDS OF GARABANDAL

Dear Friends, I send you my most affectionate greetings, and promise you my poor prayers in union with Jesus in the Tabernacle and with the Blessed Virgin. May our desire to love God and His Mother (who is also our own) grow unceasingly along with our desire to conquer our defects. I am asking for your prayers for me and my friends because we have great need of them. Pray that we may be very humble, and that we give to Jesus what he wants of us. Pray that we may succeed to become nuns some day with the purpose of serving God and helping our brothers who are in need. Such is our wish, but we are very weak and need help.

On the first of January, 1965 (apparition at "The Pines"), the Blessed Virgin told me that we Catholic Christians, do not think about the other world, of Heaven, nor of hell, and that we should think of them. In that way our lives would thus be united with Christ. We should think more about the Passion of Jesus, and meditate more about it. We must do that, and not only do it, but inspire others to do it.

We shall then feel "closer to God's glorious portals" and we would then joyously accept our crosses for the love of God.

With great affection for all, and in union of prayers.

Conchita Gonzales
12/11/65"

LV

JOURNEY TO ITALY

In spite of all the precautions that had been taken since August of 1965, many people found out that Conchita and her mother, Aniceta, had gone to Santander to pick up their passports.

As soon as the word got around, everyone began to speculate on the matter. In a short time, the more indiscreet remarks filtered through, and the shrewdest among the curious came to believe and repeat, that one day sooner or later, the two women would be leaving for Italy, which was exactly what it was all about.

*   *   *

Before relating details of this trip, it is necessary to point out certain facts. We have alluded to them previously, but now, to be thorough, it is necessary to be more explicit.

On September 8, 1965, at Torrelavega, Conchita and her mother had formally announced her departure for the convent of the Discalced Carmelite Missionaries at Pamplona, scheduled for September 29, on the feast of Saint Michael. The same day, Loli and Jacinta were to leave Garabandal for the province of Zaragoza where they were expected by the Sisters of Charity.

Why should it be precisely on the 29th of September? Because Conchita and her mother believed, for excellent reasons, that the trip to Italy would be made before the 14th of September, the date of the last session of the Council.

As events turned out otherwise, the two women had to endure several agonizing months from the time of Saint Michael's feast until the 7th of February, 1966.

Fearing the worst for them, certain opponents of Garabandal tried everything they could to prevent Conchita from being received in Rome. Others, of lesser importance, joined in with the group of detractors from the gulf of Biscayne which we mentioned earlier, to slander the adolescent. "Her head has been turned, she wears short skirts, her head is filled with radio, the rel:g:ous vocation is all off, Garabandal is finished."

During that time, Conchita felt the devil prowling around her and had to endure inner spiritual suffering known only to those more contemplative souls. She wrote of her secret distress to priests in whom she had confidence, imploring them to obtain permission from her mother to leave for Pamplona immediately.

It seems that, though she was used to leaving everything up to the Virgin, she had not immediately understood the importance of the trip to Italy. Unless she thought in her own mind—very reasonably so—that if the journey had to take place some day, it might as well be made from Pamplona as from Garabandal.

But Aniceta was on guard. And Aniceta's will is of iron. She had been convinced of the necessity and the imminence of the visit to Rome, and no one on earth could make her give in. Some day, if someone seeks a person of unusual vigor, they will find only one and her name will be Aniceta Gonzalez.

All the prayers, all the pleadings of her daughter were in vain. So were the letters which tried to make her give in to Conchita.

There is more to this. This little mountain girl closeted herself with her secret and faced up to anyone. This is the explanation for her behavior toward visitors. There is no other reason for her unshakeable steadfastness, and shyness, her rebuffs, her apparently inexplicable silences, her mental reservations before the indiscreet of all types and nationalities who came to her house, her own house, and tortured her for four months.

✻ ✻ ✻

In God's plan, "There is always a day of reckoning."

Those of us who knew why Conchita was not at Pamplona, did as Aniceta did; we kept silent. Today we can speak before the world, of the odious and perfidious conduct of the adversaries of Garabandal, both great and small. Never at any moment, in any way, did Conchita nor her mother become "deflated" as it pleased some to scandalously tell, repeat and write.

150

They simply had had to wait, with the secret they had to keep, until Providence decided.

* * *

Just about the time everyone thought that the two women were in Pamplona, the exemplary older son Serafin looked after the house while evasively answering all indiscreet questions, and Conchita, Aniceta and Father Luna were boarding a plane in Barcelona.

It was January 12, 1966.

Of this trip, we know only what we have been permitted to know. Unless God chooses at some future date to reveal it, we may never know what Conchita revealed in confidence, or the secrets which the Supreme Authorities have imposed on her. Let us not knock on doors which must remain closed. Let us respect this silence. Enough has been said publicly, known by the participants, the audience, and simple passerby to satisfy the minds and hearts of each one.

* * *

In Rome, Conchita was first welcomed at the Holy Office. Ushered in alone, evidently, she was heard and interrogated for two hours and a half. Her questioners treated her with all the kindness that her humility, simplicity and honesty warranted.

It is quite certain that all the friends of Garabandal wanted Conchita to take this trip. Particularly interested were the theologians, whose interest in this Cause arose from the conviction that upon this Providential plan depends the salvation of souls and the lives of humanity.

In their eyes, it was highly important that the first visit Conchita made would be to the Supreme Tribunal of the Holy Office, thus adhering to the correct canonical procedure prescribed by the Church. They believed the girl should make her first appearance before the legitimate Authority with jurisdiction in matters of prophetic revelation.

This correct procedure was followed, from the moment of Conchita's arrival, and is striking proof of the supernatural wisdom

151

Mari Cruz in a state of trance, 1961.

and scientific integrity of the authorities in Rome, and is a source
of immeasurable comfort to all of God's people.

❋   ❋   ❋

As had been recommended to her, among other things, Conchita prayed at length in two Roman churches. She also prayed at
the Coliseum and in one of the Catacombs. She wrote souvenir
post cards to her friends back home. We translate the one which
we happen to have here, because its message is intended for
each of us.

"Rome, 1/14/66.
For the Virgin's group of Garabandal.
My mother greets you.
From Rome where I have remembered all of you, very spe-
cially in union with the Lord.
A kiss for all.

152

Mari Cruz on June 18, 1965, near Conchita's house.

May we always keep the Message and Our Lord God in our heart.

Conchita Gonzalez."

Having attended to devotional duties, they motored on to San Giovanni Rotondo to visit Padre Pio.

* * *

When they consulted the saintly monk's personal physician, he had discouraging news. "The Padre is too tired. He absolutely needs to rest. This visit will have to be postponed till later."

Less than an hour after we heard the disappointing news, the Padre surprised them all by upsetting the customary visiting schedule, and received our friends at a time when no one is ever welcomed.

153

Conchita, her mother, and their companions entered a private parlor, next to the big church's choir loft. Joy and serenity characterized the meeting. Conchita sat beside the happy Padre, who gave her a paternal blessing. They spoke amicably for a long time, and seemed to be bathed in a celestial light, as we were told later by the Italian interpreter who assisted Padre Pio and Conchita. The interpreter, a Franciscan, compared the interview to be reported conversations between St. Francis of Assisi and St. Clare.

*　*　*

After Padre Pio's extraordinary welcome, our travelers were enthusiastic about the success of Conchita's mission to Rome. These providential meetings had taken place at a time when they were at least expected.

How Conchita reacted to the words the Holy Father addressed to her is her secret, though her Roman friends know that she treasures the Holy Father's greeting.

The Pope, on the occasion of the public audience at the Apostolic Palace on January 19, 1966 paused before Conchita to bless her in a transport of incredible joy, with the words, "I bless you, and with me, all the Church blesses you." ("Ti benedico, e con ne ti benedice tutta la Chiesa.") According to the Roman witnesses, Conchita's faithful companions, "The look on the face of His Holiness was . . . sublime."

Yes, dear readers, you have read correctly: "I, the Pope, bless you, and with me, the whole Church blesses you."

Unbelievable, yet absolutely true.

Unbelievable, yet equally true is the episode of the public audience, not forgetting that it was the last farewell of the Garabandal messenger.

*　*　*

Some minutes later in Saint Peter's square, a Roman automobile sped off toward the airport. They made it on time: the plane was waiting to carry Conchita, and her happiness through the skies.

The next day, on the 20th of January, eight days after their

154

departure for Barcelona, the three travelers, having first visited Geneva, landed in Madrid.

Aniceta finally had found peace, her task was accomplished.

As for Conchita, the first stage of her life was completely and perfectly ended; she was now free to undertake the next stage, that of keeping her promise of September 8, 1965.

LVI

TO A BOYS' CHAPLAIN

"S.S. of Garabandal
Ave Maria!
1/31/66.
Reverend Father,

I am sending you these lines through one of your boys, to tell you that on the 7th of February I am going to Pamplona, to the "Angelical college" of the convent.

Pray for me a lot, because I'm quite certain the devil is always beside me. Don't forget to pray for me and ask God to show me the way very clearly. In fact, what I want is to accomplish His holy will and give Him great Glory.

I wonder what glory I can give to Him in all my wretchedness.

The trip to Rome was very good. It could not have been better. (mejor viaje ne cabe) But I am forbidden to say anything about what happened over there. So it is necessary to obey. God will act. Everyone was very nice.

Your boys have been as good as on previous occasions. It is a pleasure to watch them praying, saying the beads and singing hymns to the Virgin.

I send my greetings to all the others. I will remember them in my poor prayers. My mother and brothers also send their greetings, they think of you a great deal. In union of prayers.
Conchita Gonzalez."

LVII

THE ANGELICAL COLLEGE AT PAMPLONA

How did Conchita know about the Discalced Carmelite Missionaries? We don't know.

But we recall her brightened face and her joy, when on September 8, 1965, she explained to us her decision to enter this congregation.

— Yes, I am entering there on the 19th of September, because I like that kind of life, because I like black people, and because I wish to go to Africa.

On the 8th or 9th of January 1966, on arriving secretly in Barcelona, Conchita stopped at Pamplona, at her future companions' place.

Before going through the door, she said to her mother with an enchanting smile, "Mother, this is my own home."

Aniceta had said to us on the preceding September 8, with all her sincerity, "God gave her to me, he could take her back again." Yet, this woman, widowed for more than ten years, has but one daughter, the youngest of her four children who happens to be the adorable Conchita.

On hearing Conchita speak of her future dwelling in this manner, Aniceta felt her heart give a twist and she burst into tears to prevent crying out her grief.

❀   ❀   ❀

On her return from Rome to Garabandal on January 21, the adolescent whose energy, decisiveness, fearlessness and fidelity to her "voices" could remind us of Joan of Arc, hurried preparations for her departure.

She visited the venerable monk who was always her spiritual confidant, her own chaplain. She went to confession to him and received Communion from his hands.

She met another monk who had always been her best friend, in whom she had the fullest confidence.

In the solitude of her soul in the village, in spite of the graciousness she shows everyone, she went back over the path to the apparitions, withdrew for a long time at 'The Pines,' at the cemetery where her father rests, and in her beloved church.

On February 5, she graciously received the journalist to whom Germany owes thanks for knowing all the truth about Garabandal. It was his third trip to the village. He telephoned us last week from Fulda: "I found a new Conchita, her trip to Rome has made her a person of stature, of depth and formidable power. You couldn't possibly imagine what she has become."

                ✿   ✿   ✿

We do not imagine anything. What follows suffices for us who know her well from "the inside."

On the morning of February 7, 1966, an automobile left Garabandal. It was occupied by four persons. Another one was waiting in the valley. Goodbyes were said at Gabezon de la Sal, and the two automobiles drove on towards Pamplona.

What were Conchita's last remarks to her mother, to Sanchez-Ventura, and to Father Luna, three of her four travelling companions? We shall know about them later on. These were the last words she spoke before entering the convent in greeting her best friend, who evidently was there also: "Father, go in first, I am happy to receive you in my house."

                ✿   ✿   ✿

At Pamplona, she is still not a postulant in the canonical sense of the word. She has become one of the adolescents of the "angelical college" of the Discalced Carmelite Missionaries. Most of the pupils have a religious vocation and are peacefully preparing for it, in view of the final step. Like her companions, Conchita will have summer vacations which she will spend in Garabandal.

What are her thoughts today behind the walls of this convent, this daughter of the sun, wind and freedom of the Cantabrian mountains?

At least this, which are her own words:

— The Superior at Pamplona does not believe in the apparitions. I'm very pleased about it. This way, no one will try to pamper me.

* * *

We know nothing of the true feelings of the person Conchita must obey. When Bernadette arrived at Saint Gildard, at Nevers, the mistress of novices did not believe in her either. We are gladdened by this. However, we must add something while the time is still ripe, not necessarily about her sojourn at Pamplona at the present time or later. We simply wish to explain our feeling concerning the realization of her future apostolic vocation.

It has been mentioned twice before in this text that Conchita had chosen to go to the African Missions. It is to live one day among the Africans that she entered the Pamplona convent. Her present vocation calls for her to live the active life of African missionaries.

Whether her superiors believe or do not believe in Garabandal, we do not picture them—all the life of Lucy of Fatima is proof—sending her off some day where she wants to go. Can one imagine, the confidante of Our Lady of Carmel living in Africa with the freedom necessary for the realization of her vocation?

Later on, Pamplona will have to choose: either this African freedom or the seclusion and work inside the mother house in Spain. This is a formidable dilemma to resolve before God.

If this is not perceived immediately, or should the wrong decision be made someday, then it would have been better that the responsible authorities had never opened the convent doors.

As for Conchita, it suffices to consider the difficulties in which she would place her superiors one day, and the trials which will result for herself, to understand that Our Lady of Carmel did not deceive her when she told her repeatedly, in public: "You will not be happy in this world, but in heaven."

Regardless of the unfolding of her private inner world in the future, of the mediation that awaits her tortured soul, and that she will necessarily have to live anywhere, she entered the house of her sorrows on February 7, 1966.

This date February 7, 1966 was a symbolic one, for on that day Conchita was exactly 17 years old. So young and so resolute. After having accomplished the first part of her mission, after having lived four and a half years which began at the "cuadro" the road to "The Pines," and terminated in Italy.

What strikes us Frenchmen on the night of this anniversary, is the quiet and humble courage with which she smilingly over-ruled the influence of all human wisdom. Nothing, no one could stop her in her present decision.

In this matter, as in many others, she resembles our Joan of Arc in that respect as in many others. Was Joan not of the same age, when, every obstacle overcome, she came to Chinon?

✿ ✿ ✿

Conchita bears a resemblance to our national saint, but in her case, her mission is world-wide. Because of that, we are happy that she chose to go to Pamplona, one of the Spanish towns closest to our borders, and one where heroism always flowered.

Conchita always was partial towards the French. She did not forget that on June 18, 1966, Saint Michael had chosen them personally. We know that she keeps us in her heart and that even the Pyrenees cannot cut us off from her.

That is why in thought, in the name of France, we would piously place at Garabandal the miraculous sword that had been found in the church of Saint Catherine of Fierbois before the departure for Orleans.

LVIII

CONCHITA'S THEOLOGY

"This is what I have to say, myself, on my own:

"There is no point in our believing in the apparitions if we

Conchita in 1965.

do not heed the Message. To speak more clearly: if we do not accomplish what our Holy Mother the Church bids us. As we all know, the Blessed Virgin said here what she said at Lourdes and at Fatima. She has said nothing new. The Miracle will come so that we may heed the Message. It will happen also to confirm the apparitions of Garabandal. But, if we heed the Message, believing in the apparitions is of no importance. Let us realize that to believe in the apparitions is a grace which requires that we give more to God, because it is a grace which He grants us, He, Our Lord, God.

"We must pray a great deal for our brothers who still do not know God, I believe it is a wish of the Blessed Virgin.

"We must also pray for those who receive graces from God or the Blessed Virgin, and who do not thank them.

Conchita Gonzalez
December 1965."

Conchita and her mother, Aniceta, examining
a French weekly, in 1965.

LIX

THE BLOOD OF MANKIND

Whether it involves the eventual chastisement, the Miracle to come, or that of the "Forma," besides all the other things, it can easily be seen that the deep worry and constant preoccupation of the clairvoyants is the saving of souls, all the souls of the world, be they believers or non-believers, Christians or unaware of the Gospel.

Garabandal is primarily, above all else, mediation and spiritual redemption.

But it is also the worry and preoccupation of the human race that the world must not be struck by Divine wrath. Day and night, the eventual chastisement of humanity haunts the minds of the four girls from Garabandal.

❀   ❀   ❀

The apparitions of Fatima are recognized by the Church. Two popes, now deceased, both saintly, have spoken about it in particular.

First was the inspired Pope Pius XII, who consecrated the world to the Immaculate Heart of Our Lady of the Rosary in October 1942.

Then, if we study the outlines of operations during the last war, we can realize that immediately after this consecration the military situation was reversed.

Beginning with El Alamein, observe the Americans landing in North Africa, passing by Stalingrad, stop at Guadalcanal and Midway to end up at Reims on the 8th of May, 1945, on the feast of St. Michael.

Through Mary, mother of mankind, and through the rosary, Pope Pius XII, the pope so outrageously attacked and misunderstood, saved the world in this time, just as in other days, Saintly Pius the V had done for Lépanto.

The good Pope John offered his pectoral cross at Fatima, the cross which had rested on his heart which was as large as humanity and as profound as that of Jesus.

His Holiness Pope Paul VI, in proclaiming Mary Mother of the Church, on the occasion of his closing oration at the third Session of the Council, did not hesitate to offer the Golden Rose to the Fatima Sanctuary.

This should suffice, we believe for those who think seriously.

❀   ❀   ❀

What, then, was Fatima?

It is primarily the salvation of souls, to be sure: "If you do not become converted—." But it is also the fear of death for mankind, concern about bloodshed: "Chastisement will strike humanity"—.

Certainly, victory seemed in the offing since the Consecration of 1942, but what a price had to be paid.

Fifty million were killed on land, on sea, and in the air, from

162

one end of the earth to the other, including the horrible atomic massacre in Japan.

After that, Korea, Indochina, Algeria, and today, Vietnam.

Who can be directly blamed for this great slaughter in the eyes of whomever believes in the existence of God and His universal operation, and the maternal mediation of Our Lady?

Let us not be afraid to say it: it was those who worked against the Message of Fatima; those who did not propagate it as they should; those who did not do everything they could to warn the world of the threatening perils, to help in every way to escape those perils or at least lessen them.

"If my requests are obeyed," said the Virgin in 1917, "the world will know peace."

* * *

Why has no one heeded the requests of Our Lady of Fatima?

The reasons are that many Christians did not know of them or were scornful; because many people who were responsible did not make them known, worked against or ignored them.

To those people, our editorial team composed of young and old veterans, the widows of comrades killed during those wars, dare to say:

"You have blood on your hands," and we continue: "Take care, you are about to begin over again."

"For us, Garabandal is the continuation and amplification of Fatima.

If you scorn the warnings of Garabandal, as you scorned those of Fatima, you will be responsible for the numerous deaths of the predicted chastisement.

You do not want people to believe in Garabandal?

You do not want people to be converted by accomplishing the Messages of the Virgin?

You will be guiltier tomorrow than yesterday and you will be despised: your incredulity will have caused all of humanity to wallow in the blood your hands are already stained with."

* * *

Let us recall here the words of Pope Pius XI offering his life at the beginning of World War II. To avert it, he announced over

163

the air: "Yes, I give my life for peace. Now, life is the greatest of all the natural assets."

We love all men with a love that is sincere, deep and faultless. We profess that they must be helped, fed, led to social promotion, comforted and if necessary, that we die for them. But we also profess that, of all human assets, the greatest object of our preoccupation is their lives.

While we want their souls sanctified and saved, we must endeavour to save human lives by averting the Chastisement.

LX

MORE CONCERNING THE GREAT MIRACLE

Along the way we have met many prudent people. They told us: "Take care, take care, to not compromise yourselves needlessly." On the other hand, since August of 1965, we know more than others what is said in the Santander circles concerning the nature of the Miracle, of the impossibility or childishness of the latter.

All this leaves us indifferent; we smile over directed indiscretions as well as at concerted timidity.

We are not afraid to defend our strenuous work of the past four years or the book which offers part of our documentation to the public.

Before closing the matter, we wish to speak once more of the great Miracle to come.

❋   ❋   ❋

Its nature?

We have never been so indiscreet as to question Conchita on the underlying nature of the Miracle, and Providence has rewarded us for it. As she had been told in **our presence;** "Padre Luis Andreu died of joy, of having seen it, on the night of the

12 hours in the life of Conchita, end of November 1962, in our presence
(one of 8 photographs).

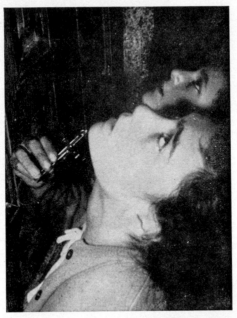

8 o'clock in the evening. The trance has ended at the door of the church.

8th of August 1961." We ventured to remark: "O, we shall also
die on the night of that great day?" The answer came in a flash:
"No, God will give us the necessary strength to bear the vision."

Since then, it has always seemed evident that if the coming
Miracle was to be but a preternatural stellar phenomenon in the
sky of Garabandal, the question of dying of joy from it could not
reasonably be considered, even though it will be, as Conchita
repeated a hundred times, incomparably greater than the miracle
of the sun, at Fatima, the 13th of October 1917.

The date?

Let us commit ourselves further.

In September of 1963, Conchita was eating with us, at the
house next door to her own.

As she seemed to be enjoying the sweets, we were teasing her

165

11 o'clock at night. The Virgin had announced that she would return to Conchita's kitchen this night.

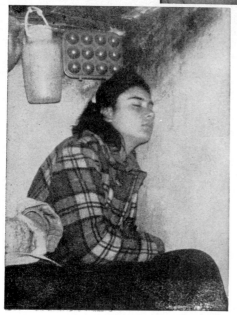

3 o'clock in the morning. All are awaiting the expected trance. Conchita is sleeping a little.

166

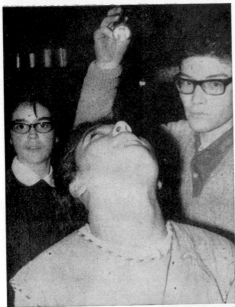

7 o'clock in the morning. As the Angelus is ringing, the Virgin returns to the kitchen.

Immediately after the ecstasy at 7 a.m., Conchita ran to the *Cuadro* to say the rosary with us and some villagers.

167

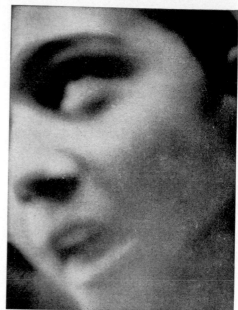

Conchita receiving Communion at the church door. The Host is not visible this time.

Immediately after receiving Communion, Conchita shows none of the fatigue of the preceding night. Conchita, completely refreshed, smiles at us.

168

The Virgin appeared near the ears of corn hanging in the kitchen, when She kissed three wedding rings that same night, at the end of November, 1962. In this 1965 photo, a picture of Padre Pio looks down paternally on Conchita.

169

about the spirit of penance recommended by the first message. She laughed heartily. Suddenly, she was silent and withdrawn. Her face then brightened up and with her hands almost joined together began:

"The Miracle will take place on the feast of a young martyr of the Eucharist. It was a boy who was carrying Holy Communion to persecuted Christians. His playmates, on seeing him go by wanted to oblige him to join in their games. When he refused, they stoned him and ran away. A Christian soldier who was passing by carried his corpse away."

"But it's Saint Tarcisius!," one of the assistants couldn't help exclaiming in a loud voice. Conchita did not react and took more cake as though she had not heard anything.

After her departure, we were discussing the matter among ourselves. The oldest member of the group came to this conclusion: "My impression is that Conchita saw the spectacle during one of her trances, and it seems to me that the Blessed Virgin did not mention the name of the martyr of whom she just spoke. In my opinion, she does not know the name."

❋ ❋ ❋

On this very precise subject of the "young" martyr of the Eucharist, we have been advised many times to maintain the greatest reserve. "Speak of a martyr of the Eucharist, in general, but do not stress the youth."

Supposing for one second that on the subject of Garabandal that we could trust human caution, it would be asking us to betray our mission. We are witnesses of facts, and testify to what we have seen, heard and touched.

On this occasion, as in others, only one thing matters to us, the words and gestures of Conchita.

We can do nothing about it. If this young Christian, whom the adolescent describes and names the martyrdom, was the Saint Tarcisius of the authentic story, the Miracle would take place on the feast day of Saint Tarcisius.

❋ ❋ ❋

We are aware that in speaking in this manner, we are multiplying the difficulties on the subject of the date of the Miracle.

170

Conchita stated to us: "It will not be on a feast day of the Virgin." She also said to one of her companions: "On that day, Mass could be celebrated in black," which means: it will not be a "double feast day" according to the language of the Roman rite, before the last liturgical reform. Now, in the Roman martyrology, that of our Occidental cities, the feast of Saint Tarcisius is celebrate on the 15th of August, feast of the Assumption of Our Lady.

The whole question comes back to finding out the exact date of the death of the "young" martyr, if he really is, as we have just noted, the authentic historical one.

In the Catholic Church, the feast of a saint is usually celebrated on the day of his or her death.

It is the "dies natalis," the birth in Heaven.

Did Saint Tarcisius die on the 15th of August, as our martyrology states?

Let the historians furnish the answer, it is their mission and duty. We have full confidence in them, since by definition, they are loyal and competent.

❀   ❀   ❀

What are we to infer as to the date and nature of the great Miracle?

Primarily, what Conchita insisted that we write at the beginning of March, 1966: "Be certain that the warning will happen and that the Miracle will follow."

Then, to quote a remark from our friend and collaborator, Doctor Apostolidès: "It would not be a prophecy if we knew ahead of time its exact meaning, and if we could guess the right date of its happening."

Since the nature and date of the Miracle are "prophetic," let us wait with minds at ease, without trying to tear away the veil which momentarily hides them from our view.

We cannot forget that the Miracle itself is directly related to the Message, and that it will be the sign of signs, consecrating the authenticity of the Message which all must accomplish immediately and spread throughout the universe as well.

171

LXI

ONE LAST WORD FROM MARI DOLORES
February 7th, 1966

I had a locution from the Blessed Virgin. She told me that I would have to suffer a great deal in this world, that I would be subject to a great many trials, and that would be the cause of most of my suffering.

I asked her to tell me if I would become a nun: she did not answer me.[1]

She told me that she was very pleased that I was here at this boarding-school.

I asked her if she would return to "speak" with me: she did not reply.

I asked her to give proof of the apparitions to my father so that he would believe in them. She told me that he would believe "very soon," and that everyone would believe also.

She told me that she was very pleased with my sacrifices, but that I must become better each day and do more penance in all things, that I recite the Rosary every day as I have been doing, a devotion which pleases her very much, that she loves us all very much, that she wants us all to be very good so that we may all be reunited with her, in heavenly glory.

Mari Loli Mazon

X boarding-school (Zaragoza province)

[1] Loli, as well, did not receive an answer concerning her vocation.

LXII

OUR BOOK IN ITALY

Conchita's trip to Italy evidently was the normal termination of the first stage of the Garabandal events. It was obviously too important for us to not miss going ourselves, humbly and conscientiously. We followed in her footsteps, and as one can take note in Chapter LV (55), Providence had us meet with the most reliable Italian witnesses, the most informed, those who were her intermediaries and interpreters on all occasions.

* * *

We are not acquainted with Rome. To be more exact, we know little or nothing of the profound spirit, the religious and mystical soul of modern Rome.

Yet its spiritual past is so extraordinary that everyone should have an inkling of the supernatural realities of today.

It is soil bathed with the blood of Peter and Paul, land of innumerable Coliseum martyrs, of Catacombs, Circus Maximus, land of confessors and virgins, land of men and women, of all ages, who during the course of centuries, generation after generation, have died, sanctifying the city and the cities of the universe, as pure water from the heights render fertile the valleys and the plains.

It is the Vatican basilica where minds are enlightened and hearts fortified by all the holy popes from the first to the last who have been buried there.

Rome? It is the prodigious, incomparable Catholic reliquary of the entire world.

Because of this past, under its immediate and able influence, the Rome of today, the secret spiritual Rome is still and ever a burning center of hidden saintliness.

173

That center had made Conchita feel welcome, miraculously facilitating her mission. We were also well received and the first drafts of our book examined. It was understood that before it could be presented to the public, it should be shown to the proper persons for correction if need be.

We were helped providentially and efficiently.

❊ ❊ ❊

In the meantime, we had made the pilgrimage to San Giovanni-Rotondo.

There, we made the acquaintance of Padre Pio, in the same parlor, we believe, as the one where he had received Conchita and her companions.

Before witnesses, we presented him with our book in the name of the editorial staff. We wished to pay him our respects and leave the book with him. He gazed fixedly at the cover, with a picture of Conchita's enraptured face, with "the Pines" of the Apparitions at the horizon, then, without hesitating another second, without even looking at the pages of the book, he opened it as though by chance to page 54, indicating with his finger the Message of June 18th, 1965. When he saw that we understood what he meant, he closed it, blessed it and then instead of keeping it, returned it to us.

❊ ❊ ❊

Thus, our book made the required trip to Italy.

Now that we know how it was received, our task seems complete.

LXIII

THE YOUNG SEMINARIST'S PRAYER

During the apparitions, adults and children followed the clairvoyants. One day, Conchita, in a rapturous trance, stopped before her first cousin, little Pepe Luis, aged 7, and told him, "you will become a priest."

Three years later, Pepe Luis, who had entered a pre-seminary in the month of October, was spending his first vacation at home at Christmas 1964. While he was playing out of doors, Conchita found a little notebook of his. She wrote these words in it "the prayer of the little seminarist."

My God, I want to be a priest, to convert sinners, Lord, with your help. In fact, I know that without your help nothing can be accomplished.

Lord, may I be a holy priest who imitates you even now; may I progress in saintliness by loving and serving you faithfully.

As of now I ask you to forgive my sins. I also ask you to forgive the world.

I promise, with your help, to become better.

Lord, you hold me now. Do with me what you wish, I accept all, provided that you accomplish your will in me.

Your son who loves you truly and prays to you, put him in your heart, and never let him out.

I want to be a saintly priest! Oh Mary, protect me!

Pepe Luis

We have seen previously, particularly in Chapters 21 and 22, that Garabandal is Eucharistic and priestly.

Those who would doubt this in 1966 could re-read this prayer which she wrote as an adolescent of fifteen for a little boy who was only ten.

Others may, on closing this book, ask God to give the Catholic priesthood of yesterday, today and tomorrow, the heart and soul of Conchita of Garabandal.

LXIV

UNUSUAL EVENTS

For several years now many unusual events have come about attributed to the intervention of Our Lady of Carmel of Garabandal, in the United States, in Spain, in Belgium and elsewhere. The most remarkable appears to us as being those of Antwerp, of California, Germany, and Neuers. We had written a chapter on this subject, destined for publication in this book. On thinking the matter over, it seemed too premature to publish it. In these cases it is necessary to apply the prudence and wisdom of the Medical Bureau of Lourdes and canonical decisions. We shall therefore wait again through all the time it requires.

However, we do not hesitate to give comfort to our readers on the effectiveness of confident prayer to the Virgin of Garabandal, by using the objects kissed by her.

A young girl, Miss Menchu Mendiolea was cured in August 1966 in the most "miraculous manner," of an incurable sickness while on her deathbed. She lives at No. 44 of the F. Palazuelos street, in Santander. The whole town was in a commotion. If the medical examinations confirmed this last-minute news, we would have to bless Heaven and thank Our Lady for her merciful passage in this episcopal city.

At the moment of re-editing this book, we have received from Madame Mendiolea personally, the mother of the happy Menchu, the following lines:

"My daughter continues to be perfectly well, as the tests made on her a month ago were very satisfactory."

This letter of November 11, 1966, from Madame Mendiolea had been preceded by authenticated reports concerning another "miracle."

It happened also in Santander, and curiously enough in the same hospital of Valdecilla, where Menchu was cured.

Here is a summary of the account:

On September 18, 1966 at 6 p.m., a little boy, Alberto Gulierrez Orena became blind, deaf and dumb as the result of a serious automobile accident, and was cured instantly. This cure took place at the precise moment that one of our medals offered by Conchita was being placed around his neck, at the moment this gesture of faith was completed, a prayer was said to Our Lady of Garabandal.

The prayer to Our Lady of Carmel was: "Cure him, this very instant, to prove that you really appeared in Garabandal." Today, at the hospital in Valdecilla, the staff refers to little Alberto as "Our little Lazarus."

Is it not now evident that everything is possible at Santander? We will speak of all that later on, of other events of another nature and of conversions.

LXV

LOCUTION OF CONCHITA WITH OUR LORD —FEBRUARY 13, 1966

On Sunday, February 13, as I was starting my act of thanksgiving after Communion—I received, suddenly, a great joy and an even greater sadness, as well as a deception.

I heard Christ's voice saying to me:

"Conchita, you came here, to college, to prepare yourself to become My bride, and you say it is to follow me. Don't you say, Conchita, that you want to do My will? Well, now, it is yours you want to accomplish. Will it be so all your life? I chose you in the world, to stay in it to face the numerous difficulties you will find because of Me. All this, I want for your sanctification and offering for the salvation of the world. You must speak of Mary to the world. Remember that in June you asked Me if you would become a nun and I answered: 'You will find a cross and sufferings everywhere.' I repeat again, Conchita, did you ever feel that I was calling you to be My bride? No, and it is because I did not call you."

Then I asked Him: "How do we feel when you are calling us to religious life?"

He said to me, "Don't worry yourself, you will never feel it."

I said to Him: "So, You don't love me, Jesus?" and He answered me, "Conchita, it is you asking Me that? Who redeemed you? Do My will and you will find My love. Examine yourself well, think more of your neighbor, and do not fear temptations. If you are loyal to My love you will conquer the numerous temptations

177

awaiting you. Understand intelligently and spiritually what I am telling you. Do not close the eyes of your soul or let yourself be deceived by anyone. Show love, humility and simplicity. Never think that what you are doing is great, but rather that it is what you have to do, must do, not especially to win Heaven, but to save the world and thus accomplish My Divine Will. Let everyone know, that each soul well-prepared, each soul well-disposed to listen to Me, will know My will. I insist in telling you, Conchita, that you will have much to suffer, from now until the Miracle, for there are few who believe you. Your own family will believe that you have deceived them. All this, I want, as I said before, for your sanctification and so that the world will accomplish the message. I want you to know that the rest of your life will be a continuous suffering. Do not waver . . . in suffering you will find Me, and also Mary whom you love so much."

Then I asked Him if Rome would believe. He did not answer me. Then He said to me: "Don't worry whether they believe or not. I will do everything, but I will also give you suffering. I am near to those who suffer for Me."

Conchita Gonzalez
February 13, 1966

LXVI

TALK GIVEN BY FATHER LAFFINEUR ON SEPTEMBER 15, 1967, FRIBOURG, SWITZERLAND

All that has been written already has never been contradicted. The book remains, and later on we shall add further facts. The essential points are there already, that is to say, the exact summary of events which took place in Garabandal between June 18, 1961 and February 7, 1966. They are unassailable, and have not been attacked to this day. This is the reality (I repeat: reality) presented to the judgment of human reason illuminated by faith and the grace of the Holy Spirit.

One can say, and it should be said, as we do in Chapters 2 and 33 of "L'Etoile . . . ." that the real problem was resolved with the departure of Conchita for Pamplona on Feb. 7, 1966. At this date we had all the relevant data concerning the most important question, that is, the subject-matter regarding the development of the apparitions, according to the testimony of qualified witnesses. Yes, with the prophecies of the Warning, of the future Miracle, of the Sign which will remain, and of the eventual punishment, Garabandal definitely belongs to history.

We knew the essential things, as well as many details of what happened at the moment these phenomena were taking place. One was able to agree with the supernatural nature of the events at Garabandal.

We must insist on this point; and since the month of March, 1963 our conviction has been strengthened. Moreover, since then we could confidently repeat and write the following: "If the seers were to come to us and say: 'We have not seen either the Blessed Virgin or the Angel . . . .' we should have replied without any hesitation: "Children, your personal judgment no longer interests us; what matters to us is the fact that the witnesses, and we are of their number, have seen, heard and touched etc. "You have neither the grace nor the mission of enlightening us on your own case, it is something which is superior to you."

That month of March, 1963 was nearly three and a half years before the happenings which we are now about to relate. We shall therefore terminate these preliminary statements by repeating, "One should read, re-read, and thoroughly digest "L'Etoile dans la Montagne" and remember all that is written therein.

Duress in Garabandal

Conchita left for Pamplona on February 7, 1966. It was her birthday and she was seventeen years old.

At that time the village had already become the prison that we had predicted it would become.

Consecrated on August 15, 1965, Monsignor Vicente Puchol Montiz was enthroned on the 17th of the same month. Before the year came to an end changes had taken place in his mountain diocese. Father Valentin Marichalar, the parish priest of Cosio

179

and Garabandal at the time of the Apparitions found himself confined to the exercise of his ministry in Cosio only and was forbidden to go up to Garabandal, to whose needs he had ministered for about the last ten years. He was succeeded there by a young priest of twenty-five, who took up residence in the village itself. The mission of this priest was absolute, to put an end to the whole affair. He made no secret of this, because he even goes so far as to say to visitors: "Even if the miracle were to take place it will prove nothing regarding that in which you are interested." Later on he was to go even further . . . .

Intelligent and active, and with the sole duty of caring for this small community of 280 docile souls living in a village consisting of 70 houses leaning one against the other—which could equally well be looked after by an elderly and less active priest—he dedicated himself cleverly and unscrupulously to manipulating the visionaries, their families and the whole village.

And he has succeeded, up to the present, at any rate, in winning over the village families through his dedication to the schoolchildren and by providing distractions and amusements for the adolescents similar to those available in cities.

He himself organizes dances which last until four o'clock in the morning, and dispenses the faithful from the Sunday obligation of rest from work—on the condition that they participate in the construction of premises to be used as a "television-club".

Thanks to all these exterior activities, the religious terror exercised in the village is less apparent. The children, the adolescents, and many of the women are won over by this young parish priest, Father Olano by name. The men, or at least the majority of them, observe all these things and keep silence.

Something was to take place in this village, until that time a village of dignified and well-mannered country folk, which all the world should now know about. . . . On June 26, 1967 four children between the ages of seven and twelve years were making fun of four visitors who were praying at "the Pines." There was a blind man among their number, and even to him they showed no consideration. It was the American, Joey Lomangino. And to make the apostolate of their parish-priest even more obvious, they even went so far as to throw dung at the tree on which the Blessed Virgin had most frequently appeared to the four visionaries. It was at the foot of this tree that Conchita had made a simple little altar out of a few rough stones. Yes, this is unfortunately true; we learned of this sacrilege the following morning. And something even worse was attempted in the "calleja" —the stony pathway which leads up to "the Pines." Fortunately they soiled the wrong slab of stone, and it was not the one upon which Conchita had knelt on June 18, 1961 and on June 18, 1965.

In this outrageously profaned prison of Garabandal, the seers tried to defend themselves as best they could. And every time they did so—and it happened very often—they came face to face with the young Father Olano, either in the sacristy or elsewhere, whether two or three of the girls were together, or one of them alone.

Duress in Pamplona

There were problems in Garabandal, as we have seen, and for Conchita, especially, in Pamplona. We knew this already (chapter 57). The Superior of the college in Pamplona to which Conchita went, did not believe in the apparitions. Conchita was glad to know this and said: "It is better so, because I shall not be favored in any way." Poor Conchita! She was not aware that we had written: "The young girl entered her house of suffering on February 7, 1966." We had also written: "We ourselves could not have suspected what was going to happen there." Please read her letters, and her insistence on going to this convent will be apparent to you.

Her mother told us that from her childhood, since she was five years old, she had always wanted to enter the religious life. At last she arrived at the door; very soon her desire to give herself completely to God would be realized, and she would become a Discalced Carmelite Missionary and would eventually be able to work among the colored peoples of Africa—her greatest wish. Her face shone with happiness and was supernaturally transfigured, as we had seen it on the previous September 8 in Torrelavega when she talked to us of her plans.

181

Well, six days after she entered, on February 13th, Jesus spoke to her. This was the interior locution which we have not spoken of until now, because an interior locution cannot be verified as can a rapture. But now we will speak of it . . . . because it is at the root of the spiritual drama of Conchita and because we have absolute and definite proof that she believed and continues to believe in it. (Conchita's Diary, Nouvelles Editions Latines, 1, rue Palatine, Paris VI, page 97.) The locution was long and had profound implications. Here are some extracts which are relevant at this point: "Did you not say, Conchita, that you wish to fulfill My Will for you? Well, at the moment you are fulfilling your own will. Is it going to be so all your life? . . . . . Have I ever said to you that I shall call you to be a religious? No. I have not called you . . . . ."

What a drama at the crossroads of life; at that very age when one chooses what one's future life is to be! And a year after this locution Conchita was still upset, disoriented in the secret depths of her soul, so much so that she told someone that after the Miracle to come she would become a cloistered Carmelite.

                    *   *   *

At this college, later on, she wept when she was present at a clothing ceremony of the Order, knowing that she would never receive the habit of the Discalced Carmelite Missionaries. And at this very moment she began to have doubts about the Real Presence in the Holy Eucharist. She confided to a friend: "I have the feeling that I have chains round my legs, as though I were being prevented from approaching the altar-rail." During her Easter holidays it took all the wisdom and doctrinal assuredness of her mother, Aniceta, to alleviate her troubled soul in this regard.

                    *   *   *

Let us see how events now gathered momentum. Easter of 1966 was on April 10th, so between that date and February 7th two months had elapsed. In these two months Providence had led Conchita from the happiness of her entry into college at Pamplona to the renunciation of her total gift of herself and to the intellectual suffering of her doubts about the Eucharist. During these two months (nine weeks, to be precise) her heart and her mind had been nailed to the Cross. But all this was but her preparation for the trial of trials.

During these same Easter holidays, at the beginning of April, she met Loli, her confidante, once again . . . and also the young parish priest of Garabandal. Loli, to whom the Blessed Virgin had said in an interior locution while she was at school in Zaragoza: "You will have doubts about your apparitions." (See 'Las Negaciones de Garabandal', by Sanchez-Ventura p. 89.) Loli, who since the month of February had been very distressed, had confided her doubts to those around her. She often spoke about them to Father Olano in the sacristy and in her own home, without realizing that she was playing into his hands. After talking to Loli, what could Conchita do but confide, as her friend had done, in the young priest who was, moreover, the only confessor in the village?

Conchita returned to Pamplona about the 20th of April. She was there, in all, for about 6 months, just the time necessary for the development of her third drama.

At the beginning of this, the third term of the school year, a three-day retreat took place, a usual occurrence in schools of this kind. The retreat was given, not by the school-chaplain, but by a thirty-five-year-old priest of the town. And he, like the Mother-Superior, did not believe in the Apparitions. This is not surprising, seeing that Pamplona is the most malicious of Garabandal's adversaries.

It was at this precise moment that Conchita, experiencing the unhappiness caused by the locution of February 13th, and her doubts regarding the Eucharist which were assailing her once more, and also upset by Loli's confidences and the interviews she had had with her parish-priest began to doubt her apparitions herself. Trustingly, seeing in him the priesthood for whom she had so much respect and affection, she opened her heart to this unknown preacher. Afterwards she went into the confessional. . . . The answer he gave was: "If you do not promise to tell the village and those who visit the village that you have deceived them, I shall not give you absolution. . . ."

Yes, you may open your eyes wide, you may not believe your ears: 'Conchita, if you do not promise to tell the village and those who visit the village that you have deceived them, I shall not give you absolution."

Did he say this unconsciously, lightly, was it lack of experience, abuse of his position, profanation? . . . . Yes, all of these at the same time. And we shall demonstrate this, showing you the sentiments you would have felt in your reaction as good Catholics.

Referring to these doubts about the Real Presence in the Holy Eucharist, the regular confessor associated with the college would have answered Conchita: "Temptations to which you do not acquiesce are not sin. Wait a while. Light will return when you have become a mediatrix for the unbelievers." But what would you have thought if he had replied: "If you do not promise to tell the village and all who visit the village that Jesus is present in the Consecrated Host, I shall not give you absolution."?

You would be flabbergasted at the idea of such an eventuality. But this is a parallel attitude to that taken by the retreat-giver in Pamplona, when he gave his blasphemous answer. Whether he was an adversary of Garabandal or not, he should have said: "Doubt is not a sin. Wait, reflect, ask advice of experienced priests. If Garabandal is true, it is normal that you should pay the price. If it is untrue, we shall see it to be so. Carry your Cross patiently. . . . Go in peace, I will pray for you."

Not only was he lacking in elementary prudence and brotherly charity but after having chosen this course, he pursued it even further.

First of all, Conchita was forbidden to speak of her doubts to her family or to any of her friends, or to her companions at the time of the Apparitions. When she returned to Garabandal after she left the college she received three or four letters reminding her of her promise, signifying to her that she was absolved only in conscience while she kept her promise. Try to imagine, if you can, the distressing spiritual situation in which she found herself at being forbidden to speak to her mother, to her brothers, to priests who were favorable to Garabandal; and at having no adviser or consoler other than the parish priest, Father Olano, who was at that time twenty-six years old.

Duress in Garabandal

And he, and there can be no doubt about this, was to give secret support to the orders which came from his colleague in Pamplona. "Yes, Conchita, he is right and you must swear on the Bible that you have lied."

We know all the foregoing with the fullest certainty, and we accept total responsibility in making it known. We can even add something further. In the middle of July, 1966 we went up to Garabandal, knowing absolutely nothing of what had happened since the previous February 7th. We were charged with the delivery of a message to Conchita from Rome. It was very short, just a few words: "You should choose an 'old' confessor, that is to say, a priest of mature years and with much experience. There should be no coercion, but rather a spiritual direction which is wisdom itself." When Conchita received the message she opened her eyes wide, looked at us in silence, and wept. . . .

At that time, of course, we did not understand those tears; but today they throw light upon the past and enlighten the future.

In Conchita's locution on February 13th Jesus had in fact insisted: "Do you not tell me that you wish to follow My Will for you? Well, it is your own will that you are following now. Will it be thus all your life?" Later on He added: "Be intelligent and very spiritual in order that you may understand what I have said to you. Do not close the eyes of your soul. Do not let any one deceive you." (Conchita's Diary, p. 99.)

Do not let any one deceive you! Conchita, listen to Jesus, listen to Rome. Also take heed of the words that came to you from Italy at the beginning of August: Be careful of the two young priests who are abusing their priesthood, and abusing you. Be on your guard, Conchita!

August 15, 1966—10 o'clock in the morning.

To a person who asked her about Loli, whose spiritual state at that moment was known to her, Conchita replied: "Loli has doubts." "And you, Conchita?" asked her questioner. "Inside me, I don't doubt, but here (she put a finger on her forehead) I also have doubts." Thus for the first time, and only to this one ques-

185

tioner aside from the two young priests we have mentioned, the young girl revealed her terrible secret. Her questioner, out of tact, let the matter rest there, and they parted immediately. Later on, the same day, witnesses told us: "At four o'clock this afternoon Conchita appeared to be quite serene and was her usual smiling self."

August 15, 1966—5 o'clock in the afternoon.

Listen to the same witnesses: "At this time, one hour later, when she and Loli were taking leave of the parish priest there was anguish on Conchita's face; she appeared nervous and troubled and said to us as she passed: 'Say a prayer for me, I need it badly.'"

What had happened? The following is what happened—and nobody knew about it until several months had elapsed. . . .

There had been a conversation, at the end of which Conchita, to free her conscience from the weight of her confession in Pamplona (the absolution of which had been made conditional) and following the recent counsels of Father Olano, had chosen to undergo a trial of fire: a meeting with Bishop Puchol Montiz, on which occasion she was finally to uphold the promise which had been sacrilegiously extracted from her by force—by reason of her good faith.

And here, we must repeat once again, neither her mother, Aniceta, her brothers Serafin and Miguel, the friends of Garabandal, nobody at all in fact knew anything of all this—especially of her momentous decision.

Duress in Pamplona

August 28, 1966.

Accompanied by her mother, Conchita returned to Pamplona with her secret. As on the previous February 7th, Aniceta gave the Mother Superior strict instructions that nobody was to be allowed to see her daughter without Aniceta's own authorization. Poor Aniceta! She knew nothing, she was unaware even of the existence of the preacher who had given the retreat at the school, and therefore could not suspect what was going to happen, the following morning, in spite of her instructions.

August 30, 1966.

Five and a half months after the locution of February 13th, accompanied by his Vicar-General (a priest of Pamplona, by the way), by one of his secretaries and, as if by coincidence, by the parish priest of Garabandal, Bishop Puchol Montiz arrived at the door of the school. The bishop was outside the boundaries of his own diocese; and furthermore he was unable to produce Aniceta's authorization when asked by the Mother Superior. "It is not necessary," he said. "But Conchita is a minor, Your Excellency! She cannot be questioned on her own, alone," replied the Mother Superior. "That is of little importance" he replied. So the door of the college opened, Aniceta's formal instructions were thrown to the winds . . . and the interview began. The interview was to last seven hours.

In anticipation of the publication of what will come to be known eventually to the shame of those who are guilty we shall now summarize the affair very briefly, taking, as always, as far as we are concerned, the position least favorable to us.

"Your Excellency, I don't remember now having seen the Virgin, but the Diary (my 54-page diary in which I told everything) is the truth." And the young girl recited this diary from memory, without any mistakes. . . .

"Your Excellency, I have not seen the Virgin, but the Message is true, the Miracle of the Host is true, the great Miracle will happen. . . ."

During the course of this interminable interrogation, interrupted only for the mid-day meal, the Bishop's eyes were more than once filled with tears. . . .

Finally, pointing to a ring Conchita was wearing on her finger, he asked her: "And that ring, Conchita?" "The Virgin kissed it, Your Excellency" "Give it to me." "But (a little maliciously this time) why? I haven't seen Her?" "I will kiss it anyway, who knows!"

This was what was immediately made known in Santander and elsewhere as the "denials" of Conchita. . . . What an error!

Rather should it have been stated and reiterated with the greatest firmness that these were the "contradictions" of Conchita in the hour of her torment.

Between a "denial" and a "contradiction" there is, in fact, an essential difference. Above all, as we shall explain later on, it is necessary to take account of what happened between the February 7th and this August 30th (we have just outlined the summary): the bad faith of the adversaries, the silence which they were to impose on Conchita from this August 30 (and the other girls several days later), the visible intervention of the devil, the foibles of the seers and of their families, the shortcomings of certain friends of Garabandal, the prophecy of the Blessed Virgin herself during a rapture of the four girls in 1961, and the mysterious designs of Divine Providence. Divine Providence spoke clearly in the locution which ended with this little dialogue: "I asked Jesus if Rome already believed. He did not reply." Afterwards He said to me: "Do not worry about whether they believe you or not. It is I who will do everything; but I shall also send you suffering. I am close to those who suffer for Me." (Conchita's Diary, p. 100) We shall return to this later on.

Duress in Santander and Garabandal

September 5, 1966.

During the night someone knocked on the door of the little grocer's shop in the village. Father Olano, who lodges there, came down in his pajamas.

"All right, I'm coming," he answered the mysterious caller.

A quarter of an hour later two motor-bicycles went down the valley. This time it was to do with the organizing of some visits to the Bishop of Santander.

The following morning Loli and her father Ceferino, Jacinta and her mother Maria went down to Cosio. A car from the Bishopric was waiting for them. The parish priest of Garabandal accompanied them. At his age one does not yet experience tiredness. . . .

On their arrival in Santander their interrogators explained to the seers the customary mechanism regarding the events at Garabandal. The "vision" was explained as a "dream"; the "call" as an "excitability" . . . and so on as regards all the rest. The victory would supposedly be quite easy seeing that the two of them, especially Loli, were talking in the same way as Conchita was in Pamplona.

A person who saw them all when they got back to Cosio told us: "Ceferino was looking somewhat ashamed at what had happened." Loli blushed, Jacinta had her arms crossed in front of her, kept her eyes on the ground and appeared to be dumb. Maria made herself scarce. The parish priest, on the other hand, was looking at the four members of his flock with an air of triumph. He had won the contest . . . (or at least so it seemed to him).

September 7, 1966.

Around six o'clock in the evening Aniceta came down from the pastures. She showed us—we were in the village—the summons from Santander for that day.

"I did not want to go."

"Why not?"

"The day before yesterday Ceferino and Maria were summoned with their daughters. Today Pilar has gone down with Mari-Cruz. They should treat me as they do the others, they should not have called me alone, but with Conchita."

"You are right; you have done well to stay at home."

"Of course. Tomorrow I am going, as I do every year on Our Lady's Birthday, to the traditional pilgrimage to the 'Virgen de la Luz'; ten hours of walking there and back."

September 10, 1966.

A letter from Conchita arrived in the village.

"Mama, I was interrogated here for seven hours by the Bishop on August 30."

Aniceta did not believe her eyes. Her anger was enough to make the mountains tremble. She hired a taxi with Serafin, her eldest son, and went to the college in Pamplona.

"Reverend Mother, did I not forbid all visits to Conchita without my formal authorization?"

189

"Could I oppose a Bishop?"

"You have betrayed the promise you gave me; I shall take my daughter home with me at once."

It was for this reason and none other that Conchita left this college run by the Discalced Carmelite Missionaries in Pamplona where, in our opinion, she should never have gone.

The chains of her second prison have finally been broken. And thanks to Bishop Puchol who, without even having thought about it and surely without wishing it, had fulfilled the Will of Jesus expressed in the locution of February 13th to Conchita. . . . In seven months the matter was all over.

Mid-September to mid-October, 1966.

We will summarize briefly. The four girls went down again, in turn, to Santander. Ridiculously and certainly uselessly, Aniceta was threatened with canonical sanctions if she did not obey this time. Along with a lady who was a friend of hers she accompanied Conchita, who said to them as they were entering the Bishop's house:

"I will tell the Bishop the date of the Miracle."

They were received by the Bishop—and the parish priest of Garabandal: "Conchita, sign your recantation." Conchita signed.

And what was the text? "I did not see the Virgin." But the reservations which constituted the "contradictions," namely; "But the Diary is true . . . the Message is true . . . the Miracle will happen . . . and a sign will be left at the Pines . . . etc., etc.," did not figure in the document she signed.

"Aniceta, sign also, please."

"I saw what I saw, I am not signing."

When they were outside, the lady who was accompanying them asked:

"And the date of the Miracle that you said you were going to tell those gentlemen?"

"I couldn't remember it when I was standing in front of the Bishop."

"And now?"

"Yes, I remember it."

"Shall we go in again?"

"No."

"But since you didn't see the Blessed Virgin tell us the date; it's not important any more."

"No, only eight days before the Miracle, as the Virgin made me promise."

Let us not forget the other visionaries; Jacinta has also signed. So has Loli. So has Mari-Cruz.

Jacinta, in front of the Bishop, said to her mother Maria:

"You sign too, Mama."

"Yes, I will if you can fall into rapture here, now."

"But Mama, you know that that's impossible."

"Then I'm not signing."

In Garabandal, Loli remains silent, at least in front of us. Why? Because, like the others, she has had strict orders from Santander . . . especially if she meets that priest from Nevers who, as Bishop Puchol was to say publicly in a televised press conference on March 17th, "had committed the crime of declaring himself an 'enthusiastic advocate of Garabandal.' He is the number one enemy. . . ."

Loli also remains silent because she is strictly supervised by her family and by her parish priest. Except in Balmori, where we met her alone, she can never be with us on her own. And yet, even without words, she makes her deepest thoughts known to us. In our presence, her face lights up; a smile illuminates it; she thanks us with her eyes; she knows that her doubts do not weaken our absolute certainty. In front of her family, who has never let us be alone with her, Loli thanks us in silence for not abandoning her.

It was not long ago that she took us by the arm, near the Church, as she had done on June 18, 1965, in order to tell us again: "You know that of course I have seen the Blessed Virgin. Do not doubt it!"

Did Ceferino sign, like his daughter Loli? We shall know one day. In any case, at the end of June, 1967 he appeared to have aged by ten years and he seemed to be bearing a very heavy Cross. Six weeks later, on reading the report of Brigadier Alvarez, his reflections and his attitude seemed to be a confession.

Mari-Cruz, for her part, had to sign with her two hands, so to

191

speak. She went to such lengths that it seemed to have gone to her head: "We hurt ourselves very much when we fell on our knees, but we managed to hide it." Does she know that this lie drew a round denial from Conchita, who wrote to us immediately?

Did Pilar sign? It would be logical if she did, seeing her past attitude, but as she now seems to be less triumphant than before . . . who knows?

This is the summary and in the hope of making it all known, the Truth about what happened between February 7th and October 14, 1966. . . . Eight months.

We are deceiving nobody; because, faithful to our method, we once more repeat that we have chosen the position least favorable to us. The proof? We have stated the fact of the words: "I did not see the Virgin." And also what Conchita also said: "I have forgotten if I saw her." We don't accept only "a loss of memory" (this is quite certain), we also accept the denial. *With* the reservations of "but . . . but . . . but . . ." which prove that Conchita has not denied, but rather that she put before the Bishop the "contradition" of her state of mind.

God grant that Santander, on sending their report to Rome on October 16, 1966, has not imitated those who judged Joan of Arc in the cemetery at Saint Ouen. If they have, they knowingly deceived the Church and the whole world; and in eternity where Bishop Puchol now finds himself he will have encountered the Procurator D'Estivet and Bishop Cauchon. . . . (Bishop who judged Joan of Arc.)

❋ ❋ ❋

Not only has Santander imposed absolute silence on the visionaries and their families, but it has offered to find Conchita, and the others, too, no doubt, a new boarding-school, all fees paid. In this manner they will have her safely out of the way. In addition to this the vigilance of the parish priest has been reinforced by more exacting orders—perfectly logical and justified because the seers, they say, have denied everything.

All the visitors who go to the village know the mocking smile of Father Olano and his childish arguments against the reality of the events. What they often do not know, if they are not Spaniards, is the incredible reverence that the young boys and girls of these mountain districts have for a Bishop. It is a certain kind of terror of the clergy that can be created by a young Spanish priest.

Here are two examples: Since October 16, 1966 Santander has announced that the whole affair is finished. All Garabandal was aware of this, and they knew that the Bishop's Note (subsequently published March, 1967) was going to be made public, resolving the case once and for all. They were told to expect a visit from the Bishop. When it became known that he was going to visit the village on April 9, 1967, everybody trembled and said: "This is it . . . he's going to come and excommunicate us!" Yes,— nothing less, nothing less!

The tragic death of Bishop Puchol on the feast-day of St. Michael of Monte Gargano the following May 8th certainly relieved their anxieties a little. (Bishop Puchol died in an auto accident 30 miles north of Madrid on May 8, 1967.) But what fetters still remain over the seers, their families, and over the whole of this small village! One proof is that at the beginning of August, 1967, Jacinta refused to allow a drawing to be made of her, or to give her autograph. "No," she said, "they have forbidden me to allow this."

Intellectual Childishness

We have prophesied the pressures and duress. The refusal to allow priests to go up to the village was obvious, but we were far from imagining that this would conceal so much priestly bad faith, so much clerical hostility, so much mysterious blindness, so much childish imprudence.

We have already sketched an outline of the first two. We shall now deal with the others.

We could, of course, proceed illuminated by the light of Conchita and resolve the whole affair in two minutes by the words she said to us personally: "Child's play? No—because we can't begin it again."

This reply is, undoubtedly, quite conclusive and we take it as such. But it gives us too easy a victory and everybody knows that

193

we don't like to have a victory without risks and without working for it. . . .

We shall explain, then, and prove it—forgetting that Conchita with her few words has solved the question conclusively. In this way we do more honor to human intelligence, involved in this affair on a world-wide scale; more honor to the Catholic Church (which should not be confused with Santander and which should not be accused of having stopped where Santander has stopped). We shall not allow Santander to create a new "Galileo" affair.

Honesty, Wisdom, ancient Roman virtues!

In Catholicism, philosophical and theological exactitude must be added to these. One should re-read the chapter called "Before the Commission" (of Santander). It will serve as an introduction to what we added today regarding the philosophy and theology practiced by Santander. There they are convinced of two things: (1) apparitions in the sense indicated belong to another age— to that of the ingenuity of a Catholicism of the past; (2) certainty in the face of events of this kind can only be assured through evidence. . . .

That the evidence belongs to the visionaries alone we have shown in Chapter 33. The witnesses, whether from Santander or elsewhere, have been given only signs, motives for believing. Just as Jesus taught, when He said: "If you do not believe in My words, at least believe in My works. . . ." Our book relates the "works" of Garabandal, the photographs etc., confirm them.

Bishop Puchol has publicly denied the possibility of the supernatural nature of the events in his Note on March 17th, in which he wrote what he was later to repeat to journalists, on the radio and on television regarding the Magisterium of the Church. Obviously, he is totally unaware of the existence of Lourdes, of Beauraing, of Fatima, not to mention other apparitions.

❊   ❊   ❊

As well as honesty and exactitude in doctrine, common sense must also be added. We are even tempted to write that common sense precedes both of them.

We have seen what went on in Conchita's soul between February 7 and October 14, 1966. Her anxiety and perturba-

194

tion before and after the interior locution of February 13th; the diabolical temptations regarding the Holy Eucharist; the drama —the third in two months—of her doubts about her apparitions; the net woven by the preacher of Pamplona and the young parish priest of Garabandal (or, if you prefer, the concerted action of these two beaters, directing their frightened quarry towards the hunters of Santander).

All these things bring us face to face with a superhuman tragedy, the victims being Conchita and her companions. And therefore when the hour of clarifications comes—and it is fast approaching—the thing which will give the most scandal is the intellectual childishness of the adversaries. At the height of their supreme malevolence and before the whole world they are dishonoring human intelligence, and are trampling underfoot the simple common-sense of the Catholic people.

At the moment when seventeen-year-old girls, hounded like rabbits, don't know which side to take, they have the audacity to attribute this to a state of psychosis for which they, and they alone, are responsible. In so doing they seek to confirm their own judgment and proclaim it to the whole world. Having scorned the events in Garabandal when they were taking place, with the development proper to them, they are now taking advantage of the upset state of mind of these young girls in order to draw conclusions favorable to their own judgment.

They are even rejecting a five-year-old prophecy according to which "a day will come in which the seers will contradict themselves; in which members of their families will not behave as they should in regard to the apparitions; in which they will even deny having seen the Blessed Virgin—thereby creating a confusion concerning Garabandal similar to the confusion which will reign in the Church."

They have read in Conchita's "Diary" that she asked forgiveness of the Virgin for having allowed herself to be deceived by them. That was as long ago as the end of July, 1961, in Santander. . . .

And they have read in the same "Diary" that at the beginning of 1963, because of a crisis of conscience which unfolded itself in our presence, the girls saw clearly that their doubts had not

195

reached the depths of their souls, but rather that the devil had worked on their senses, their imagination, their memory and that it was in these that they had experienced their doubts. This was, in fact, written by Conchita herself: "We have in a certain sense allowed ourselves to be dominated by Satan."

According to these adversaries there is nothing to be done, all is useless; Garabandal no longer exists, no celestial personage came down to the village.

Their blindness is such that they do not surmise that the devil has obscured the light of the preceding years among the visionaries, and they do not even realize that they themselves have helped Satan personally in his diabolical task.

❋   ❋   ❋

A Rude Awakening

Well, Santander, this is what you have had the audacity to lay before the common-sense of Catholics, and before the whole world . . . at your Tribunal. In the future there will be a rude awakening—we have been convinced of this for a long time now.

In the first place, you have not shown yourselves to be judges of integrity; you have not accepted full declarations; you have accepted only that which aided your own designs. You have suppressed all Conchita's "buts . . . ," "but the Diary is true . . . ; but the Message is true . . . ; but the Miracle will happen . . . etc.," You have given the name of "denials" to what were no more than "contradictions." And you have also begun again the scandalous game you played in July–August, 1961.

And above all, because you based yourselves solely on the state of soul of the girls during the period from August 30 to October 14, 1966 you have laid yourselves open to all kinds of surprises. How? Because it only needs a change in these states for you to find yourselves obliged, of necessity, to modify your conclusions. And this is precisely what has happened; they have already changed and very much so, even before the Note of March 17, 1967.

Yes, even before you passed judgment your conclusions were already invalid.

196

On January 1, 1967, only two and a half months after October 14, 1966, Conchita composed the wonderful prayer which can be found on page 124 of the book entitled "Conchita's Diary.". . . Here are a few lines:

"Lord, I beseech You for those who are spreading the Message,
For those who are not fulfilling the Message,
For those who do not want to know anything about the Message,
Lord, I pray that Your Message might be made ever more
widely known . . ."

So . . . is Conchita confirming the existence of the Message? Yes or No?

At the end of February, 1967, we showed both Conchita and Loli two different leaflets (pictures) which claimed to represent Our Lady of Garabandal. The two girls were 135 miles away from each other, but both made a complete and definite criticism of the pictures, pointing out various details and saying: "but no, not like that . . . our vision was like this."

Do you fully understand? "No celestial personage had been in the village," but "the Virgin that we saw is quite different from the picture you are showing us."

❋   ❋   ❋

About the same time there was a rumor in Spain and elsewhere that the Miracle would take place on the following April 13th, which would be the feast-day of St. Hermenegild and would fall on a Thursday. It was believed possible because St. Hermenegild was a martyr of the Holy Eucharist and was a native of Spain.

But Conchita's reply when questioned about it was: "To guess at dates regarding the Miracle shows a lack of faith in the Blessed Virgin. As she told me, I shall anounce it eight days beforehand."

. . . "There have been no Apparitions . . ." but the Miracle has been prophesied and will take place.

Easter Holidays, 1967

In Fatima, Conchita met her great friend, Joey Lomangino, the blind American who is the great apostle of Garabandal in the U.S.A.

197

A companion of Joey's, a well-known Fatima apostle from America, asked Conchita:

"Conchita, the Virgin promised you in two of your raptures that Joey would be cured. Will he regain his sight on the day of the Great Miracle? She replied immediately "Yes."

"Doubt of having seen the Virgin". . . but on two occasions, on account of two raptures, she has even prophesied the cure of a blind man, on a certain date . . .

The following conversation took place on the same date or thereabouts:

Taking advantage of an opportunity, and in order to see her reaction, somebody said to Conchita with a certain irony: "But isn't it you yourself who have fabricated the whole affair?" Her reply came as quick as lightning: "No." "Then it was from God, something altogether above and beyond you?" "Yes." "You realize that the Virgin appeared to you, and you believe it?" "Yes."

And Conchita proceeded to relate things quite normally, as though she had never had any doubts at all.

Yes, since April, 1967, only six months after October 14th and no more than a few weeks after the Note of March 17th, 1967, Conchita was relating things in a normal fashion, as though she had never had any doubts.

And it was just before Bishop Puchol went up to the village, on Sunday, April 9th, a month before his tragic death on the following May 8th, the feast of the Apparition of St. Michael on Monte Gargano (Italy).

A Last Comment

We could, and we should, add still more things. Noting their dates we shall have a thread of inflexible testimonies, but this is for later on. Today we only announce them in order to console our hearers and our readers . . . Conchita's answer to the 'Gaceta Illustrada' in May; our meeting in her house in the village with Joey Lomangino on June 26th; the little picture painted under Conchita's guidance in May–June; Jacinta at "the Pines" with our friend Bernardo in July; Conchita, Loli and Jacinta among the visitors at "the Pines" and elsewhere. . . . The visionaries are living in a new world, their confidence restored.

We shall end with two conclusions:

First of all is Conchita's, of course. It dates from the end of March, 1967, when she heard of the Note of the 17th:

"—If the Bishop has acted in good faith, God will take this into consideration. But as regards his Note, I think this: those who already believe in Garabandal will believe more from now on . . . and by reason of this more visitors will come to the village in the future."

Divine Providence, as always, does all things well.

Lastly, our own conclusion: The common-sense of the people of God can never be mocked with impunity.

He who permits himself to judge the state of a soul when that soul is in the "dark night" is obliged, in advance, to condemn himself when light comes to that soul again. In this case, whoever it is, is like the weathervane on our houses—always at the mercy of the four winds.

Fribourg
September 15, 1967

Note: Additional information on March 7, 1967 Note of Bishop Vincent Puchol to be found on page 276.

LXVII

CONFERENCE IN CANADA

Such is our conference in Switzerland, which we wrote while traveling on the roads of this small country.

We are completing it with another conference that we wrote on the roads of Canada. We do not have on hand, notes left in France, but we certify as absolutely authentic, at least in their real sense, all the following news. This way our book will keep all the qualities that have never been contested, the absolute truth of our testimony, the positive, straightforward narration of the facts.

199

May 1967

We are always surprised that Garabandal's adversaries have not published their reasoning concerning the facts, thus, willingly depriving us of their knowledge. We believe they have failed in brotherly charity towards us because they owed us, they owed the entire world, to prevent us from making errors, from deceiving the world.

In a family, those who withhold the truth owe it to the other members (of the family) who, in their opinion, would be in error. We know the books which are favorable to the apparitions. We point out: "Dios en la Sombra" published in Spain, and written by a theologian of long standing in the diocese of Santander. Not only does he reveal facts unknown until this time, but he proves that nothing was canonical in the inquest which resulted in the note of March 17, 1967. May we recommend that everyone read this very important volume which can be ordered from: Editorial Circula, Agustino Simon I, at Zaragoza, Spain. (Available only in Spanish, at present.)

❈ ❈ ❈

Yes, we are still waiting for *"Le Livre Blanc"* (the White Book) from the official commission of Santander. As St. Thomas of Aquinas said: "In such matters, the argument of authority cannot suffice."

We suppose that the article of the *Gaceta Illustrada* (a Spanish publication), inspired by the note of March 17, does not sum up the argumentation of the commission. If this is the case, we could send them the dialogue we personally had with Conchita at Burgos in mid-May 1967.

We pass it on to you:

— "Conchita, here is the article of the *Gaceta Illustrada,* which pretends to justify the note condemning Garabandal.

— I know, and I intend answering it myself.

— So, all this was child's play.

— No!

— Why no?

— Because we cannot start over again.

— You are going to answer this article yourself?

— Yes.

— Give me a summary of your answers.

— Come tomorrow."

And the next day Conchita handed us, typewritten with her own fingers, ten petrifying phrases which would pulverize the ten ridiculous affirmations made by the journalist on the weekly paper.

We will mention but one, which to us is the most essential:

"No, I didn't deceive anyone at the occasion of the Miracle (of the *Forma*) of Holy Communion on the 18th of July, 1962." Let's resume with the same conclusion: "I didn't see the Virgin, but the ten arguments of the adversaries are false, and the Miracle of the Host is true now, and was true then."

* * *

June 26, 1967

Our great friend, Joey Lomangino, the blind American, writes to us, through his secretary: "I will be in Garabandal until June 28th." Immediately, we decide, if he crosses the Atlantic we should travel the 625 miles to join him and Conchita on vacation in her village.

On the afternoon of June 26th, we found Serafin, Aniceta's eldest son, alone in the kitchen. We talked together for two informative hours. This handsome man, past his thirties, displayed the supernatural, quiet wisdom of the perfect mountaineer. He humbly related many brilliant things concerning the apparitions of the visionaries.

We especially remember this one:

"In my opinion, The Miracle will come when confusion in the church will be even greater." This reflection of Serafin, which impressed us so much, cannot be understood by the reader unless it is considered as an historic fact, which is absolutely incontestable. Not only will it enlighten the deep thought of Conchita's eldest brother, but it will prove that the doubts of the visionaries were predicted by the Virgin of Carmel and themselves, five years in advance.

It was in 1961, at the time of the absolute certitude and inexpressible joy for the children, concerning their apparitions.

So, in 1961, as they emerged from a trance, all four were questioned as usual.

— This time, what did the Virgin tell you?

They looked at each other as if for consultation.

— Well, tell us.

— We don't understand too well.

— Talk just the same.

— The Virgin said: A time will come when all four of you will contradict yourselves about the apparitions; when your families will not behave well about them; when even you will doubt the apparitions, even deny them.

— Is that all?

— No, she added: Thus you will establish among you the same confusion that now exists in the church.

A priest was present and he vigorously protested.—"It's not the Virgin appearing. In fact, there is no confusion in the church. It is the Devil talking." Because of their respect for the clergy, the people dispersed in silence, since they could not answer him. They did not know that Our Lady was not mistaken. The actual confusion in the church, the confusion in this year 1967, which is now so noticeable in the Christian people, already existed in 1961, and probably even before, among the theologians and their listeners.

In the silence and solitude of his stable on the pastureland of Garabandal, Serafin, the very wise mountaineer, has been clearly aware of this situation for a long time.

* * *

On the night of June 26, 1967, the family is all present. We are sitting at the family table, Conchita facing us, Joey Lomangino at our right. The face of the adolescent is resplendent with Christian beauty.

We were glancing at her, when Joey touched us with his elbow, his hand on a book, which Conchita had just dedicated to him. We read: "In fond remembrance and in union of prayers, so God will make use of these apparitions for the salvation of souls."

Return in May, 1967

Many visitors to Garabandal could show the same quotation given to them on papers, pictures and books which they had presented to her to autograph. As to what she wrote for us at Burgos, in May 1967, it is: "At Santander I said I didn't see the Virgin, I should have said, I doubt that I have seen the Virgin. Yes, I signed what I said but did not swear to it. By the grace of God may our apparitions contribute to the salvation of souls and prevent humanity from being struck by the chastisement."

✻ ✻ ✻

Conchita! Conchita! So! in spite of what your young pastor, Father Jose Olano, in connivance with Father Emiliano from Pamplona, and the others, and in spite of Father Olano repeating: "You must swear on the Bible that you deceived the village and the world," you did not swear, you did not take an oath.

Listen to us, attentively.

First, you should write and sign, and declare: "I doubt that I have seen the Virgin," and not what you wrote and signed: "I did not see the Virgin."

You should state your evidence more clearly, and add all the "buts," all the known restrictions. "But, the Miracle of the Host is true," "but, all the messages are true," "but the Miracle will come," and the rest. You should say this, because, all this you have said and repeated to your interrogators of Santander.

Again, listen, listen well to this, for you could not know it. You could not understand it. When, after years of inquest, we were called to give evidence to the Canonical Commission, who were to study the apparitions at Beauraing, thirty-five years ago, we faced a real Canonical Commission, organized and proceeding according to canonical laws. It consisted of a president, his assessors, a lawyer, and a notary. They were the same priests, named by the Bishop of the diocese where the apparitions occurred, and confirmed in the dignity of their mission.

203

At Santander, from April 30 to October 14, 1967, you, Conchita, and the others—you didn't even appear before an official Commission, but in front of priests and a bishop, who, for the occasion, improvised themselves as your judges.

Before questioning us at Beauraing, we took the oath with our hand on the Bible. You, Conchita, just confirmed that you did not take an oath.

Conchita, the whole world must know it, for these two reasons alone, though there are many more—not only your interrogation, but that of your companions, was not, and is not canonically valid, and your deposition is not, either. Everything must be dismissed and begun anew. Yes, Conchita, everything must be dismissed and begun anew. Another tribunal must take over, as we say in civil law.

Above all, it proves clearly that the defenders of Garabandal, not only have the right, but also are obliged in conscience to continue their battle.

This also proves the eminent wisdom of the Congregation for the Doctrine of the Faith, which ended its note of March 10, 1967 with these words, clear for everyone: "As for us, we abstain."

July, 1967

Conchita is on vacation, and the French pilgrims profit by the opportunity to go up to the village. We can follow the four visionaries, day by day, each of our friends having sent us their testimonies. We are summing up.

The first week Conchita and Jacinta are withdrawn. They are asked for autographs, to photograph them. They hesitate, and we are surprised, they answer: "We do not have the permission." Permission from whom? From Santander? From the pastor of Garabandal? We will know later.

It suffices, for now, to ascertain that the religious intimidation still remains more than a year after the abominable actions of Father Emiliano, the occasional confessor at Pamplona.

Nevertheless, at the end of the same month, For a French priest, passing through, Conchita undertook to write a whole page in Spanish. When it was translated for him, he brought back to us what could be called the picture of a priest, drawn by the adolescent. It is a touching picture and all supernatural, which, seen with the prayer of the young seminarian Pepe Luis would enable a retreat master to bring back to this audience the evangelical vision, and perfectly visible, the state and apostleship of the priesthood.

And, here, is the copy:

What the Virgin wants of the priest.—?

First, his own sanctification. Fulfill his vows for love of God. Pursue, win many souls by example and prayers, because in our time it is difficult to do it otherwise. May he be saintly, by love of the soul, through Christ. To seclude themselves, once in a while, in silence so they may listen to God, who continually speaks to them.

To meditate often on the Passion of Jesus, so their life can be in greater union to Christ, the Priest. Thus, they will inspire souls to penance, to sacrifice. They will help them to carry the cross better, which Christ asks us all to carry.

To speak of Mary, who is sure to carry us to Christ.

Also speak to souls and make them believe, that since there is Heaven there is also a Hell.

I believe this is what Heaven wants of her priests.

Conchita Gonzalez
July 29, 1967

In reality, not only were the visionaries forbidden to give autographs or to be photographed, they were also forbidden to return to the *Cuadro*, especially to "the Pines."

Conchita told a French nun, familiar with Spanish: "Mother, I haven't returned for a year."

And the French, without knowing, will be the occasion of the liberation of Conchita and Jacinta. Let's give them, here, the homage they deserve. If, as Venerable and dear Padre Rodrigo, Spanish Jesuit, willingly repeats:

— "The Virgin appeared in Spain, but it's the French who received and welcomed her."

Everyone also knows that at the time of the last apparition of St. Michael on June 18, 1965, alone, three pilgrims from France had the privilege of kissing Conchita's crucifix.

It was befitting that, their return to Garabandal in 1967, in spite of Father Jose Olano's supervision, recreated the atmosphere of freedom which the visionaries needed.

One of the Frenchmen had the privilege to be accompanied by Jacinta to the *Cuadro*, where she showed him the exact spot of the Angel's first apparition. Shortly after, other Frenchmen were praying at "the Pines." All of a sudden, light footsteps claimed their attention. They turned around; Conchita was smiling at them. They finished the rosary, and then, Conchita talked to them of the apparitions at "the Pines," pointing out the tree where Our Lady of Mt. Carmel appeared most frequently. However, like Jacinta at the *Cuadro*, she stopped suddenly, and confessed: "I do not have permission to say more."

❊ ❊ ❊

Then, it was Jacinta who led friends to the rock above which, with Loli first, then with Loli and Conchita, she witnessed the terrible vision of the chastisement during the Corpus Christi Novena in 1962.

❊ ❊ ❊

As for Loli, she was staying home. Not that she wasn't tempted to accompany the pilgrims, but her father, Ceferino, prevented her from going out because the pastor of the village punctually visited his "little bar" and because her mother, Julia, feared her pastor as much as her husband feared him.

The French (them again!), were reserving an unusual surprise for those terrorized parents.

One morning, one of them brought a weekly paper which he had found at a merchant's in Cabezon de la Sol. It referred to an article two months old. The journalist had met Mr. Alvarez, the commandant of the armed police of Puentenansa—on which—Garabandal depends.

It is he, at the time of the apparitions, who was at the village every day, alone or with his men. We know him very well, for he witnessed one of Conchita's ecstasies with us, in Conchita's kitchen.

In the article in this weekly paper, he was telling briefly what he had seen hundreds of times, and proclaimed his fervent faith. For him, the supernaturality of the facts was evident. With natural ease, our French friend placed this old document on the table in the little bar. Ceferino noticed it and looked through it. Little by little, the look on his face changed, and we saw affirmative nods of the head. Deeply moved, he retired to his kitchen. There, face in his hands, tears came to his eyes. The past filed through his memory, he must have remembered the notes he had given us in bygone days, that little notebook, in which he had written in his own hand all the ecstasies of the month of August, 1962.

Very dear, grieving Ceferino, sturdy as an oak, who saved "the Pines," by ridding them of caterpillars, once consented to surrender at Santander, and again in the presence of a young priest only twenty-six years old.

✿ ✿ ✿

St. Michael's Chapel

We had dozens of such testimonies in our files concerning the months of August and September. They point out that the visionaries were regaining their freedom of behavior and their understanding.

Let's review the last days of September, 1967. Let us recall a fact which is at first thought, amazing.

At Garabandal, our Lady of Carmel is not preoccupied with herself. She hasn't mentioned a sanctuary to be dedicated to her. We understand this easily. In reality, as long as she led the children everywhere—to the *Cuadro*, at "the Pines," through the whole village, at the cemetery, at church, around the church, in almost every home in Garabandal (unprecedented in the annals of apparitions)—the temple of the Virgin, if we dare express ourselves this way, already exists; it is everywhere; it's the whole village. It would be a great mistake to enclose it with walls.

So, the Virgin asked for the construction of a small chapel dedicated to St. Michael. Queen of Heaven, she wants to honor her loyal Knight, the Archangel who intercedes to her for us, the Archangel who is her medium to humanity.

207

More than others, the Barcelonians were thinking about the chapel to St. Michael and especially Mr. Sanchez-Ventura, author of the book, "The Apparitions of Garabandal." Within a few days, a group of masons picked up the prefabricated chapel, in Zaragoza.

On the evening of September 28th, about one hundred pilgrims were going up, on foot, from Cosio, carrying, in turn, a statue of St. Michael. Let's skip over the incidents provoked by Santander and the pastor of Garabandal. We will come back to them some day when the ridicule dies out in Spain and in the village as well.

We remember three things: at the laying of the first stone for this chapel, erected between the *Cuadro* and "the Pines," evidently on private ground, Conchita was present and smiling. Again on September 28th, at 8 o'clock in the evening, Conchita and Jacinta were at "the Pines" among the pilgrims in prayer. Jacinta was crying with happiness, while Conchita, calm and happy, was looking at the dearest of her trees, the one under which Father Luis Andreu saw the Miracle to come.

At our last visit to Garabandal we were talking with Aniceta in front of her home. Suddenly she turned towards "the Pines" and said, "See, from here I can see the chapel and even the statue of St. Michael. It gives a good feeling to be looking at them while reciting my rosary."

October 30, 1967

On that day a Spanish woman was at Loli's. The conversation was especially cordial. Suddenly the young girl got up, went upstairs and came back with her big missal in her hands.

"Señora, I'm giving it to you. Take it."

When the visitor refused, Loli insisted.

"Yes, take it. But there is a condition: that you will disperse the pages throughout the entire world. This way the Virgin's kiss will reach the whole universe."

"Loli, I don't understand too well. I know that Our Lady kissed your missal, at least the cover."

"When Our Lady kissed my missal, she not only kissed the cover, but every page; yes, each page. Here, look at these two pages of the Canon. They are my favorites because they represent

208

Jesus crucified and the angels receiving His blood in a chalice. These pages I give to the young girl accompanying you."

"Loli, Loli . . ."

"On the condition that all the pages carry the Virgin's kiss to all humanity."

November, 1967

We could not miss the anniversary of the last apparition at "the Pines," November 13, 1965. We were escorted by a French friend—again a Frenchman—to whom Conchita had offered the rosary kissed by Our Lady of Mt. Carmel on this solemn occasion, the 13th of November, 1965. Before and after this pilgrimage of love, we saw Conchita at Burgos, for three days. We were four witnesses from France, plus an artist well known in Spain. There are so many things we should relate!

Let's sum up our conversation with the artist.

— "Look at these sketches I've just finished at Conchita's direc-tion."

— The first, the Virgin alone.

— The second, the Virgin and the Infant Jesus.

— The third, the Virgin, the Eye of God, and the twin angels.

— The fourth, the Archangel St. Michael alone.

— "Hundreds of times Conchita corrected my work, making me retouch this or that. Don't worry; she hasn't forgotten one single detail of the apparitions."

Facing such affirmation, we could ony answer, "Dear artist, we have known it since February, 1967, and Conchita proved it to us, right here at Burgos, on that date, as Loli proved the same thing, in what concerned her, at Bolmori, the day after our visit to Burgos. But I like to have you say so yourself. Then, the whole world will know that Conchita Gonzalez, in spite of assertions, is completely back to the truth."

Let's not be afraid to repeat ourselves, as it is a subject of great importance.

We address ourselves directly to Santander.

"Santander, your note of March 17th is nothing more than the conclusion, which you made public, of the inquest which you brought to a close, on October 14, 1966. But, on these last dates the girls were in 'spiritual obscurity' (or confusion). So, you have judged a state of soul and not the facts of Garabandal as they happened, at the time they were happening, following attentively as they unfolded.

"Universal good sense, elementary logic, demands of you that true to your intellectual method, you judge them under their new state of soul: their return to 'the light,' to the truth. Certainly, it will be humiliating to contradict yourself publicly, to attest to the world that your move of March 17, 1967, has absolutely no value, that you are obliged to proclaim the contrary; to proclaim that the apparitions are true and supernatural. We understand very well the situation which binds you, and we do not wish you the most terrible public confusion. We are suggesting this, with a real fraternal love—the usual procedure of civil law which is also the canonical law.

"You have judged the happenings at Garabandal in an inferior court. Your Commission was the tribunal (or Court of Justice?). As long as this one was mistaken, it must be dismissed and you must organize another which will begin from the beginning and following the method indicated in Chapter 2 of the "Star on the Mountain." An obvious condition is that your new judges will be completely just and, contrary to what went on previously, that all witnesses of Garabandal, favorable or not, will be heard in accordance with canon law.

"You will start with Father Valentin Marichalar, pastor at the time of the apparitions. Surely the real solution would be the tribunal of appeal, but we won't even go as far as to claim it. In the meantime we, the witnesses who believe in Garabandal, have the strict duty to prove the whole truth. Rest assured that we will never fail to do so, no, never."

✿   ✿   ✿

Our Pretentious Ignorance

If we all reflected deeply we would blush at our ridiculous pretentions. We, ourselves, not being authentic visionaries, have the incredible "naivete" to impose, on those who are, our very in-

210

adequate logic. How? By pretending that the "real" visionaries must carry to their death, always and everywhere, the evidence of their visions. But we know nothing of this realism, which is beyond us, and because of this ignorance we cannot establish laws to govern the "preternatural." We cannot establish those laws, by our own personal knowledge, of a world which escapes us.

In order to talk wisely about it and benefit by it, we must refer to authentic confidences of uncontested visionaries in the history of the New Testament. They are legion. From the Virgin of the Annunciation to the children of Fatima, to stop there, coming by way of the shepherds of Christmas and St. Teresa of Avila.

* * *

Let's examine three recent cases: Melanie of LaSalette, St. Bernadette of Lourdes, Lucy of Fatima.

At Dion, at the road of Mars-on-Allier at Paray-le Monial, Melanie had lived a few years under the protection and guidance of Father Combes, pastor of the region. Usually, Father would receive, orally or written, the answers to questions he would put to her. There came a day that Melanie let the good but imperious interrogator wait longer than he wished to and he was surprised, indeed impatient, about it. This is an interesting passage of the conversation.

"Reverend Father, when I sat down at my table to write, my mind became cloudy, my memory disordered, confused. I couldn't see anything, remember anything."

* * *

St. Bernadette, a year preceding her death, is in her convent of St. Gildard, at Nevers. At this moment she is consumed by holiness, or almost. A French Bishop, who became a Cardinal later, interrogated her:

— "Sister Marie Bernard, and your apparitions?"

— "Ah! Your Grace, I don't like to go back to it. What if I had been mistaken."

— "What happened over there?"

211

— "In a great light, the Lady in a white robe, blue sash, roses on the feet, etc. . . ."

* * *

Lucy of Fatima.

The French specialist on Fatima, the most competent and universally esteemed on the subject of Fatima, was telling us, in our home, this year:

— "Don't be surprised by the momentary obscurities of the children of Garabandal, the faltering of their minds, of their memories."

— "Why?"

— "It was the mysterious case of Lucy. She, too, was doubtful of her apparitions for a time."

* * *

The conclusion is obvious in the face of these three particular cases which enlighten us on the logic of a world which is not ours. And in that world, the minds and memories of the true visionaries belong to God, and to Him alone.

To be astonished by this would be as ridiculous as to think that authentic apparitions emerge not from Divine pleasure, but from the free determination of His human creatures. Listen here to the echo of Conchita's reflection made to us at Burgos, and mentioned in another chapter: "No, Garabandal is not child's play, because we cannot begin over again!"

* * *

November 13, at Garabandal

In the village an American is visiting for the second time. The first time we thought he believed in the apparitions. We were mistaken, for he wrote us later from Palestine that there was nothing to them. Back from the Orient, we met him again, at Garabandal, in June, 1967, at which time he was still searching for the truth.

November 13, 1967, he seemed to have found it.

In any case, he was very enthusiastic when he was telling us, that day in Conchita's home, what he called his three miracles.

He said,—"Mari Cruz gave me a piece of one of her rosaries kissed by the Virgin during the apparitions. Here it is. I detached a few links from the chain, right here. I sent them to the United States to a woman suffering from cancer for whom all hope had been abandoned by her doctors, who were giving her but 15 days to live. She placed these precious links on herself, prayed to our Lady of Carmel of Garabandal, and was suddenly cured."

— "You have the documents?"

— "Not yet. But it is not difficult to verify the truth of such a cure."

— "Your conclusion?"

— "I like to believe that the Blessed Mother remembered Mari Cruz too."

* * *

November 14 at Burgos.

As of November 11, we just spent long hours with Conchita. This time, her mother is present, relaxed and happy. The artist is there also, with four Frenchmen, one of whom is a priest friend of ours. We ask Conchita, first, for messages for this last one (the priest), and for the Spreaders of the Message, for each person present, and for a few absentees.

While everyone is chatting, through the noise of a very animated conversation, Conchita places herself in the center of our group. Ten minutes later her task is finished, and we read. The writing is more a "scribbling" for she did as soldiers do, writing in their trenches. She wrote on her knees.

But what treasures! They are more and better than at the time of the ecstasies. She looked into consciences, she enlightened the clergy, she explained the apostolate of the Garabandalists, she determined the Christianity of teaching and how to educate the children.

Having providentially found the copy among our papers, on our trip to Canada, we are most happy to publish it.

213

I. To a (reliable) priest interested in Garabandal:

"Dear Father, I wish you great happiness while you sacrifice to work for Mary, and I, in my poor prayers, will intercede so that you'll never get discouraged in the work of the Virgin. She'll help you while you work with good will. Pray for us (the four girls) so we'll not close the eyes of our souls. Pray and ask that we may accept God's will, that we may forget ourselves and think more of others. Nothing more, Father. May the Virgin triumph at Garabandal, so everyone will be crowned with graces, so everyone will glorify God, and love Him above everything else.

Conchita Gonzales"

II. To priests and lay people of sub-centers, to secretaries, officers, to lecturers, to propagators:

"Give thanks to God for having been chosen to help the Virgin to 'carry' souls to God. Pray much for priests, who are the salt of the earth and the 'well-loved' of Christ.

I pray much for all of you so you will give to the Father and Mother (God and Mary) what they are asking of you.

We are in the last warnings. Why 'bargain' with the Lord? Pray for us. Ask that we may be humble.

With much affection,
Conchita"

III. To a lady who had explained to her that we must offer doubts on faith and the darkness of the soul, for the unbelievers:

"This holy picture in gratitude for your conversation, which helps me to struggle against doubts of faith. I embrace you.

Your very grateful
Conchita"

IV. To a soul desiring a deep and true spiritual life:

"I unite myself to you, to the true Love, who is Christ, and to Truth, who is Himself. May the Virgin enlighten you and help you to serve Him in all things.

Conchita"

V. To teachers:

"I ask God that you may be shepherds of your pupils."

VI. To a sick woman:

"I have learned of your infirmity. To those He loves, the Lord makes them a gift of suffering.

With Conchita's affection"

VII. To another priest:

"I will write you a long letter, day after tomorrow. For tonight, this holy picture. God will not abandon you, either in sufferings, or in joy.

Conchita"

        ❄   ❄   ❄

Camillas, November 1967

The previous day, at Garabandal, we had talked for two hours, in her home, with Jacinta, her mother, Maria, and her father, Simon. With the greatest mutual confidence we recalled all the past, our former conversations, doubts of the visionaries, the Miracle to come.

Leaning on the fireplace of the kitchen, never had Jacinta looked more pure nor more beautiful, in every respect.

However, it was Reverend Father Rodrigo, S.J., of the Pontifical University of Camillas, who resumed this conversation on Garabandal.

"After two years of silence," he said, "Jacinta paid me a visit here at my home. We talked for three hours."

Without breaking the secrecy, which trait we regard highly, Father resumed this conversation. Then, joining the thumb and index finger, which are long and so aristocratic, raising his hand very high in a gesture which suggests a man who is about to drop on the living room carpet a very precious object,

"Jacinta? She's a little angel, from before the Fall, which the Virgin let fall on our poor earth, to console and comfort it."

        ❄   ❄   ❄

Final Word.

We are in Montreal. We were about to give our fifth conference, in particularly difficult and humiliating conditions, and at

215

the same time so supernaturally effectual, when we received (on the morning of December 27) a letter from Madrid.

"I forgot to write before part of my conversation with Loli on October 31, 1967, in her home, when she made me the extraordinary gift of her missal, and I admit that I was extremely surprised! Here is what she also said:

— If I were to talk to you of my apparitions of the Virgin and the angel I would have to lie to you.

— Lie to me?

— Yes, I wouldn't be able to tell you as they were.

— Why?

— Because I was forbidden to.

— You were forbidden to tell the truth?

— Yes.

— Who forbade you?

— (Loli, all confused) I cannot tell you.

— Yes, Loli, who forbade you? Your father? Santander? your pastor? a confessor? Answer me, who?

— I cannot tell you.

✿ ✿ ✿

Dear readers, perhaps when in our conferences we would bring up the religious, the clerical intimidation, you were shocked and scandalized by the audacious words we were writing?

Here is the moment to rally to the truth.

Inventing nothing, we are simply giving proof of that stability of character, that intellectual serenity, loyalty, which requires that we call things by their right names.

We didn't substitute ourselves for Conchita or Jacinta, who in July and August, 1967, could no longer bear the truth of the secret in which they were being enclosed.

Read over the above lines. If you add to them Loli's poignant confession of October 31, 1967, you'll understand that the jails we talked about in our conferences in Switzerland, were of small importance in the face of the infernal secret in which they dared to fetter their consciences.

216

Behind the walls of this obnoxious pact, four girls were desperately crying out towards heaven; in front of those locked doors, we, the Christian people, claim their liberation, even if we deliver them ourselves and throw in their executioners, for always!

* * *

Conclusion

Such is the absolute truth of the apparitions of Garabandal.

Surely, the conference in Canada was not written with the application that the importance of the subject required. As for the one in Switzerland, it was drawn up haphazardly at whatever stops we made along the way. It also has the same tone.

In following the chronological order of our accounts we have necessarily missed the opportunity for a logical summary, for a sympathetic presentation of the facts, which would have impressed the reader even more. May the reader take time to read both conferences twice, and so make up for the imperfection of our work as a pilgrim of Garabandal.

The essential aim was to deliver to the reader, even though taken "on the run," testimonies which were absolutely sure and which, with our book "The Star on the Mountain" constitute "our sign of credibility."

This is why we do not hesitate to avail ourselves of the inspiration of the words of Reverend Laurence, Bishop of Lourdes, recommending the apparitions of St. Bernadette, to the great Pope Benedict XIV:

"Knowing that these proofs of credibility are incontestable and uncontested, we think it is reasonable to believe, on human faith, that Our Lady of Carmel and the Archangel Michael have really appeared at San Sebastian of Garabandal, to the four visionaries, Conchita, Loli, Jacinta and Mari Cruz."

Montreal, December 28, 1967

LXVIII

A CURE IN THE UNITED STATES

We are publishing the following testimony because it is accompanied by a duly signed and notarized document. However, we would be remiss in our duty if we would not confirm that, quite often, the mail which we receive on the subject is absolutely amazing. The letters might be from France, where these cases are most numerous, or from Austria, America, Germany—in fact, from everywhere.

In New York, those who are interested in the subject have told us eagerly of the incredible favors that they have obtained, and have signed their depositions in our presence.

This has been an extremely moving experience for us because these cures have been the occasion of profound conversions, and occasionally entire families have been converted.

It would seem that Our Lady of Garabandal is interested especially in persons stricken with cancer.

When She does not obtain the cure which is requested, God will often ease the suffering of the afflicted, or will stop the pain entirely. In the terminal cases, we have seen that She helps even those whose death seems certain.

All the reports mention the use of religious objects which have been either kissed or touched by the Virgin during an apparition.

The religious object used is almost always a medal.

76 Norman Road
Brockton, Massachusetts 02402
U. S. A.

AVE MARIA
November 30, 1966
His Eminence Alfredo Cardinal Ottaviani, Pro-Prefect
Sacred Congregatin For The Doctrine of the Faith

VATICAN CITY
THROUGH THE VIRGIN MOTHER MAY THE LORD GRANT US SALVATION AND PEACE!

In obedience and submission to the Hierarchy, the following account is placed unconditionally in the hands of the proper Ecclesiastical Authority, and I declare before the world that I accept their final decision, in advance, whatever it may be.

Here is the testimony written by the doctor of a lady who was cured by a *Rosary Kissed by Our Lady of Carmel of Garabandal.*

The daughter and I touched the woman's foot with the *Kissed Rosary,* and as sick as she was, I asked her to pray as many Rosaries as she felt she could.

The woman knew nothing about the Reported Apparitions that have been taking place since 1961, in the little village of *San Sebastian de Garabandal, Spain,* she had simply been told that the Rosary had been *Kissed by Our Blessed Mother.* I left the *Kissed Rosary* with her until the next night when I returned to the hospital to get them.

In the meantime, we had asked many people to *Pray* that she would not have to have her leg amputated. *We Begged Our Lady of Carmel of Garabandal to "Put Her Under Her Mantle" and to Give All of Us the Grace to Accept, with Love, the Holy Will of God. . . . All For His Honor and Glory. . . .*

May the Virgin Mary, with Her Loving Child, in the company of St. Joseph and St. Michael, The Archangel, Bless *All* of Mankind and the entire world.

Asking for your special prayers and blessings.

Maria Carmela Saraco

Francis Emmet Smith, M.D.
418 WASHINGTON ST.
BRIGHTON, MASS. 02135
—
TELEPHONE 782-8316

November 1, 1966

Mrs. Eleanor Dekes
110 Bigelow Street
Brighton, Massachusetts

Re: Mrs. Clementine Cedrone
110 Bigelow Street
Brighton, Massachusetts

Dear Mrs. Dekes,

Your mother, Mrs. Clementine Cedrone, who has been diabetic for nine years, was admitted to St. Elizabeth's Hospital on November 27, 1965 because of osteomyelitis of the right foot. X-rays showed destructive changes involving the proximal aspect of the proximal phalanx of the middle toe as well as the proximal head of the third metatarsal. Although it is regarded as quite normal and usual procedure to amputate the limb above the knee under these conditions, Dr. Joseph Mullane decided not to perform this operation for two reasons:

1. Your mother would not accept an amputation.
2. He felt that your mother might as well walk on it until the infection spread.

He was unwilling to do any local removal of bone because healing is not expected to occur at her age with the amount of hardening of the arteries which she has.

I had several doctors take a look at her films, including Drs. Marks, Kellett, and Bailey at the Deaconess Medical Building in Boston. It was the opinion of everyone that no healing could be expected to occur. Your mother was given 20 million units of penicillin per day until January 11, 1966, when she went into acute pulmonary failure. This was treated in the usual fashion. She recovered and was discharged. Subsequent X-rays showed that the bones on the right foot were healing.

On September 28, 1966, it was evident that the osteomyelitis had completely healed. Drs. Marks, Kellett, and Bailey had seen films in March of 1966. The conclusion was that she had healed osteomyelitis of the right third metatarsal.

It is my conclusion that your mother has been very fortunate to be, at this time, walking on two legs. It had been the judgment of many who saw her and her X-ray films, that she should have had an amputation last November.

Sincerely Yours,

Francis E. Smith M.D.

Francis E. Smith, M.D.

FES/jac

Subscribed and sworn before me this 21ST of
December 1966

Benjamin A. Bannister Notary

My Commission Expires 9/28/73

220

LXIX

MYSTICAL ROSE
AN AMERICAN VISIT TO GARABANDAL

Plans for our pilgrimage to the shrines of Our Lord and Our Lady were started almost one year before the actual date of departure, which was on September 9, 1965. On that day twenty American pilgrims left Kennedy International Airport for Lisbon.

In the early days of the planning of the pilgrimage, some thought had been given to our going to Garabandal, since we had heard of the reported apparitions of Our Lady there. However, because of the difficulty in getting there and the long distance that it would take us out of our way, we decided not to go. In June, however, because of the reported apparition of St. Michael and the great interest this caused throughout the world, we gave more thought to going. The decision to go was made and much of our original itinerary had to be re-routed and several places left out.

On September 15, 1965 we left Madrid to go to Santander and stay overnight before our journey to Garabandal on September 16, 1965. Here I wish to state that we went with the full knowledge that the Church had not made any official pronouncement on these reported apparitions and thus we went as an act of Faith and Love to honor Jesus and Mary and to offer the sacrifice of this journey for the salvation of souls. Before we left the United States a letter was sent to the then Bishop of Santander explaining our purpose and leaving in his hands the decision as to our going. Since we did not receive an answer from the Bishop and thus did not have a denial to our going, the journey was made— as stated in the letter, as a private journey made by private individuals not representing any organization or group.

We arrived at the small town at the foot of the mountain about 11:30 a.m. From this town of Cosio we proceeded to take our people up the mountain by car. Because we had twenty people, it took about two hours and four trips of the car to bring them to Garabandal.

I was in the first car. When I arrived, my first thought was to contact Miss Eloise Duiga who had made many of the necessary arrangements for our group. A young boy from the village led me up the hill to "the Pines" where Eloise was, along with Mr. Joe Lomangino and his mother from Long Island, N. Y., and several other people. Miss Duiga greeted me and, after a short explanation about "the Pines" and where it is said that Our Lady has appeared, we proceeded down the hill to see to my people who were sitting in the Inn owned by the man who is mayor of Garabandal and father of Maria Dolores.

By this time it was close to 1:00 p.m. After seeing that the people were taken care of, I went with Eloise to the home of Conchita. She had just returned from working on her family's farm. When I arrived at Conchita's home she was speaking with some people who had come to visit her. The people were a German couple. The husband was a professor of science and told me that he only believed in things that he could see proof— here, he said, I have seen such proof. I observed Conchita while she talked to this couple—she appeared most at ease and most friendly and warm in her manner. About this time several others of our group came to the house and soon Conchita was being asked to pose for pictures. All through this time she remained most at ease, most submissive to the requests and above all, carried them all out with a spirit of humility. During the time the pictures were being taken one of the people who had been staying in Garabandal noticed that Jacinta was walking down the road away from the village on her way to work in the fields. They called to her. She, however, gave a definite appearance of wanting to go on and not return. Some prevailed on Conchita to call Jacinta. This she did and Jacinta came as Conchita asked. She allowed her picture to be taken with Conchita as she was asked but gave the appearance of wishing not to be given attention. Soon after the pictures were taken and those present were engaged in conversation, Jacinta slipped away to work.

As it was time for Conchita and her family to eat, we left to return to the Inn with our people and to welcome the last of

The American group near the Pine Tree where Our Lady appeared most frequently.

our group to Garabandal. After they arrived it was decided that we would go up to "the Pines" with Miss Duiga. As we started up the hill, we began to say the Rosary. At several places Miss Duiga explained to the people that at these spots Our Lady had appeared to the children. As we proceeded up the hill the slope becomes very steep and some of our people were unable to climb the rest of the way to "the Pines." For those of us who could, we knelt in "the Pines" to say the last decade of the Rosary. When the Rosary was finished the people began to gather some of the pine needles, bark from "the Pines" and a few roots from the ground. To the surprise of all, these objects gave off the fra-

223

Conchita praying the rosary with the American group at the site of the June 18, 1965 apparition of St. Michael. This is the statue of Fatima from which emanated the fragrance of roses.

grance of roses—not pines. Many of these items still give off the same fragrance even after our return to the United States.

After coming back down from "the Pines," Miss Duiga began to take the people to the various homes in the village where they would stay the night. We later learned that some of these people of Garabandal slept in the stables that night to make room for our people. The kindness of these people is hard to put into words.

After the people had been shown where they were to stay for the night, they were instructed to meet at the home of Conchita to say the Rosary with her. She was to return from her work on the farm at about 5:30 p.m. The plan was to say the Rosary in the field in front of her home. When Conchita was told of this plan she said she did not wish to say it there but up at "the Pines." She wished this for two reasons: 1. to say the Rosary in the field in front of her home would be too much show; and 2. she stated that Our Lady said we must make sacrifice. Because of the steep slope up to "the Pines" and since our people were not all able to make the first journey up to them, Conchita was asked if she would consider not going so far. She agreed to go to the spot about half way to "the Pines" where St. Michael had appeared on June 18th of that year.

Before we left to say the Rosary, I presented to Conchita for her veneration a statue of the Pilgrim Virgin which I had brought from Fatima. I held the box containing the statue as she kissed its feet. To my surprise, I experienced the fragrance of roses. This lasted only for a short time but the fragrance was very strong. Shortly after this we started up the hill to say the Rosary.

When we reached the spot, Conchita knelt down to begin the Rosary. Conchita used my father's Rosary since he asked her to do so. Throughout the Rosary, Conchita kept her eyes closed and never moved although she was kneeling on small stones. When she got back up after the Rosary these small stones remained imbedded in her knees for some time. She said the Rosary at a normal moderate rate, with much reverence. Her voice was soft and almost seemed to have a musical quality about it.

After the Rosary the people asked Conchita to pose for some pictures and to sign the backs of religious cards or other such items. Throughout this she remained calm, obliging and humble. I remember looking at her during this time and feeling sorry for her—for all the inconvenience she was often put through by well-meaning people. At one point she looked up at me and I shook my head and smiled as much as to say your burden is heavy. She smiled back and one could almost read the answer—this I must do—this is part of my cross.

Upon my return with the others to the village, many of our people came to me and asked if I had received the same fragrance of the roses as they had during the time they were going up the hill with Conchita and during the recitation of the Rosary or at "the Pines" the first time. They wondered what it meant. I told them that I had only received the fragrance when Conchita kissed the statue. As to what it meant, I could only say I felt it indicated the presence of God and Our Lady. When I returned home I mentioned the fragrance to a priest-friend seeking the meaning—he said to me "Bob, isn't one of Our Lady's titles Mystical Rose?" Most of my people had received the fragrance but not all at the same time. This gave us the indication that the fragrance was something that was given to individuals at various times but not the group as a whole—therefore, it could not have been a general fragrance in the air or all would have received it at the same time since the group usually stayed close together.

About 7:30 p.m. that evening we went to the church to say the Rosary with the people of Garabandal, as is their custom. A young boy led the Rosary. Conchita was in the church but knelt with the other people of the village and said the Rosary along with them. I do not remember seeing the other girls in the church but think they were there. The next day the wife of one of the men in our group, Mrs. Fortin, told me that her husband had been kneeling toward the front of the church during the Rosary and received the fragrance of the Roses very strongly. None of the other members of our group received it in the church.

It might be noted here that when our people went to the shrine of Our Lady of the Pillar at Zaragoza, Spain, they identified the fragrance that emanates from the Pillar as the same as that experienced in Garabandal. I, as the leader of the group, knew of the fragrance at the Pillar but I did not wish to put the power of suggestion into the mind of my people and therefore did not tell them before they venerated the Pillar upon which that image of Our Lady stands (given to St. James, the patron of Spain, by Our Lady as tradition tells us). I wanted to see if they found any similarity in the two fragrances. After they venerated it, they all identified it as the same fragrance. I can remember seeing one of our members go over to another altar and kneel down after having kissed the Pillar. Seeing that she seemed a bit shaken, I went over to her and asked: "Dorothy, are you all right?" She said: "I will be all right in a few moments but I just experienced the same fragrance here as I did at Garabandal."

Now to return to our day at Garabandal. After leaving the church, our group went back to the house owned by the father of Maria Loli—the Inn. There our people ate their supper. The supper (for all twenty) was cooked by Maria Loli. She, however, did not come out of the kitchen to serve the people— this her father did. We must here make a comment on the generosity shown by Maria Loli's father. The food he served was plentiful and good. Someone had asked for cheese during the supper. He had only one large piece of cheese which he cut up and served to the whole group—not just to one person. I cannot remember the cost of the supper—only that it was very little. When the people gave me the money to pay for the meal they included a tip as is their custom. When I gave him the money, he counted it. Seeing that I had given him more than he had asked, he gave the surplus amount back to me. I then returned it to him and told him it was just a little tip and thank you from the group for his wonderful service.

Later that evening when our people had gone to the homes where they were to stay for the night, my parents and I went to the home of Conchita. There, together with Joe Lomangino and his mother, Miss Duiga, and Clyde from Brooklyn, N. Y., we spoke with Conchita and her mother for about two hours. She wrote out a few short notes to several priest-friends of mine and we talked about the apparitions and happenings of Garabandal in a general way. I asked Conchita if there was anything I should be doing to spread a Rosary devotion I promote that I was not doing presently. She smiled at this question and said she did not know of anything more I should be doing—then she added— "just continue to do all your work for the love of Jesus and Mary." I was impressed by this answer—not because it gave me anything new to do but because it was simple and she did not try to give an elaborate answer—but went straight to the needed motive for all works of God.

I, as a trained social worker, deal with people every day in my work and have been trained to pick out signs of abnormality in the personality and character of those with whom I come

in contact. I must state that I was impressed with the normality
of Conchita in every way. She seemed at ease with people,
gracious, and most of the time, smiling. This is in the face of
requests of an endless stream of visitors to Garabandal which
should tax the physical and emotional strength of a person to
near breaking.

The next morning our people began to leave the village at
5 a.m. by car. The last group left at 8:30 a.m. During the early
morning hours when it was dark, the people who stayed in the
various homes were brought to the village plaza by those with
whom they stayed. The people of Garabandal carried candles to
light the way for them and remained with them until they left.
Truly these are a gracious and a charitable people.

LXX

PROPHECY FOR AN AMERICAN

Here in the United States lives one who has become a part of
the prophecy of Garabandal. The prophecy is closely associated
with the "Great Miracle" of which Conchita has so often spoken.

The story of this man, whose name is Joe Lomangino of Lin-
denhurst, New York, would be too long to relate here in this
chapter. It will suffice to say that Joe lost his eyesight some
twenty-one years ago because of an accident. Since that time, by
the grace of God, he has come step by step closer to Him
through the guidance of Mary, the Mother of God.

In 1963 Joe was visiting the famed stigmatic priest, Padre Pio.
During one of their conversations Joe asked Padre Pio for guidance. He had heard of the reported apparitions of Our Lady at
Garabandal in Spain and wished to visit the village. He questioned Padre Pio if he should make the visit or by-pass the village. Padre Pio told Joe: "Go, Joe, but be prudent." Joe went as
Padre Pio advised and was prudent.

Joe's visits to Garabandal through the past years have brought

228

a close friendship between him and the girls, but in particular with Conchita. And it was from Conchita that prophecy made its voice known concerning him. Let us quote directly from several notes written by Conchita to Joe—the first, March 19, 1964, the feast of St. Joseph.

"For Joe Lomangino:

The Virgin has told me: "Tell Joe that the day that the Miracle for the world is performed—he will see. At first he will see the Miracle that my Son, through my intercession, will perform and then he will see for ever.' Words of the Virgin.

"Joe, much happiness for today—your saint's day—Saint Joeseph.

Conchita Gonzalez."

Later Conchita again reaffirmed this prophecy to Joe but also added admonitions to him about the use of his "new eyes." This term in the next message "new eyes" plays a part also in the prophecy. Notice that Conchita uses the words "see" and "new eyes," not eyesight, as we might expect. Why? We feel that the reason for this is that Joe's eyes over the years have atrophied—so in a sense he needs "new eyes" to see. Conchita could not be aware of this as all those who meet Joe are not— but Our Lady is aware of this.

And now we come to the second reference. As you read it keep in mind the prophecy is for him as is the admonition, but in the admonition we, who see, can also take from it words for our selves.

"For Joe Lomangino:

"May your new eyes be for the greater glory of God and the good of many souls.

"God gives them to you because He loves you and wishes that you use them for His glory. You ought to pray for those who do not know God that they may love Him and for those who know Him that they may love Him and make reparation to Him."

"Pray for me."

Conchita Gonzalez
10/9/65."

Joe Lomangino with Conchita at Garabandal on June 18, 1965.

230

LXXI

THE UNTIRING MATERNAL COMPASSION

Garabandal has the same spiritual tones of the other great Marian apparitions recognized by the Church.

Once more, Our Lady has returned to earth because She is a Mother, not merely for the clairvoyants, nor for a few chosen souls, but for the entire world, this world which is getting more evil, as Loli told us!

At San Sebastian, the Virgin did not shed any tears; those she shed at La Salette and at Syracuse seem to have been in vain. But she chose to bear with Jesus the cross of redemption, four innocent little girls who will never again be happy on earth, four little—mediators.

Certainly, through these children, all the generous souls are called upon to share in a certain manner the Virgin's concern for the world!

One day, in one of her trances, Conchita was reciting the rosary when, inspired by the Virgin, she recited: "Holy Mary, Mother of God *and our Mother,* pray for us, miserable sinners, etc. . . ."

Mary, Mother of God, Mother of Jesus, lived from the manger to Calvary with Her Son, for Her Son.

She knew the prophecies and Simon had informed her about the sword of sorrow which would one day pierce her heart.

Thus, all of the time during the life of Jesus, Mary lived with both a serenity of soul and an anguished heart.

Is it not so with every mother who lives with a child, suffering morally and physically, and is powerless to prevent it?

The "Compassion" of Mary for her Son is something so profoundly touching that one must have been as sorrowful a mother as She to understand Her.

More than elsewhere, the tragic soul of the Spanish seems to have penetrated this mystery. In Spain, statues of the Virgin can be seen, clad in black, and the Virgin crowned with her seven swords, holds within her hands a handkerchief in which to shed her tears!

For whom does she weep?

Mary, the Gospel says in speaking of the birth of Jesus: "Brought forth her first-born Son at Bethlehem."

In fact, her maternity did not stop with Jesus, since, at the cross, she became the mother of all of sinful mankind.

After being a sorrowing mother at the foot of the Cross, she remains the distressed mother who fears to lose the children that Jesus gave to her at Calvary.

More than at any other period in history, she now sees the dechristianization of whole nations.

She had shown to the children of Fatima so many souls falling into hell. So few men and women have heeded her! Could we not understand why she beseeched the world at Garabandal to listen to her message, so as to avoid the chastisement she fears for it?

There could still have been time in 1917, after hearing Lucy, Francisco and Jacinta, the little children of Fatima, to avert the dangers of communism that Our Lady announced on the hour it was born! Unfortunately, the warnings of Fatima never crossed the borders of Portugal before 1942! What has been done since, now that the same communist threat assails us from everywhere?

LXXII

WITH OUR LADY OF CARMEL OF GARABANDAL AND THE CLAIRVOYANTS

One day at Garabandal, the children were astonished by the attitude of the Virgin, and Maria Dolores asked her: "You, too, are praying?" They had not yet understood that after having praised the Virgin full of grace, our Hail Marys asked her to "pray for us sinners." It seems to be part of human nature to not take notice of spiritual realities.

From top to bottom: Loli, Jacinta, Mari Cruz and Conchita, in 1961. They are with Father Valentin Marichalar, parish priest of Cosio, in the valley, who also serves their parish. This kindly priest, both dignified and humble, has known many difficulties. In the Spanish civil war, he miraculously escaped from a firing squad!

Our Lady does not wish to obtain graces from her Son or Our Father in Heaven, unless we pray with Her!

She knows that a terrible chastisement could strike down her children on earth if they do not change. Through the many, many apparitions in the past, we have learned that she is trying to "restrain her Son's arm."

She has been making almost desperate efforts to warn us, to ask us to prevent souls from deserving everlasting punishment

233

Father Luis Andreu, in his library in 1961.

and bodies from chastisement! She pleads with us to pray with
her for the world!

It could remind us of Moses up on the mountain, interceding
for his people, holding in his raised arms the fate of the battle
being fought down on the plains. Whenever he paused for an
instant, thus interrupting his intercession, the tide of battle would
turn against his army. Two men had to support his arms in a
raised position till victory was final.

In the same way, Our Mother in Heaven remains before God's
throne. She asks that all faithful souls, little children and those
like them, sustain her prayer, and pray with Her, to win the
battle against Satan, which Jesus wishes so much to grant Her.

Our Father in Heaven wants us to be insistent! It is the eternal
struggle of Jacob and the angel. It is God's glory, as that of Mary
and our own, when we shall be victors in that mysterious struggle
in which He wants to see His mercy win over His justice.

It is therefore necessary that the "spiritual battle" of the mediation of the children of the Virgin be fought not solely by the
four young girls of Garabandal. We must join with the clairvoyants in prayer and sacrifice.

I

DOCUMENTS

THE DEATH OF PADRE LUIS ANDREU

AND THE OPINION OF REV. FATHER ROYO-MARIN, O.P.

The first part of our book stopped in 1963.

At that time, we were not in possession of a document which we have since received. It reports the exact circumstances of the visit to Garabandal, on the 8th of August 1961, of Father Luis Andreu and of his death the next morning, at four o'clock, at Reinosa.

It was written by Rafael Fontaneda Ruplicado, an eyewitness to the facts.

Here is the literal translation:

      ❋   ❋   ❋

"On the 8th of August 1961, we went up to San Sebastian of Garabandal with Father Luis Maria Andreu, S.J., who was going there for the third time since the 29th of July. Our trip coincided with that of Father Royo Marin, a celebrated Dominican Spanish theologian.

Father Luis seemed keenly interested in the events of Garabandal, and in the little girls, though without showing what he thought of them. He spoke to us about visions in general, of the varieties of them and the importance of being knowledgeable in psychology in order to pass a sound judgment.

On the 8th of August, we met Father Valentin Marichalar, the parish priest. He had to leave for Torrelavega, and so left the keys of the Garabandal church to Father Luis, requesting that he serve as parish priest during his absence.

The Padre was very cheerful and joked with me happily, remarking: "There now, I'm parish priest of Garabandal."

The Mass celebrated by the Padre was extraordinarily touching, and all the congregation was moved.

❀　❀　❀

During this morning, the girls had a trance. The Padre was near them; as he had done the other times, he noted attentively everything they said and did. During this trance, the Padre seemed engrossed; those who were placed nearest to him noticed tears coursing down his cheeks. He was obviously in the presence of something extraordinary.

In speaking of these tears the next day, his brother, Father Ramon Andreu, S.J., expressed his amazement; he had never known Padre Luis to be so emotional; he had never seen him cry.

On the evening of the same day, the children in trance state, went up to "the Pines" and hastened down at an unheard-of rate. In the moment they had stopped at "The Pines," the Padre observed them minutely.

We could see that he did not want to miss a single detail of what was going on.

Very quickly, a powerful emotion seemed to go over him and he repeated four times in a high voice the word Milagro! Milagro! (Miracle, Miracle).

While the girls, still in their trance state, began their descent towards the village, they said that they were going to the church, while continuing their dialogue with the Virgin.

If the climb was a fast one, the descent was vertiginous.

Father Royo Marin advised those who were present to run to the church, for, as he said, the children seemed to have wings on their feet.

It was after this descent that Father Royo Marin took a stand on the matter:

"I am not infallible, but I specialize on such matters, and I state that the children's vision is true. I have observed four signs of which there is no reason to doubt."

I went up to him and said: "Father, if it is as serious as you

236

say, why would you not remain here a few more days?" He answered me: "It is impossible for me to stay, but this is so clear that it cannot be anything but true."

❋   ❋   ❋

When everything was over, some came back down from San Sebastian to Cosio on foot while others returned in jeeps. Through deference, we wanted Father Luis to ride in a jeep.

He appeared particularly happy and so were all those who shared the jeep with him. Several times, Father Luis clearly expressed his elation to me, and his certainty that the children were speaking the truth.

On arriving at Cosio, we took our places in the different automobiles which had brought us and had made up the expedition. Though my brother wanted Father Luis to get in with him, the Padre preferred to motor with me, as he had done when we came. I was sitting in the back seat, with my wife Carmen and my eight-year-old daughter, Maria Carmen.

Father Luis got in next to the chauffeur, José Salceda.

All during the trip, each one commented on what they had seen.

Father Luis stated that he had spoken with Father Royo Marin, and was in agreement with him on all points.

My wife and I, as well as José Salceda, were struck by the deep and intense elation shown by the Padre, as well as a deep happiness which he manifested.

As he spoke, his breathing was quite normal, but he would often repeat: "How happy I am! I'm overflowing with happiness! The Virgin gave me such a gift! I do not harbour the slightest doubt about the reality of what has happened to the children! It is the truth!"

And so we conversed when, on arriving at Puentenansa we wished to stop for some refreshment.

Padre Luis would accept only a cold drink.

On arriving at Torrelevega, we met the jeep which had brought us from Cosio to Garabandal. It was filled with people from Aguilar del Campo. Our chauffeur, José Salceda, asked them if they needed help.

237

Father Luis and he spoke with them for a few moments.

* * *

During the second part of the trip, we resumed our conversation, and I asked him: "Father, would you not like to sleep for a while?" Which he did for about an hour.

Shortly before arriving at Reinosa, on awakening, he told us: "What a sound sleep! How well I feel, I no longer feel tired!"

Nevertheless, the rest of us were all sleepy, as it was already four o'clock in the morning. We stopped near a fountain to have a drink.

Father Luis asked the chauffeur if he had drunk and he replied that he had his eyes drink because they were more thirsty!

The trip was then resumed, and Father Luis began to repeat what he had said previously: "I am full of joy, of happiness! What a gift the Virgin has given me! How fortunate it is to have a Mother in heaven! We need not fear supernatural life! We must treat the Virgin as the four children do! They are an example to us! I cannot have the slightest doubt about their visions. Why should the Virgin have chosen us? This is the happiest day of my life!!!"

On finishing this sentence he remained silent. I asked him a question to which he did not reply. "Father, what is going on?" I thought he was feeling nauseated. He answered: "No, nothing, I feel drowsy." Bowing his head, he emitted a slight gasp.

* * *

As he turned towards him, José Salceda noticed that the Padre's eyes had changed. He called to us: "The Padre is very ill." My wife tried to feel his pulse. "Stop," she said, "he doesn't seem to have any pulse. There is a clinic here." (It was at Reinosa.)

Thinking that it was nothing more than nausea, I tried to open the door when the car stopped.

"There is nothing to worry about, Padre, it will pass off, everything is going to be all right." My wife insisted: "Let us drive him to the clinic." I told her: "Don't be silly." But, he was already unconscious.

238

We had stopped a few feet away from the clinic.

We rang the doorbell at once and the nurse who answered the doorbell could tell that the Padre was dead. My wife answered that it was impossible, and that something should be done. The nurse gave him an injection while the driver went to seek a priest and a doctor. The latter arrived within 10 minutes. It was Doctor D. Vincente Gonzalez. He could only confirm the death. Immediately, the parish priest from the neighboring parish administered the last rites.

* * *

After the first few moments of uncertainty and nervousness had passed, we telephoned to Father Ramon, his brother, who was preaching the spiritual exercises of Saint Ignatius to the nuns of Valladolid. A few hours afterwards, Father Royo Marin arrived to keep us company and console us; then my brothers and cousins of Aguilar del Campo, and by mid-morning, Father Ramon had arrived.

We could not stop commenting with my wife on this terribly impressive event for us, though in another sense, we had an indescribable feeling of peace and serenity.

The only answer we could give to those who asked: "Of what did the Padre die," was: "He died from joy."

Though only a fraction of a second had elapsed between normal life and death, his lips continued to smile.

The only sign of his passing on was a slight hiccough before replying: "No, I feel drowsy."

According to his brother, Father Ramon Andreu, Father Luis had never experienced any pain or cardiac trouble. His only illness was a bout with hay fever every spring. His only medication was pills for his allergy.

On the 8th of August, he had come down from Garabandal by jeep, thus his fatigue could not have been greater than that of the pilgrims who had walked all day at Garabandal, then had spent the night walking back down the 3 miles to Cosio.

During the preceding year, he was a theology professor. He frequently participated in sports, and often went out to the country in the company of other colleagues on holidays.

I returned to Garabandal a few days later.

The little girls spoke to me of the Padre's death.

The Blessed Virgin had told them that Padre Luis saw Her, when he said, "Milagro, Milagro," at "the Pines." He would also speak to them during a trance state. They would hear his voice, but not see him.

When I attended the first of the many dialogues they had with him up to that day, the painful moments of the dawn of the 9th of August, 1961 were filled with a very special meaning for me, in which God's Providence and Mary's love played important roles.

Father Royo Marin's comments on Padre Luis' last words pronounced in this world came back to my mind.

"This is the happiest day of my life!" Padre Luis had said. What could have been the meaning of such an affirmation, when the happiest day in a priest's life is usually the day of his ordination?

Did these words not seem to be an anticipation of the joy of entering into eternal felicity?

Father Royo Marin had said to us: "Truly, the day we arrive into God's arms is the happiest day in a life!"

That day was to arrive for Father Luis Andreu on the 9th of August, 1961 at twenty past four in the morning, on returning from Garabandal. We could measure the smoothness of this passing on by observing that our eight-year-old daughter, who had travelled with us, went to bed on our arrival at Aguilar del Campo, and then slept alone all night without the slightest fear or nervousness.

My crucifix, which I had pressed to Father Luis' lips and which had been kissed beforehand by the vision of Garabandal I gave in turn to Father Ramon Marie, who thanked me as though he had received the most precious gift.

Rafael Fontaneda Ruplicado."

❁ ❁ ❁

To sum up what is essential in this long report, the details of which we thought would interest the reader, we would leave it up to his brother, Father Ramon Marie, also a Jesuit, to narrate in a more exact way the details concerning Padre Luis.

"On the 8th of August 1961, Father Luis returned to Garabandal. He celebrated Mass in the village church. In the evening, he was present when the little girls had their long walk in trance state—their first of this type—going from the church to "The Pines." There, he participated for several minutes in their trance. He pronounced the word 'Miracle' four times. This was the only case in Garabandal where the children had seen someone besides themselves while in their trance state.

"They stated that they had seen him on his knees, which was the position he was in at that moment. The Virgin, who was looking at him, seemed to say to him: 'You will soon be with me.'

"The clairvoyants also said that the Virgin told them that Father Luis had seen the great Miracle ahead of time, which Conchita, without having seen it herself, announces for some unknown date.

"This happened around ten o'clock at night.

"A few hours later, Father Luis died without any agony, at Reinosa, on the Aguilar del Campo route.

"His last words were: 'What an example these children show us in the way they behave themselves towards the Virgin! What a good Mother we have in heaven! This is the happiest day of my life!'

"He was in an absolutely normal state when he pronounced these words, then he bowed his head, and stopped speaking.

"One of the persons with him said: 'Is there anything wrong, Padre?' He replied: 'No, nothing.' Then he seemed to doze off! He was dead.

"Father Luis did not suffer from any heart condition, nor from any other illness. His only health problem was hay fever.

"Since his death, on several occasions, the children have spoken with him in their trances, just as the Virgin told them he would. However, they never see him, they can only hear his voice. During these mysterious conversations, he gave them advice.

"Conchita says that the Virgin told her that the body of Father Luis will be found intact, just as it was at the clinic at Reinosa,

241

on the day it will be exhumed, which will be the day after the Miracle. He is buried at Ona."

* * *

As we have seen, Mr. Rafael Fontaneda Ruplicado speaks also of the Rev. Royo Marin, the celebrated Spanish Dominican, in his report. The latter wrote a book which is very important in every respect, on mystical theology and is the successor to that great theologian who was another Dominican of Salamanca, the Rev. Father Arintero, friend of the great French Dominican, the

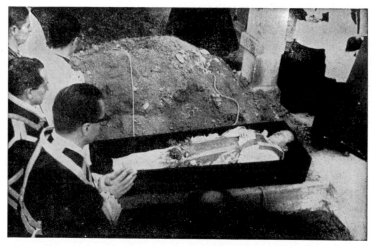

Burial of Father Luis Andreu, on Aug. 11th, 1961. His body is expected to be found uncorrupted the day following the great Miracle.

Rev. Father Garrigou-Lagrange, whose opinion on the apparitions at Garabandal is of the highest importance.

Let us read once more the remarks Father Marin made at Garabandal on the 8th of August 1961, and the following day at Reinosa.

"If the ascent to 'The Pines' was rapid, then the descent was vertiginous."

Father Royo Marin advised those present to run to the church, because as he said, the children seemed to have wings on their feet.

It was after this descent, that Father Royo Marin took a stand on pronouncing these essential words: "I'm not infallible, but I am a specialist in these matters, and am able to state that the vision the children have is genuine. Four different signs indicate to me that there is no reason for doubt."

Then, Mr. Fontaneda interrupted, saying: "Father, if it is as serious as you say, why do you not remain here a few days longer?"

The Padre concluded: "I cannot remain, but this is clear and cannot be anything but the truth."

* * *

Not many hours after the death of Padre Luis, continued Mr. Fontaneda, Father Royo Marin arrived at the clinic of Reinosa, to keep us company and console us.

We had thought that for a priest, the happiest day of his life was his ordination to priesthood. Father Royo Marin set us right by saying: "The day we arrive into God's arms, that is truly the happiest day in a life!"

* * *

Like a true Dominican, Father Royo Marin did not let the matter lie. Having learned that a group of witnesses wished to go down to Santander to make a report to a competent authority, he took a position again: "I am sick in bed with a temperature of 102°. To my regret, I am unable to accompany you. You may say for my part I believe the apparitions to be genuine. I also think that it is a serious duty for the religious authorities to go up to Garabandal immediately."

* * *

At the beginning of 1965, the same Dominican came to preach and say Mass in the church of Santander. In the vestry, friends from Garabandal asked him: "Father, what do you think of the apparitions?"

"I have not been able to return to Garabandal. Therefore, I have not formed any opinion as to what happened since my last visit, but when I was there, they were genuine."

243

II

A SPANISH DOCTOR

Following the letter we received from Doctor Apostolidès, we now give the translation of a very documented medical report which was sent to us by Doctor Celestino Ortiz Perez of Santander, pediatrician, specializing in child psychology.

* * *

"I think that it would be in order to add the medical information to the theological, concerning the children of Garabandal, before passing the judgment the problem calls for.

This study is based on my own direct personal observation on those days dating from the 15th to the 25th of August, September 13th, from the 5th to the 24th of October, of the 23rd of November to the 24th of December of 1961.

On January 23rd—February 18th—March 13th—April 18th—May 5th—June 16th—July 18th—August 23rd—September 5th to 21st—October 1st—of the 4th and 25th of November of the year 1962.

* * *

Actual child psychiatry is an active psychiatry whose fundamental basis is experimental child psychology, so that a knowledge of this psychology is absolutely indispensable to us.

Family history:

I know of no cases of psychological trouble in their family. There have been no intermarriages between the parents.

Personal history:

They have had the usual infectious childhood diseases.

As an odd fact, I noted that in October 1961, Maria Dolores and Conchita had whooping cough; they had fits of coughing

244

during their trance state, and that the disease which was mild, lasted about a month.

Present state:

Since the beginning, these children have shown that their general condition is the very best. They have grown and developed normally, showing through their remarks a normal psychology.

Age:

Conchita, Loli and Jacinta were 13 and Mari Cruz 12.

Their intellectual development corresponds to that of eight-year-old children in our cities.

They passed through the (Hickder Garden Hetzer) phase which precedes puberty, without the slightest disorder.

We have not been able to notice any tendency to be impertinent towards their elders, nor a propensity to disobedience, etc.

Jacinta and Conchita arrived at puberty at the beginning of the winter of 1961, without showing any observable change in behavior nor in their trances.

Previous social behavior in their milieu:

Their behavior was and has remained irreproachable, like that of children who receive Holy Communion each time there is a Mass in the village.

Actually two of them received Communion, while in a state of trance, from the hands of the Angel—usually when there is no Mass—by observing all the rules of preparation and thanksgiving.

From the point of view of their psychology, it should be noted that they did not form the usual coterie of friends before the events. Another detail to note is that they did not always agree to play marbles with the other clairvoyants on coming out of school.

In school, their behavior was no different from that of the other children, with the exception of Maria Dolores who was remarked on for her goodness.

Their behavior with their families, their obedience towards their parents and superiors improved after the apparitions began.

Character:

One outstanding trait in the four children is their good naturedness; they have remained as they were, gay and mischievous.

However, in reactive psychopathy of childhood there are always changes of feeling, instinct, of will and character.

Psychological reactions with these girls are perfectly normal.

Maria Dolores and Conchita are very communicative, whereas, Jacinta and Mari Cruz are more reserved. They have all remained very timid, as little village girls tend to be, although they have become more sociable from meeting with the strangers who have invaded their mountain.

In all of them may be noted their particular smile which is a special sign of goodness, the smile that has caught the attention of all those who have had occasion to talk with them.

Their natural good manners should be pointed out and especially their goodwill which they have shown on many occasions, even towards their worst detractors.

Their humility is exemplary.

Intellectual developments:

Their intellectual quotient is slightly higher than other children of their age and condition, though their intelligence has not been developed.

This is especially true of Conchita who is superior to the others.

The lack of intellectual development in these mountain children is due to the insufficient number of years they spent in school, though they attended class regularly.

The children cannot be blamed in any way for this backwardness. The climatological conditions and other contributing factors create many a hiatus during their school year. They are not responsible for this.

Their religious education is due partly to the parish priest of Cosio, and partly to the school or to their families. It has nothing to do with mysticism.

❊   ❊   ❊

Behaviour during sleep:

After being present and having studied the matter many times, I can assert that these children showed no signs of disturbance in the rhythm nor in the depth of their slumber.

246

Now, changes in this matter, are precisely a premonitory characteristic sign which accompanies psychic disturbances in children.

Reflexes:

Motor reflexes together with the sensitive and psychic reflexes in all of the four girls, all appeared to me to be perfectly normal.

Even during their trances, the greater part of their motor reflexes remain normal.

Their pupils remained normal-sized and their pupillary reflexes did not change.

Immediately after the trances, there was no trace of motor hyperexcitability, either sensitive or psychic. On the contrary, all that can be observed is the most complete normality.

Description of their trance state:

This always begins very abruptly. They fall on their knees wherever they are. It would be nearer the description to say that they "drop" because they fall down with the whole weight of their bodies.

From the start they show great tranquility. Their eyes remain open, and their pupils stare upwards, without any blinking or trembling, their heads hyperextended, with an expression of infinite sweetness on their faces.

Their bodies remain rigid, without any spasm, trembling, or perspiration. Their pulse rate is faster in the beginning, but promptly becomes normal again. As for the rhythm of their breathing, it remains constantly normal.

At the same moment, that they enter into their trance state, they present Peiper's reflex—an attitude of hyperextension of the nape of the neck, especially with Conchita—which consists of holding her head back, in response to a sudden brilliant beam of light.

That which compels attention considering the great number of trances they have experienced, is that they have not developed a conditioned reflex; that each time their pupils received a flash of light, they have not gone into a trance. Now, they have been photographed with flash bulbs many times, often with high precision cameras and 1000-watt bulbs and there was not an instance where they went into a trance.

247

As for the rigidity they show, it is very different from lethargical contraction, as well as cataleptic tonicity.

In fact, despite this muscular rigidity, their articulations remain completely flexible and normal.

In this state, as they begin their trance walk, they show a special characteristic: their feet seem to do some sort of dance.

With their gaze fixed upward, their heads thrown backward, hyperextended, they advance over the most irregular terrain, or the most abrupt places; they can move forward or backward without ever faltering in their steps.

If they fell at times, it seemed as though they had done it purposely without ever showing the slightest hurt.

They have walked barefoot for hours without any sign of erythema redness on the soles of their feet.

❊   ❊   ❊

They maintain a dialogue mostly in low tones with the image they perceive. They rarely raise their voices so that they can be heard by those attending. It becomes necessary then to use a tape recorder.

They recite the rosary and sing hymns at the top of their voices.

Their reciting of the Ave Maria is incomparably beautiful. The length of this prayer is not the same with each girl (20, 23, 24 or 25 seconds), which proves that there is no existing telepathic influence between them.

In this state, they give proof that they are beyond medical science and all natural laws.

They show no reaction to pain, pinpricks, etc. . . .

Once out of their trance, however, they react immediately. It usually ends after a Sign of the Cross and they smile in an exquisite natural manner.

They have then returned to their normal state, without showing any sign of mental or physical fatigue, despite the length of the trances which, at times, lasted four hours.

All this is contrary to what happens in hysterical, hypnotic or telepathic states.

Conclusion:

There follow after this several pages of a scientific nature by

Doctor Ortiz on hysteria, hypnotism, catalepsy and nervous disorders in children.

The author clearly shows the differences which exist between states of psychic illness and the trances of the Garabandal children.

As our book was intended as a means of cursory information, and Doctor Ortiz having given information which is very technical and scientific, we will go on directly to the conclusions of him who was—by far—the most regular and thorough of all the qualified observers, from a medical standpoint, of the happenings at Garabandal.

1) The four little girls, from a pediatric and psychiatric point of view, have always been and continue to be, normal.

2) The trances in which we have observed these young girls do not fit into the framework of any psychic or physiological pathology presently known.

3) Considering the length of time in which the phenomena was observed, had there been any pathological character of any type, we would have detected the indications very easily.

4) In child psychology, normal as well as pathological, I can find no explanation which could present as natural events, phenomena which, according to our present knowledge, escape all natural reality.

     ❖ ❖ ❖

Our conceitedness falls apart when we are faced with this kind of dilemma, such as God bestows on us to point out to us our own medical limitations.

All attempts to try and rationalize phenomena which are beyond the rational, are in themselves irrational and absurd.

Doctor Celestino Ortiz Perez
Pediatrician, Isabel 11, 3–1°
Santander, October 1962.

249

III

WITH THE CLAIRVOYANTS IN THE TRANCE STATE

We have previously seen what Conchita says concerning the apparitions, compared to the doctrine and commandments of our Holy Mother the Church, about the Message and the achievement of this Message. We believe as she does and as she says concerning the matter. Her conclusions of what happened in Garabandal are very close to our own.

However, we feel that the reader would like to take a closer look at what went on in some of the past trance states of the clairvoyants. We believe that apart from the personality and mission of each of them, the experience must have been about the same for each one, as the tape recorder tells us what happened to Conchita on December 8, 1962.

This, then, is a faithful transcription of the words from a tape recording of which there are copies, some of them not very exact, circulating around the world. This tape evidently gives only Conchita's questions, answers and speech. The numerous dashes indicate the words that the tape recorder missed, that is, the words, the silences, the affirmative or negative signs, the smiles or remarks of the Blessed Virgin. This should be enough to show anyone the "intimacy of the clairvoyants of Garabandal during their trances." It is an example of what we called in Chapter VII, the "contents" of the apparitions.

Conchita's conversation with the Blessed Virgin, in a trance state on December 8th, 1962:

Yes, our Mother Mary, all those who are here know that today is your feast day—but you must have celebrated it up there!

Oh! yes, they all hear you, yes, they hear you, yes, they are recording you (on tape), yes . . .

Listen, when you will come here, you will come like that? Please say so.

And now, since you are Mother of all, you will give a present to each one, will you not?—

We will give one to you—

Listen, please make it so—

* * *

About the Miracle, I no longer speak to you about it since I know everything—eh?—I have such a longing for the day to arrive to be able to tell it—they want to know the day—

Listen—(incomprehensible phrase)—

* * *

Oh, listen: do you know who came today? The "fat little man" [1] —that one did not ask me to bring you greetings, no—

Oh, Mother, but you are Immaculate!—

Listen, today, someone brought me a little baby, a very wee one, who does not at all resemble the one you bring today—

But, but, how long is it since the baby came—your Baby?— And he has not grown at all, at all, he is exactly as he was before—

Where was he?—Where was he?—Where is the Baby when He doesn't come?—in heaven? or in a cradle?—Where is he?—

Oh!—You can be here and there at the same time!—Oh, yes!—

* * *

Listen, they say that it will not happen, because they do not want to believe me—Eh, why is it so?

Oh, listen, listen, what can I tell the people, to those who do not believe?—who talk and wonder if we should believe—

Anyway, as we, we know it already—that—

How much time will it take for the Miracle to come when the people will know about it?—a week will be enough?—Oh! Could I tell that?—and no—Oh!—

* * *

They are taking your voice too—No the tape-recorder was not here at my house, it was not here, oh, no, it was not at my place—

[1] It refers to Mr. Placido Ruiloba, of Santander, "the man with the tape-recorder."

251

it did not belong to this man, it belonged to the one who is called—

(This concerns the tape-recorder owned by Doctor Gasca.)

* * *

He doesn't have wings, does he? Let me see—

* * *

When will I be able to enter the convent, because they would be willing to admit me now, but my mother will not let me go yet—Listen to what certain people say, that they will not want to have me there—I will, won't I? Yes?—

You tell me yes—but not yet—And the Baby says nothing.[1]

* * *

What do you call him, Jesus—the Infant, what name do you give Him too? Do you know what the people here call Him, the Baby?—The Infant Jesus.

* * *

And you? We call you the Virgin, the Mother of God, they give you many names.

When will the people be able to see you? One does not know when? . . .

* * *

While we were in church praying today, afterwards, this Frenchman who had been at my house began to cry out, "Mary, our Mother!" and You, you did not answer—

* * *

You are laughing, Blessed, yes you love me, you love me—
Listen, everyone loves you very much—
Oh, they are calling you also. Listen, listen, people tell me—

* * *

Do you sometimes have snow over there in heaven?—Cold such as we have? Like when it snows or something like that?

[1] What is Jesus' will concerning Conchita's definitive vocation?

252

Because snow falls from up there—Oh, why is it cold here then
—Eh! it is not cold up there?—

❀   ❀   ❀

Listen, all those people who came today, came to see if you
would perform the Miracle today, and I believe that—
They should all have wished you a good feast day, it is not so?
You should know that they were all pressed close together
to hear you—they have been there a long time.

❀   ❀   ❀

Well, listen: it's all the same to me if they hear what I say,
because they can hear you as well—Just as they hear me, they
can hear you too—just as—just as—because your voice is clear—
Besides, listen, listen! Do you know why they cannot hear?
Because, listen, when I began to see the Virgin, when I began
to see you, they were not there (at the beginning of the trance)
and they all went out from over there, out of the kitchen—well,
if they have the tape-recorder from the table, no one brought it
along—ah—? Besides, it doesn't matter to me if they do hear
me—

❀   ❀   ❀

Listen, do you remember last year when you said to me:
"Happy Birthday!" I didn't dare wish you yours—but this year,
yes, oh but yes—"Happy Birthday!"

❀   ❀   ❀

You are leaving already? Wait another little while longer.
Oh! wait—
N.B. The closeness of Conchita and the Blessed Virgin is such
that Conchita uses the familiar "tu" form of address, as one
would in a mother-daughter relationship.

253

FOUR THEOLOGICAL LESSONS

I

MARY AND THE CHURCH

First Lesson

Pope Paul VI, Vicar of Christ, issued the letter, SIGNUM MAGNUM (The Great Sign) on May 13, 1967. This great Pope introduces the letter with the words: "The Great Sign which the Apostle John saw in Heaven, 'a woman clothed with the sun' is interpreted by the Sacred Liturgy, not without foundation, as referring to the Most Blessed Mary, the Mother of all men by the Grace of Christ the Redeemer." St. Peter's successor goes on to say that: "Proclaiming the August Mother of God as the Spiritual Mother of the Church as the crowning of the Third Session of the Second Vatican Council."

Continuing, the Supreme Pontiff says: "On the occasion of the religious ceremonies which are taking place at this time in honor of the Virgin Mother of God in Fatima, where she is venerated by countless numbers of the faithful for her Motherly and Compassionate Heart, we wish to call the attention of all sons of the Church once more to the indissoluble link between the spiritual Motherhood of Mary, so amply illustrated in the (Council's) Dogmatic Constitution on the Church and the duties of redeemed men toward Her, the Mother of the Church."

Later in SIGNUM MAGNUM, the Teacher of Christendom states that by Her unceasing prayers, Mary "makes herself their Advocate, Auxiliatress, Adjutress and Mediatress." He then mentions the Marian message of invitation to prayer and penance, declaring that: "Our era may well be called the Marian era." Pope Paul continues by referring to the "Hope that this pastoral exhortation of ours for an even more fervid and more fruitful Marian devotion piety will be received with generous acceptance." He ends SIGNUM MAGNUM by recalling the consecration of the Church and mankind to Mary, the Mother of God and to her Immaculate Heart by his predecessor of venerated memory, Pius XII, on October 31, 1942, stating that he renewed this consecration on November 21, 1964. Finally, the Visible Head of all Christians writes: "We exhort all the sons of the Church to renew personally, their consecration to the Immaculate Heart of the Mother of the Church."

Some years ago, we witnessed the degrading of the man who ridiculed and laughed at the influence and power of the Pope, saying: "The Pope?—how many Divisions does he have?" What happened in Russia years later we now refer to as "the process of de-Stalinization." Today, they are not lacking those in the Church who speak of the "de-Stalinization of the Woman, Mary" —that is supposedly taking place in the Catholic Church. If we are truthful, we cannot but admit that there are those within the Church who de-emphasize the role of Mary in modern Christian living. To them, Mary is a source of embarrassment in their ecumenical efforts. They would like Mary "to get lost" for a few years and then after Christendom has been united by their brilliant minds and zealous activity, Mary could be let in the back door when no one is looking. People such as these claim they are very interested in Jesus Christ and the spread of His Kingdom. They would indeed separate Jesus from Mary in the cause of Christian Unity. To the deposers of Mary who claim Pope John XXIII as the Patron, one would suggest the prayerful reading of his diary; THE JOURNAL OF A SOUL. There, one encounters not the legendary John XXIII, but the real Angelo Giuseppe Roncalli, who was most devoted to Mary and who daily prayed the Rosary.

Many are asking this serious question: "WHAT IS THE ROLE OF MARY IN TODAY'S CHURCH AND IN THE MODERN WORLD?" The above excerpts from Pope Paul's SIGNUM MAGNUM leave very little room for doubt about Her importance in today's affairs. The same Pope gave a heartwarming answer to this question when he made his pilgrimage to Fatima in commemoration of the Fiftieth Anniversary of the Apparitions which took place from May to October of 1917. How many of us rejoiced to see him on television on the platform with Sister Lucia, the only survivor of the Apparitions!

For those who look back to Vatican II for their authoritative answer to Mary's role, one need not look any further than that work that is known as: "The Decree of the Dogmatic Constitution on the Church." The last chapter of this decree is titled: "THE ROLE OF THE BLESSED VIRGIN MARY, MOTHER OF GOD, IN THE MYSTERY OF CHRIST AND THE CHURCH." One encounters there the following:

> "In this Church, adhering to Christ the Head, and having communion with all His saints, the faithful must also venerate the memory—above all, of the Glorious and Perpetual Virgin Mary, Mother of our God and Lord Jesus Christ."
>
> "In an utterly and singular way She cooperated by obedience, Faith, Hope and Burning Charity in the Savior's work of restoring supernatural life of souls. For this reason, She (Mary) is a Mother to us in the order of Grace."
>
> "For, taken up in Heaven, She did not lay aside this saving role, but by Her manifold acts of intercession, continues to win for us gifts of eternal salvation. Therefore, the Blessed Virgin is invoked of the Church under the titles of Advocate, Auxiliatrix, Adjutrix and Mediatrix."
>
> "Hence, when She is being preached and venerated She summons the faithful to Her Son and His Sacrifice and to love for the Father."

What are we to say about the Apparitions of the Mother of God that have taken place from time to time throughout history? We know that the Church has pronounced favorably on many of Mary's Apparitions; (just to mention a few): LaRue De Bac—in Paris (1830), La Salette—(1846), Lourdes (1858), Pontmain (1871), Fatima (1917), Beauraing (1932), and Banneux (1933). All the Popes since Pope Pius IX, namely, Leo XII, St. Pius X, Benedict XV, Pius XI, and more than all the others, Pius XII, have proclaimed Mary and Her Apparitions and have had recourse to Her as their final hope in the calamities of the times.

Listen to the words of Pius XII, written on September 24, 1951, to Cardinal Tedeschini, appointing him his personal representative at the special Holy Year Solemnities to be held at Fatima on

October 13th of that year: "We, from the first years of our Pontificate, have again and again urged the good faithful of Portugal and other regions of the earth to go with every greater confidence and more ardent prayer. . . ."

To all past proven Apparitions of the Virgin Mary, one could well use Duns Scotus' Syllogism: God and Mary could do it. It was fitting that they should do it. Therefore, they did it. That Mary should appear to people living today, a person of Faith may well say: So be it.

II

THE PLACE AND THE ROLE OF MARY IN GOD'S CHURCH

Second Lesson

Dear Friends:

You are all, no doubt, familiar with the magnificent words pronounced by our Holy Father Pope Paul VI, in the Dogmatic Constitution "Lumen Gentium," proclaimed on the 21st of November, 1964, during the Vatican Council II, concerning Our Holy Mother.

I can only enumerate here the titles that the council document gives to the Virgin Mary, considered in her relationship with Christ, and with the Church, the Mystical Body of Christ.

In the general economy of the salvation, she has played a role of the first order by the fact that She has been the Mother of the Messiah; that She consented to the Incarnation of the Son of God, thus becoming not only the Mother of Jesus, but also the Mother of God, the title from which flows all the other privileges of the Virgin. She watched over His Childhood and His Secret Life, as She will watch, after the Ascension, the infancy and the first developments of the Church.

She inaugurated in some way the public ministry of Jesus by inducing by her discreet prayer, His first miracle.

After the Resurrection, her presence alone brought together the little group of Apostles, which had dispersed during the drama of the Passion. After the Ascension, She prepared to receive the visit of the Holy Spirit, who will confirm them in grace and will make of them the unshakeable pillars of the Church.

Ever since, her role, in order to be more veiled and more discreet, has not changed.

Also, the same Paul VI proclaimed her the model of all Christians by the sublimity of all her virtues, and the Mother of the Church by her universal Mediation.

We already know all these things, but it will be good to reread them and to think about them in the very text, in this eighth chapter of the above Constitution, exclusively devoted to the Virgin Mary.

Here I would like to insist more particularly, in this first conference on Mary's role in the life of each Christian and each apostle in particular, be he priest or lay, monk or nun.

1) I would like to speak to you especially about her role as Mediator for souls.

The universal Mediation of Mary is a truth approaching the faith, that is to say, that this truth is not only certain and recognized by the Church, but that it is quite near being solemnly defined by the supreme magistracy of the Church (Pope or a future council).

At the first Vatican Council in 1870 on the preparatory schema of the Council only the sudden declaration of the Franco-Prussian War prevented truth from being defined, in hastily dispersing the Fathers of the Council.

It was without doubt also on the preparatory schema of Vatican II, but some stormy interventions coming from diverse currents in the Church and outside of the Church, and also, we believe, from an intervention, not veiled, from Satan, forced the Fathers of the Council to relegate this truth to the background, in order to go to the more pressing matters, as said by several Fathers and several theologians waiting in the "wings."

But Paul VI, the great Pilot, was watching. Intervening on time in the deliberations which were heading toward confusion, precisely on the subject of the Virgin Mary whose role, in the Church and for the souls, they wanted to minimize, he had explicitly introduced into this same Chapter VIII of the Constitution, the lines which we are going to report and which make of this truth the equal of a dogma of faith.

2) "This maternity of Mary's, says the Constitution, 'Lumen Gentium,' she endured without cease, in the economy of grace, since the consent which her faith had given to her at the Ascension and that she maintained without hesitation under the Cross, until the ascension of all the chosen ones to eternal glory. In fact, elevated to heaven, She did not discontinue this salvation function, but She continues, by Her urgent intercession, to obtain grace for us, for our eternal salvation. In Her maternal charity, She is concerned, until they have arrived at the happiness of the Fatherland, with the brothers of her Son, who are still pilgrims and are exposed to dangers and miseries. Also, the Virgin is invoked in the Church under the titles—Lawyer, Auxiliary, and Mediator."

Thus is defined without equivocation, this very consoling truth —to know that the Virgin Mary is the obligatory intermediary indispensable to our unique Intermediary Jesus Christ, Our Lord.

But we must go farther and ask ourselves how the Marian mediation operates. Here, Catholic theology will be of great help to us, for its role is not to reveal new truths, but to clarify those which already exist and to seek to make us understand that which Faith and divine Revelation teach us, as far as a natural mystery can be explained and understood.

A mediator (man or woman) is a person who is between two dissidents and who tries to reconcile them. In our case, the dissident parties are mankind and Christ.

Here, there is a possible confusion to set aside, a confusion which disheartens some Protestants of good faith and even some Catholics.

We have not said and we cannot say that Mary is Co-Mediator with Christ between God and man, for St. Paul has told us: "There is only one Mediator between God and men, this intermediary is Christ alone. It is between Jesus his Son, and us, that Mary is mediator: She is Intermediary for the Mediator. It is for that, that the Constitution 'Lumen Gentium' has added as soon after the passage cited a while ago, the following sentence: 'All that must, however, be understood in such a manner that one neither removes nor adds anything to the dignity and to the action of Christ, the only Intermediary.' Two paragraphs later, the same document adds: "Thanks to this subordinate function of Mary . . . supported by her maternal help, the faithful cling more closely to the Intermediary and Saviour Jesus."

Let us go a little further and ask ourselves what is the nature of Mary's intervention or mediation.

Mary's mediation is, at first, moral, as, for example the intervention of a Queen in behalf of the King to influence him to grant a favor to a subject. We have a beautiful example of this mediation in the Old Testament. Queen Esther seeing her people condemned to death as a result of the intrigues of the arrogant and impious Haman, approaches the all-powerful monarch and implores his mercy and not allow her people to perish. And indeed her all-powerful moral intercession is granted and those condemned to death are saved.

This role of moral supplication, the Queen of Angels and of Men filled continually in favor of sinners in order to obtain mercy and pardon for them principally at the hour of death. And such is her efficacy that St. Bernard, the last of the Fathers of the Church, did not hesitate to call Mary, "All Powerful Intercession: Omnipotentia supplex."

But that does not exhaust all the Marian Mediation which extends much further.

Just as the Holy Humanity of Christ exercises a universal and physical causality in the bestowing of sanctifying grace on each soul in particular, thus there is, in the intervention of Mary, a certain physical causality which reaches each soul in particular, whether adults or children, Christians or pagans and in whatever manner grace is given to us: by the sacraments, by personal prayer or by the prayers of others.

And She does it, not in the manner of Christ, whose humanity united to divinity acts like a welded instrument, that is, not only in the manner of a chisel between the hands of the sculptor, but in the manner of the hand and even the brain of the sculptor, the brain being a part of the very being of the artist, while the chisel is united to him accidentally at the very moment of the action and only at this moment. The instrumental causality of the Virgin is entirely different.

Her role of Mediatrix is, we have said, derived from her divine Maternity.

It is therefore as Mother that She participates in giving us grace. Now, in procreation, the mother does not intervene as an active principal; She only furnishes the matter; she prepares it and provides for it at the generation by the Father.

In the same way, each time that sanctifying grace is given to a soul by the sacraments or otherwise, the Virgin Mother actively prepares us to receive it, whether by leading us to the dispositions required for contrition, for faith, for trust and love, or by giving us the Actual Graces of illumination and inspiration.

In the case of the Sacraments for example, you all know that it is not enough, in order to receive the specific grace of this sacrament, to receive or to accomplish the external rite, that is, to receive the water of Baptism, the Unctions in Confirmation or the Extreme Unction and to hear the words pronounced by the minister, one must also have the required dispositions. And it is precisely in the acquisition of these dispositions that the Virgin Mediatrix intervenes, and that, each time, without exception, we receive grace. Thus the beautiful title attributed to the Virgin by the Church in the Litanies of "*Mater Divinae Gratiae,* Mother of Divine Grace." This title must be taken here in its proper sense and not only in a metaphoric sense, as when we say that she is a "Mystical Rose." Mary is the Mother of Grace in the sense that she cooperates like a mother to give it (grace) to us after having prepared us for it.

Because this doctrine is beautiful and because it is right to make us love our Celestial Mother upon whom we totally depend, we must not only be born to the supernatural life of grace, but also must increase it and persevere in it.

I shall conclude by citing this beautiful prayer of St. Bernard, (he has been named the Cantor of Mary, so well has he spoken of her):

"Consider, Oh man, the design of God, recognize a design of wisdom, a design of kindness. Wishing to spread the celestial dew of grace in this manner He pours it all at first on the

261

fleece; before redeeming mankind He puts the entire price on Mary . . . He put into her the plenitude of all good in such a way that if there is in us some hope, if there is in us some grace, if there is in us some hope of salvation, we know that our abundance comes from her. Let us venerate therefore, from the very bottom of our hearts with all our affection and with all our wishes the venerable Mary, for such is the will of the One who wanted us to have everything through Mary. (Office of Mary Mediatrix, 6th lesson.)

III

THE INTERVENTIONS IN THE CHURCH OF THE MOTHER OF THE CHURCH

Third Lesson

It is said in the Books of Divine Revelation that the Prophet Jonas was sent by God to the Ninivites in order to warn them that because of their wickedness and the universal corruption which raged among them, God was irritated and had resolved to destroy their nation. Moved to repentance, everyone, from the youngest to the oldest, began to do penance and to weep for their sins. And God, "who does not wish the death of the sinner but wishes that he repent and that he live," was moved, pardoned them and saved this city, wicked but repentant, from imminent ruin.

For a hundred years, Noah warned his fellowmen, who steeped themselves in the ways of corruption, to change their lives and to convert. They mocked the warnings of God's envoy. We know what happened to them: a frightful flood destroyed them all in a few days. Some progressives have tried to make us believe that the Flood never existed over all the world, but a more profound and more objective study is engaged in giving ground again to the text of the Bible; the universal Deluge really occurred.

We also know the fate reserved for the unfortunate cities of

262

Sodom and Gomorrah, whose corruption among the individuals surpassed everything that one can imagine. A rain of fire and brimstone consumed them.

With us, in our so-called free regions, the disruptive forces of evil are at work and their action in order to be more hidden is neither less insidious nor less effective. It assumes all kinds of forms, subversion of the minds by communist and atheistic propaganda which invades the most enlightened minds and endeavors to undermine the Catholic Faith at its most profound bases: Birth control practices to which they tend to give a legal appearance and for which they plead with the Pope to accept and even to encourage. Conjugal infidelities, abortions and practices of homosexuality of which some have undertaken to legalize. Grave negligence in the education of children, on the part of the parents and teachers, is still worse, in a sense, than to refuse them entrance into life, since one thus throws them, without mercy, into a brutal world where they will be incapable of fighting and defending themselves against the invading evil. Disobedience and the independence of children toward their parents when this is not contempt or open rebellion. . . .

In the face of these grave dangers which menace us, before these gnawing erosions of our wonderful French Canadian families (and we might add those of America and all parts of the world), before this invading corruption, let us not be surprised if God, who is always compassionate, and who wants to save us at all costs, once again begins his warnings which are formally entrusted to his prophets.

In 1954 the Church commemorated the Centennial of the Apparitions of La Salette in which the Blessed Virgin had implored men to stop offending God, adding that the arm of her Son had become so weighted down that she could no longer restrain or prevent it from striking.

In 1967 our sovereign Pontiff went to Fatima to thank the Virgin for having come to visit us and to implore her to continue her help for us which is more necessary than ever.

Just as in the time of Noah we have arrived at a critical period in the history of mankind. For more than a hundred years God has been increasing his warnings.

But His Messenger, this time, is not an ordinary mortal or even a Prophet as in former times: it is His own Mother, the incarnation of His tender kindness and compassion.

On La Rue du Bac, Paris, 1830; at La Salette, 1846; at Lourdes, 1858; at Pontmain, 1871; at Fatima, 1917; at Beauraing, 1932; at Banneux, 1933; at Syracuse, 1953; and in many other places, although of a less official character; and most recently, at Garabandal, in Spain (from 1961–1965), the Virgin has increased her visits. Her voice has become more and more urgent to request us to do penance and to pray more.

Will we still remain deaf to her voice? We have for a long time. We must realize it is the destiny of all of us that is at stake and that if the misfortunes which threaten us come true, it will not be the fault of God, who could not do more, without going beyond the limits of Faith.

Here, I am permitting myself to relate to you a very significant fact.

Toward the end of the Franco-Prussian War, several German priests, who had been military chaplains, then taken prisoners by the Allies, have affirmed under oath, that they have seen in the thick of battle, quite high in the sky, above the French Army, a great majestic Lady, who seemed to preside over the fighting. According to their testimony hardly suspect of partiality, She had Her back turned to the German Army and She was encouraging the Allied soldiers. At certain moments, Her extended arms made gestures of retreat. At the same instant the entire enemy army retreated, dispersing as if by an insurmountable force. Until then, the victory had remained uncertain and the losses were immense on both sides. From that moment on, victory began to take shape for the Allied side, and it was emphasized until the final triumph.

This fact was related in some important ecclesiastical reviews, as for example, "L'Ami du Clerge," but with the same delay which has been noticed in the transmission of almost all the Marian Messages, the delay due, we think, to the conspiracy of silence. Mr. Sanchez Ventura clearly made reference to it in his book "Stigmatises et Apparitions" on pages 195 and 196, in the following terms: "one reads in the newspaper of the German General Staff: 'On the nights of the 17th and 18th of January, 1871 Prince Frederick-Charles, commanding the Ninth Army, stopped his forward march. King William of Prussia called for one of his army corps for his operations on the Seine. General Von Schmidt, who knows that the French Army is in full retreat, finds this order deplorable and demands permission to advance in reconnaissance as far as Laval, on January 20th. This permission is refused, and on the 22nd of January his detachment is dissolved.'"

This abrupt change of tactics is inexplicable for the Germans as well as for the French. The historians of Pontmain quote these sentences attributed to General Von Schmidt, on the morning of the 18th of January: "It is finished, we will go no farther; yonder in the direction of Brittany, an invisible Lady has barred the way to us. . . ." On the 28th of January, without the Germans making one further step, the armistice was signed.

Although there is truth in this account, we believe that it illustrates and symbolizes wonderfully the constant intervention of the Mother of God in the great combat which a militant humanity undertakes against the infernal hordes. Without Mary, everything that has long been good, beautiful and divine in the Church, and perhaps humanity itself would be destroyed forever. How true is this word from the Holy Scripture: "Mary is more fearsome than an army in battle array."

I have listed the principal apparitions with which the Virgin has deigned to honor us for more than a century.

If you have read these accounts, you have no doubt noticed that they all resemble each other, at least in certain respects and in especially the contents of the message and its purpose.

All of the messages urge us to prayer, to penitence and to the frequent reception of the Holy Eucharist and to an invincible faith in supernatural realities. Almost all have a universal purpose: they speak to all Catholics at first, then to all men through and by means of some privileged children who have received them.

Some have wanted to see in this type of uniformity in the manner in which the Virgin manifested herself, a proof of the non-authenticity of these apparitions.

We see on the contrary, a non-equivocal proof of veracity. For Mary, like her Son Jesus and even like God, is perfect. Having once adopted a manner of acting, they do not, as we must, have to perfect it from one time to the next. With the first stroke they have attained perfection and they have no further reason to change.

One of these traits common to all the apparitions of the Blessed Virgin is their great simplicity and the fact that almost all of them, especially those which are destined for all humanity are directed to young children and to some poor children having nothing about themselves which could attract any kind of popularity.

It is not our place to give the reasons that God and the Virgin have had to make this choice, but in reflecting upon it, it pleases us to see in this choice a divine characteristic which authenticates these apparitions. "I thank thee, O Father, that you have concealed these things (the divine mysteries) from the great and from the wise, and that you have revealed them to the little ones," The Divine Master declares.

At all times, indeed, God has preferred the humble and the ordinary to the scholars and to the favorites of the world. Even from the simply human point of view, it is easy for us to see why God chose to act in this way because of the simplicity and honesty of a child's mind. The child is direct and straightforward. That which he knows he says with frankness, without adding or subtracting anything. Because of this, is a child not the ideal instrument for transmitting a message? He is unaware of our subtle reasonings, our selfish reckonings, our human deferences, our cleverly embroidered lies, which distort the truth and often make it say exactly the opposite of what it means.

Children have still another quality that we can envy. Still possessing baptismal innocence, they are better prepared than adults to receive these extraordinary graces.

Finally, they who are weakness itself, are, at least as much as we, capable of heroism. Indeed, we know that all those who have been chosen as prophets and missionaries of the Virgin Mary, have accomplished their mission with a heroic fidelity, even before those who have presented themselves to them as severe judges and sometimes as executioners. That which we call "the little story" will tell us much later, when the passage of years will have muffled passions and prejudices, that this new type of executioner was no more absent from Garabandal than from

266

Fatima, from Lourdes, from La Salette and all the other places where the Virgin had to confront the malice of the devil and his followers.

Finally, a last trait common to all the true Marian Apparitions is that, in spite of the variations of circumstance, of time and of place there are not and there never have been, any contradictions between the various contents of the messages of the Blessed Virgin, if one makes comparisons between them. All, although they belong to different times and are expressed in different dialects, coincide entirely as to their essential tenor and even to their manner of expression.

(See the development of these ideas in the book of Sanchez-Ventura y Pascual: "Did the Virgin Appear at Garabandal?")

IV

PROPHECIES IN THE CHURCH

Fourth Lesson

In our first two conferences we have spoken of apparitions, of celestial messages, of prophecies. And we have spoken of them as if they came from themselves, as we would speak about a different fact, of any kind of event reported in the newspapers. But, you may well suspect that that goes without raising any great theological questions before priests, specialists in these things and the Bishops who have the special mission of safeguarding the faith in the Church, wrinkle their brows and take on an anxious air and show surprise and anxiety.

Of these cares, of these surprises, of these anxieties you have heard echoes while reading all the books and publications which have spoken of these extraordinary facts. It runs quite a gamut of sentiments and reactions ranging from simple distrust to the most categoric denial.

We must not be surprised with these defensive reactions on

the part of the Authorities, reactions which have perhaps dampened our enthusiasm that we had at first experienced upon learning that the opaque wall which separates us from the beyond had partly opened, but which will have the final result of basing our belief not only on sentiments, but on a reasoned and enlightened conviction.

In this third conference, I would like to make a brief incursion into the sub-stratum theology underlying these extraordinary facts.

In fact, apparitions are not a new occurrence in the Church and they have not taken any theologian unawares, or even any priest who has even basic knowledge of theology.

St. Thomas Aquinas, Doctor of the Church, who is more than ever of topical interest in accordance with the fathers of the Church and in following the teaching of the Apostle St. Paul, speaks to us at length and gives us illuminating explanations on this subject.

All the Marian Apparitions which have taken place in our century, and the very important messages and predictions that they contain, can be included in that which St. Thomas calls "The Charisma" and more specially "The Prophecy."

Charisma is a free gift from God given to someone, not primarily for his own sanctification, as for example, the Sanctifying Grace, the virtues and the gifts of the Holy Spirit, but for the good of the community of which he is a part. It always has in view the sanctification of souls, but it does not necessarily presuppose the personal sanctity in the one who receives it and who exercises it.

Charismas were very frequent in the first centuries of the Church, for the Church had in order to implant herself, to conquer many obstacles, the principal ones being general incredulity, obstinacy, blindness, and the infidelity of the Jewish people. The Holy Spirit was to strike with great blows and accomplish spectacular marvels in order to open up a road to the dawning Church, devoid of all human means of penetration.

Today, these Charismas have become more rare, without stopping altogether as we shall see in a little while, because the

Church is universally known, but also, we believe because Christians are less fervent and less radiant and have even become less amenable to the action of the Holy Spirit, who can hardly use them anymore to manifest itself and to accomplish its work of love and of mercy.

In his first Epistle to the Corinthians, Ch. XII, St. Paul enumerates the principal Charismas: "The manifestation of the Spirit, said he, is given to each one with a view to its common usefulness: To one the Spirit gives a word of wisdom, to another is given a word of science . . . ; to another faith . . . the gift of curing . . . the gift of miracles . . . prophecy . . . the discernment of the spirits . . . the gift of diversity and interpretation of languages. All of that is the work of one and the same Spirit who distributes his gifts to each one in particular, as he pleases. . . ."

As one sees it, the gifts of the Spirit are most diverse, as are diverse the ministries in the Church and the activities of men. What assures their deep unity is that they come from the one and the same Spirit of God.

Even today Charismas are not an exceptional thing, even if certain ones are gifts out of sequence, as the power of performing miracles or of having visions as we are considering now. Christian life and the entire function of the institutions of the Church depend entirely upon them. It is through them that the Church governs the people of God, giving power to some and grace to accomplish their functions of teaching, of exhortation, of acts of mercy (Rom. XII, 7 etc.); to others the power and grace to answer their proper vocation and to be useful, each one in his sphere, to the family, to the parish to the ecclesiastic community (Eph. IV 12). All the special vocations of Christians are founded upon Charismas. The priest, the nun, the monk who have embraced and who faithfully observe celibacy do so by virtue of the Charisma of Chastity. Married people who wholeheartedly practice their duties as spouse and as educators enjoy just as valuable Charismas on which they can always count. Each one then receives his Charisma according to his particular vocation. Among these Charismas, there is one which I would like to stress especially, because it touches most closely upon the Marian Apparitions which are the principal object of the study of our present conference; this Charisma is the one of Prophecy.

The Charisma of Prophecy

There have always been prophets since man has existed on earth. All the nations, all the religions, have boasted of having their prophets. They may be called soothsayers, sorcerers, magicians or men of God. They are men and women whom one consults in order to know what must be done to appease the gods and to render them favorable; in order to know the distant or immediate future.

Our twentieth century, so proud of its science and of its progress and which claims to be able to do without God, also has its prophets whom it consults in secret. These prophets are called fortunetellers, mediums, soothsayers, natural clairvoyants, with or without hypnotic influence; and all doing very good business.

This is all the more reason, we believe, to learn to carefully distinguish true prophecy from its many counterfeits.

Authentic prophecy began with the Hebrew people in the Old Testament. Our early Old Testament History—which has unfortunately disappeared from our schools to give place to a so-called scientific interpretation of the Bible, but which leads to nothing less than to deny everything supernatural in the Bible— our Little Old Testament History, I say, spoke to us about great and little prophets who all had, in varying degrees, the mission to announce in advance the future Messiah and to prepare men for His coming. "To announce the coming of God and to prepare us for it," that is the essence of all true prophecy, whether it be made by Moses, by Isaiah, or by Melanie, Lucy of Fatima or by Bernadette of Lourdes.

It is in fact in the Church that the prophecies are continuing. "Prophecies will disappear one day," explains Paul (I Col. XII, 8), but it will only be at the end of time. The coming of Christ down here, rather than eliminating Charisma from Prophecy, on the contrary provoked its extension, which had been predicted. "May all the people be prophets," wished Moses, who himself had been one of the greatest prophets of the Old Testament. And Joel saw this wish come true in a vision, "In the last days" (Joel III, 1-4). On the day of Pentecost, Peter declared Joel's prophecy accomplished, when he said, "The Spirit of Jesus has been spread over all Flesh." Yes, visions and prophecies are common things in the new people of God. In the Churches that he founds, St. Paul wishes this Charisma of Prophecy be not underrated (I Thes. V, 20). He places it well above the gift of languages (I Cor. XIV, 1-5); but he holds nevertheless that one exercise it in orderly fashion and for the good of the Community (XIV, 29-32), and that one remain submissive to authority (I Cor. XIV, 37). In addition authentic prophecy is always recognizable thanks to the rules of discernment of the spirits.

Let us see now how things happen in the person who receives the gift of prophecy. At first, this gift is neither a habit nor a permanent quality given once and for all, and which one would then use at will, as is the case, for example, for the sanctifying grace and instilled virtues.

It is a momentary (or fleeting) impression that the soul receives for a well-defined time and which totally and exclusively depends on God, to whom alone it belongs to actualize or to make it cease. Reread the accounts of all the authentic apparitions. You will inevitably find there, these characteristics of passivity in the prophets, sudden beginning and cessation; profound transformation of the chosen person during the time that the supernatural phenomenon lasts; his sudden return to normal, as soon as the Divine intervention ceases.

Most of the time, the prophet is warned some time before the phenomenon occurs. Thus, with the prophetesses of Garabandal, the warning is ordinarily made in three stages. The young girls were at first warned, several hours in advance, that they would soon be the object of a celestial visit. They have, then, an apprehension or hunch accompanied by an absolute certainty of the favor that they are going to receive, and they prepare for it. In this book in Document I, one sees Conchita in a state of expectancy. Having been warned the night before that she would soon be visited, she puts on her coat and keeps herself in readiness to leave. But while waiting for the Moment, she falls peacefully asleep—which, frankly, is an indication that she is not of nervous temperament. The waiting lasts all night.

271

A second warning informs her that the visit is imminent and will happen in a certain place. She leaves immediately, moved as if by an invincible force, although perfectly free and (this force) which she feels she would be able to resist, but which she does not want to resist for anything in the world (indication of an effective and working grace).

Finally, the third stage; she enters into ecstasy and finds herself before the apparition. It is only then that the Charisma of the Prophet takes place. The warnings are preliminary phenomena which leave the prophet in his normal, usual state, during which he can speak, eat or sleep; tease, laugh or cry if anyone thus affects him, he can be cold or warm, in a word—behave himself like any other human being.

The state of ecstasy or of prophecy stops as suddenly as it began and no force or human skill is capable of making it last any longer. The privileged can regret it and, indeed, our little prophetesses from Garabandal sweetly complain to the Virgin that the ecstasy did not last long enough; it lasted only a very short minute, as they say, but they can do nothing about it; as soon as the Divine intervention has stopped, they return (fall back into) their natural state, experiencing a great nostalgia about the departure of the celestial Visitor. They feel that no desire, no effort of the imagination, can detain Her one instant longer.

What happens while the phenomenon of prophecy lasts?— Only the privileged ones who have experienced it can tell us, and still rather imperfectly, for, after the phenomenon has ceased, they have only human words to express the Divine marvels seen in the light of God. All their descriptions remain inadequate, and are only stammerings. They retain, above all, a negative knowledge (remembrance of it): "No, it is not at all like anything that we see or can see on earth. . . ."

But theology comes to our aid and teaches us the following:

During these privileged moments, the soul leaves the body, so to speak, and enters in direct communication with the heavenly personage who visits it. The latter, by an illuminative act, in which the senses have no part, enlightens the mind of the seer on one or more truths. Although she immediately believes it, she does not always understand its meaning or comprehend it fully.

272

When Bernadette Soubirous hears the Beautiful Lady say: "I am the Immaculate Conception," she is convinced that the Virgin received such a privilege, but does not understand its nature. To the seers of Fatima and Garabandal, the Virgin affirms the existence of Hell and the possibility of terrible forthcoming chastisements. They believe it with all their hearts, but will not understand it, unless further enlightenment is given to them on the nature of the chastisement and Hell. The enlightenment was concerned with the mysteries revealed, not with their nature, at least not before they witnessed it.

Is it possible that the seers or prophets doubt the things they hear or see during the ecstasy?

They can entertain absolutely no doubt during the illuminative process, for at that moment God acts in them and makes them perfectly aware of the reality of the vision; the action of God is always effective, it carries its own enlightenment.

But when the illuminative process has ceased and the seers are again living the simple life of faith required of all Catholics, they may be beset by doubts concerning things they were absolutely sure, especially if they have to face contradiction; if they must ascertain things they have heard and seen in opposition to denials or threats suggested by people they love or respect. Their state of soul may change then, for we must remember that the will and emotions play a great part in the act of faith, precisely because we do not see directly what we believe.

Let us quote the perfect answer (theologically speaking) of a seer of Garabandal when asked if she still believed in her visions: "Yes, while they last, but after, this is something else." While unaware of it, she condensed in a single sentence what I explained above. We may find an example of this in the life of Our Lady herself. It was clearly revealed to her that Her Son would be God. At the time of this marvelous revelation, there was no possible doubt in her mind, for the Divine inspiration carried with it the absolute certainty of the divinity of her future child. But such illumination lasted only an instant. Immediately after, the Virgin Mary was again surrounded by the shadows of faith. To keep believing that her Son was God, she had to remind herself of the marvelous things she has heard and seen at the

273

time of her miraculous conception. St. Luke states this explicitly: "Mary kept all these things and pondered them in her heart," implying that this was her way of keeping and sustaining her faith.

But her faith was subjected to severe trials. The Child to whom she gave birth and whom the Angel said was God, was weak and powerless as any other child in the neighborhood; he depended completely upon her for food and care. In order to save his life threatened by the impious Herod, she had to flee with him into Egypt. During their hidden life at Nazareth, her Son was like any other young man; he did nothing extraordinary; he obeyed his mother and his foster-father, St. Joseph, and prayed with them every day to his Heavenly Father in a simple and human manner, as did every true Israelite. Finally, after an attempt to found a Church destined to last until the end of time, he died a shameful death upon the cross as the lowest of criminals.

If Our Lady did not lose faith in the divinity of her Son, it is because she was sustained by extraordinary grace which she must have obtained through constant prayer.

The same applies to seers and prophets. The divine favors and privileges of which they have been the object did not shield them from the ordinary living conditions. Neither were they shielded from doubt or danger of losing the faith, even in the messages entrusted to them. Therefore, and this applies both to them and to us, it is through humble and constant prayer that they must continue to sustain and strengthen their faith.

If the seers of Garabandal have been beset by doubts and if the faith in their mission has seemed to be shaken, let us not condemn them, let us pray with them and for them so that they may persevere to the end to be witnesses and messengers of Our Lady who chose them in preference to others.

One more question: *Should we wish to have visions or receive prophecies?* Although the Apostle St. Paul spoke highly on the charisma of prophecies and its great usefulness to the Church, the general trend among Catholics has always been that we should not aspire to these extraordinary graces that put the recipients in a conspicuous position. This tradition goes back to

St. Paul, who, after having enumerated all the charisms enjoyed by the first Christians, states: "But, I ask you to aspire to something higher than all these extraordinary gifts: above all, aspire for charity and sanctifying grace that goes with it."

This is also the doctrine of the great Doctor of the Church, St. John of the Cross. More than anyone, he knew the grandeur and sublimity of Charisms that God can grant souls. With a Master hand, he described them in "The Ascension of Carmel," the first of his spiritual books. But more than anyone, he warned souls against desiring these extraordinary gifts because they carry a great danger of illusion. Moreover, they are not a proof of sanctity, only a means among many others to attain it. He considered the practice of the three theological virtues of faith, hope and charity as the means "par excellence" to attain high sanctity and the gift of contemplation. He stressed the naked faith, stripped from all miraculous support, the faith of little children satisfied to believe blindly the Word of the Heavenly Father, with unshakable confidence.

Recently, I received a letter from a young lady, very devoted to the Blessed Virgin. She confided to me a project she had made with her husband. They decided to buy a small property, mostly because it contained a lovely grove where they would build a grotto, similar to the one of Lourdes, so that Our Lady could come and make a pilgrimage center. I told her: "No, do not do it, and do not wish to have apparitions. We do not attract Our Lady by building a grotto as we attract swallows with prefabricated nests. It is God Himself and the Virgin who choose the places where they want to appear and they manifest themselves to whom they please and only to those. From a simple human point of view, we could say that they often baffle us with their choice of places and persons. There is one more reason not to interfere. If ever one or several of you were favored with this kind of privilege, I would certainly not envy you, rather I would pity you with all my heart, because it would be the beginning of a real calvary of which neither you nor I could foresee the outcome. It is so much surer to follow the common path of faith: common by the number of those who are called in it, but in reality, sublime and extremely sanctifying: "Blessed are those who believe and have not seen" said Jesus to the Apostle Thomas who demanded from His Master tangible proofs of His Resurrection.

The end

Rev. Charles Bourgeois

On May 6, 1968 additional information was obtained from Rome concerning the March 7, 1967 note issued by the Bishop of Santander. This information was obtained by Father Gustavo Morelos, a priest from Mexico interested in the events of Garabandal and founder of the White Legion.

When Bishop Vincent Puchol issued the statement or note saying that there were no apparitions at Garabandal . . . that all could be explained naturally, it was printed in the newspapers. When this statement was printed there was also printed along with it a letter from Cardinal Ottaviani which had been recently sent to the Bishop. If anyone read these two letters together they would come to the conclusion that the Cardinal, speaking in the name of Rome, had agreed with the Bishop and that was the end of the matter. It was known, however, that this was not the case but much harm was done because of this misuse of association of these two statements under one heading in the paper.

The news from Father Morelos is as follows as taken from a letter sent by him to Manuel Romero the then director of the Garabandal Center in Mexico:

"It is now 11:45, on May 6, 1968——

I am about to leave the office of the Sacred Congregation of the Holy Office, actually the Congregation for the Doctrine of the Faith. I had a meeting with Msgr. Plentida, of whom I clearly asked the following question.

'The letter sent to Bishop Vincent Puchol, Bishop of Santander (R.I.P.) by this Sacred Congregation (March 7, 1967), did it signify that the Vatican had declared itself (on the matter of Garabandal)?'

He answered me thusly:

'The Vatican, in all matters of this type, walks with leaden feet. The letter (March 7, 1967) therefore was not a pronouncement of this subject.' Here he observed with circumspection (translators note: He was attentive; discreet). 'It was a *private letter*, addressed to the Bishop of Santander.— These words suffice—Rome leaves to the Bishop the responsibility of his acts.'

Certainly, I have already been cautioned personally of this position—and directly by His Eminence Cardinal Ottaviani himself. But, I have wished to listen to the news from another member of the Sacred Congregation in order to be able to thus affirm one more time—and with fuller knowledge of the reality—*that Rome has not declared itself in the case of Garabandal*, that Rome continues to keep itself up-to-date on what happens, that Rome studies the question and waits."

THE MESSAGE

"The Message that the Holy Virgin has given to the world through the intercession of St. Michael.

The Angel said: Because my Message of the 18th of October, 1961 has not been complied with and little has been done to make it known to the world, I tell you that this is the last one.

Before (on October 18, 1961) the Chalice was filling, now it is overflowing. (The Chalice of Divine Wrath.)

Many priests are on the road of perdition and they take many souls with them.

To the Eucharist, there is given less and less importance.

We must make every effort to avoid Divine Wrath which is pressing on us.

If you ask Him for His forgiveness with a sincere soul, He (God) will forgive you.

It is I, your Mother, who through the intercession and mediation of St. Michael, want to say that you must amend. You are already in the last warnings.

I love you very much and do not want your condemnation.

Pray to us sincerely and We shall give it to you (what you ask us) (We: God and Our Lady.)

You must sacrifice yourselves more.

Meditate on the Passion of Jesus."

(Signed) Conchita Gonzalez
June 18, 1965

Thirty Witnesses
Spanish, French, Belgian, German, English, and American
March 7th, 1966
on the feast of Saint Thomas Aquinas.
A norma dei decreti di Urbano VIII a quanto di soprannaturale viene narrato nel presente opusculo deve essere prestata unicamente fede umana.

———

About the considerations of a French theologian concerning the
Appearance, the nature of the Apparitions, the Miracle of the
Forma, the End of Times which is not the end of the World,
Conchita's remark that "one is more or less loved," Mari Cruz's
case, please refer to the original French book: "L'Etoile dans la
Montagne."

APPENDIX

[Preface from the original French book]

Apparitions are not essentials of our faith; they lead to belief or they strengthen faith. They belong to the category of outward signs; also, they are placed under the administration and control of the Church, which establishes, at least by her perpetuity, the foremost signs of credibility. Apparitions that have not received the official approval of the Church do not deserve the same credence as those which have been recognized by the Church as being of a supernatural origin.

❉   ❉   ❉

Apparitions are held, and justifiably so, only for "extraordinary" people. Few people are thus favored, and among the sincere persons who think they see or perceive invisible realities, many see as objective realities things which are more or less only imaginative impressions. There are those who are able, somehow, to be benefited supernaturally, provided that they live the faith, and never topple from the solid rock of sound doctrine.

Nevertheless, the waves of Modernist-like conceit which dash even into the Church blind its "enlightened" followers and skeptics, if they neglect the consideration of apparitions. This is precisely the aim of the Modernist-like view. But, if one takes that point of view, if one considers the intervals of time, if one sees humanity but not each human being, then apparitions become ordinary events.

God has never ceased to manifest Himself visibly. The presence of Jesus on earth established, in this respect as in all others, a transcendent achievement, and a point of departure which does not correspond to any other past event.

It is difficult to see why God's visible manifestations which belong to the New Covenant are the targets of such critical suspicion, while those of the Old Testament do not raise any problems. The brilliant scholars who explain Scripture deem it so, and wish to charge that the Archangel Gabriel is a mental projection of "hagiography," (the stories of saints' lives; the veneration of saints) but the scholars admit the real existence of the angel who stayed the arm of Abraham . . . God, then, not yet having found a better way of obtaining that result. Should you smile at them, or take pity on them?

* * *

Yet, the truth is very simple. To practice one's faith is very difficult. God, who is Merciful, has always helped His children, the believers, in manifesting Himself to them in a visible way. Then, if one considers the rapport between God and mankind, one must state A POSTERIORI (another word for "by experience"), and A PRIORI (another word meaning "by reason"), that, by virtue of the Loving Author of Faith, apparitions are a part of the Church, a living and permanent thing.

That is strengthened somewhat by the practical standards whose basis we have already discussed. That position is good, because the apparitions are integrated, by right, into the life of the Church, that it belongs to the Church, which is first in the scheme of things, to decide on the worth of the apparitions, which themselves are part of the scheme of things. Or else, in expressing the same idea in a negative manner: if the apparitions did not make up a vital part of the Church, the Church would not be qualified to decide as She does in matters which concern reality, somehow appear covered by standards which render them self-sufficient.

The Modernist attitude is false, then, from all points of view— dogmatically, ecclesiastically, even humanly. It consists of not professing exclusively that suspicion is a part of all apparitions. (The Church has factions which represent the views of the right, the left, and the middle-of-the-road. Why must there also be a closed-mindedness concerning God Himself?)

Our purpose is not to analyze the nature of the apparition, but to recall its significance. We then conclude: apparitions ought not to come as a surprise to Christians, if they are really true believers, and are thus familiar with the arduous way to Heaven, and if they really believe in Divine Love and thus discover, at the same time, the Presence of God in the manifestation of His Mercy. A faith which is strong and essentially confident, liberally welcomes anything which God gives in addition.

It is proper to say, in view of what follows, that the qualification of the apparitions by the Church does not uniformly raise the same voices anew. When an apparition has brought a prediction which is to come to pass, as was the case at Fatima (and is the case at Garabandal), it is the Pope and the Congregation for the Defense of the Faith, of which the Pope is head, which is responsible and who decides upon the apparition and anything else which concerns the supernatural aspects of such an apparition. The decisions which prudence can dictate to the Ordinaries (Bishops) have only temporary value as judgments. They are not, either by right or by fact, of any value concerning the supernaturality of the apparition. This is a provision of common law, a judgment handed down by a tribunal, or an assembly who has no authority to render it NULL and VOID. It is NON-EXISTENT AS A JUDGMENT.

Neither the Bishop of Santander, nor all the Bishops of Spain, can decide the facts concerning Garabandal, and if they would pretend to decide, they would encroach upon the power of the Pope.

❊   ❊   ❊

The second observation regarding the facts of the apparitions, arises from the first. Apparitions are a living part of the life of the Church. To repeat, apparitions are not included in the depository whose safekeeping and promulgation are commissioned by the Church. This situation involves, at least for the theologians, an obstacle better known by the name "dogmatic facts."

There is an enlightening comparison, between the existence of the apparitions on one hand, and the existence of saints, on the other hand. God, here and there, manifests Himself within the Church. Who would dispute His right to do so? But, He manifests Himself in unexpected ways. It is not likely to attribute to the Apostles any knowledge whatsoever of the apparitions of the Blessed Virgin at Lourdes in 1858, although they knew implicitly of the Immaculate Conception. It is not likely that the Apostles had had the revelation of the existence of a Frenchman named Benedict Joseph Labre, who was very close to God, although the Apostles had the assurance of permanent sanctity and eternal fruitfulness of the Church. The difficulties arising from that become apparent: on what basis does the Church support its claim to authority, to see implicitly or explicitly, its authority, whether it be in qualifying an apparition or whether it be in the act of canonization? The infallibility of the Church, which is founded upon the promise of Christ—has it not had as an aim that which is transmittable and transmitted by tradition?

We do no intend to debate this quesion here. At least, it puts an important distinction in evidence.

The power of discernment is exercised only on the occasion of the former; the Church proclaims, by virtue of Divine favors which was given to it, that such a fact, observed and unexpected, really is God, or He would be better to remain remote.

But the Church does not have to promulgate these facts upon which She judges and qualifies almost (casually). And even when the Church solemnly declares its authority, as in the canonization of a saint, She does not add to the Truth of Revelation.

That is why the power of discernment which the Church adds is not only practiced for the sake of deposition; *this power is expressly directed to the preservation and the promulgation of truth* of which the Church is guardian, ruler, and mother (Custos, et magistra, et mater).

The Church then exercises a power which is uniform in its execution, because it is still founded on the same Divine Authority; but the methods of applying it are different; discernment is proper, by right; promulgation is incumbent to the Magistrate in matters concerning apparitions. From that, results an important consequence concerning the *event,* the "apparition."

The apparition can really have an ecclesiastical significance. It is true, in this particular case, when a message, expressly destined to be spread, is associated with the apparition itself; the apparition is, in general, the privilege of the very few, or else of one person alone.

Such was the case at La Salette, at Lourdes, and at Fatima, apparitions which have been positively sanctioned by the Supreme Authority of the Church. Such is also the case for the apparitions at Garabandal, on which subject the sole authority, in this instance, is the decision of the Pope himself, and this has not yet been given. A message destined for the greatest diffusion possible is associated with the apparition; and it is manifest, for those who are nearest to the visionaries, that the message constitutes, for the girls involved, the most important thing in the whole series of apparitions of the Blessed Virgin.

Under these conditions, upon whom does it depend to spread the message? Evidently, the Authority has the right to examine the objective contents of the message which it will not know to be authentic without being consistent with sound doctrine; but it is necessary to add that this statement is perfectly satisfactory; (that is to say) from La Salette to Garabandal, the warnings are the same; they echo the Gospels and the explanation of Tradition.

Nothing which is consistent with the normal demands of Authority then, stands in the way of the diffusion of the Message.

But, again, who must spread the Message, since the authority must, in this case, remain exclusively specific on the truths, not on the signs which accompany it?

*   *   *

The answer to this question is so simple that if it were not for the obstructions to the answers which clash with each other, it would be necessary to apologize for venturing to recall them.

A new idea is spread in a village by people who are interested in it. A message which concerns all Christianity must normally be spread by the Christians themselves. It is incumbent upon those who oppose the idea, to specify the serious reasons which inspire their zeal. They must not forget that those who are spreading a message containing the rudiments of Christianity do not have the power of judgment reserved to them. On the other hand, to "be wary of" the apparitions does not justify the assertion of untruths.

Know Garabanal, for it is the subject of this book.

M. -L. Guerard Des Lauriers, O.P.